CIVIL WAR
COMMAND AND
STRATEGY

CIVIL WAR COMMAND AND STRATEGY

THE PROCESS OF VICTORY AND DEFEAT

Archer Jones

THE FREE PRESS

A Division of Macmillan, Inc.
New York

Maxwell Macmillan Canada
Toronto

Maxwell Macmillan International
New York   Oxford   Singapore   Sydney

The Free Press
A Division of Macmillan, Inc.
866 Third Avenue, New York, N.Y. 10022

Maxwell Macmillan Canada, Inc.
1200 Eglinton Avenue East
Suite 200
Don Mills, Ontario M3C 3N1

Macmillan, Inc. is part of the Maxwell Communication Group of Companies.

Printed in the United States of America

printing number
1 2 3 4 5 6 7 8 9 10

Library of Congress Cataloging-in-Publication Data

Jones, Archer
    Civil War command and strategy : the process of victory and defeat/
    Archer Jones.
        p. cm.
    Includes bibliographical references and index.
    ISBN 0-02-916635-7
    1. United States—History—Civil War, 1861–1865—Campaigns.
    2. Military art and science—United States—History—19th century.
    3. United States. Army—History—Civil War, 1861–1865.
    4. Confederate States of America. Army—History. I. Title.
    E470.J74 1992
    973.7'301—dc20   91–44224
                                                                 CIP

To my Civil War collaborators:

Thomas Lawrence Connelly (1938–1991)
Herman M. Hattaway
Jerry A. Vanderlinde
Richard E. Beringer
William N. Still, Jr.

Sorely missed in this endeavor.

CONTENTS

———————

Contents

PREFACE

When I taught at the U.S. Army Command and General Staff College in 1976–77, I offered an elective course on Civil War military history to a small group of army and air force majors. Taking an almost wholly operational approach, I based the class presentation on Herman Hattaway and my *How the North Won: A Military History of the Civil War*, then nearing completion. Toward the end of the course, when I asked the class whether they believed the Civil War well conducted, they unanimously believed it was. Later, they showed their discrimination when I asked a similar question about the United States in the Vietnam War by answering yes, except that the strategy was "awful."

Yet much writing about the Civil War seems, implicitly at least, to describe an essentially inept conduct of the war. The South frittered away its resources in local defense; it lost because of the casualties suffered in futile frontal attacks; and its best general wasted his men in a hopeless search for an annihilating victory. Although the North won the war, it has fared little better at the hands of some historians: They criticize its generals for pursuing a passé strategy of territorial conquest, and even seem to damn Grant with the faint praise of winning through attrition.

Since much of the criticism of the military conduct of the war focuses on the command and strategy, a careful analysis of these will go far toward answering the question of the level of competence in the conduct of the war. This study's answer is that both belligerents had effective systems of command and

ix

that, on the average, the civilian and military leaders gave performances of good quality. And, in making their wise strategic choices, both the Union and the Confederacy astutely balanced political and military considerations.

By grounding its understanding of the war in the art of war as the participants knew it, this work of military history adopts a good vantage point for understanding and evaluating their performance. This will probably serve us better than the method often used, adopting later wars as the standard for an appraisal. As the appendixes contain most of the historical background supporting this treatment, readers can choose between reading the appendixes first or ignoring them in whole or in part.

In assessing some of the more important battles, I have hypothesized the effect of alternative outcomes in an effort better to estimate their importance. In this respect, it will become obvious that, contrary to common expectation, the typical Civil War battle turns out like those of most other wars; a different outcome rarely would change the course of the war. The political context, war aims, and the effects on public and official opinion give most campaigns, as well as battles, the bulk of their significance.

Particularly in its interpretations of Lincoln, Grant, Halleck, Davis, and Lee, this work relies on the aforementioned *How the North Won: A Military History of the Civil War*, which contains the documentation for these. In spite of the dependence on earlier books, I hope that variation in perspective and emphasis will make this enough of a new book to reward readers of the old.

I express my gratitude to the University of Richmond for allowing me to use the library and to the always proficient staff in the reference room. I owe even greater thanks to the Tuckahoe Branch of the Henrico County Library, where the system always works the way its designers imagined that it might. I am particularly grateful to the staff, who always display a cordial alacrity in responding to every question, in bringing books from another branch, and in securing interlibrary loan items with truly miraculous resourcefulness and speed.

Among many individuals who have given me aid, I am particularly indebted to Stephen V. Ash, Richard E. Beringer, Herman M. Hattaway, Coleman Jones, Howard Jones, Michael R. Terry, Richard P. Weinert, Everett L. Wheeler, and Tommy R. Young, II. I am especially grateful to Joanne L. Jones and Chérie Weitzner for their editing and to Joseph T. Glatthaar, Warren W. Hassler, Jr., Craig L. Symonds, and Guy Swanson for the many valuable suggestions they made as a result of reading the manuscript. I owe a similar debt to my old friend Virgil P. Randolph, III, for his superb crash program of editing and commentary on the final draft. The character of the book owes much to the leadership and wisdom of Joyce Seltzer of the Free Press. When I had failed to find anyone to execute the campaign diagrams, Marie-Christine Jones, my new daughter-in-law, earned my special gratitude by undertaking the unfamiliar task, completing it promptly and well, and thus displaying the versatility and competence of a French-educated engineer. Defects in her diagrams, like all errors of fact and interpretation, are my own responsibility.

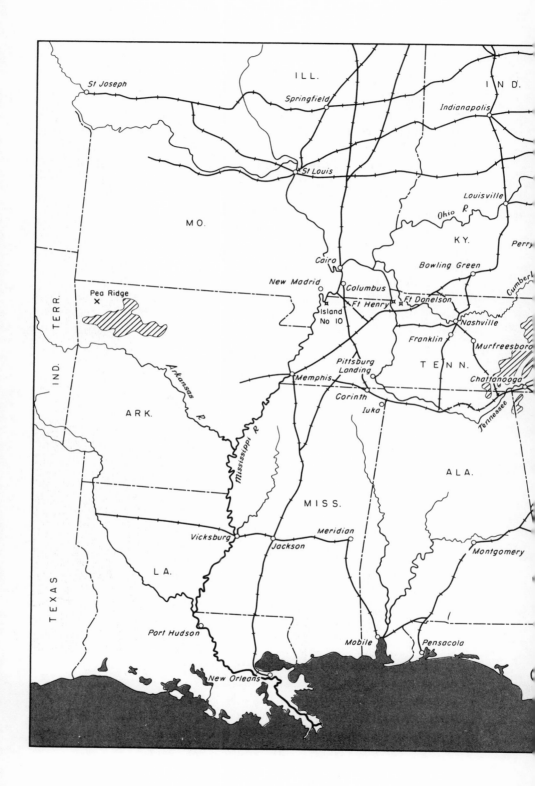

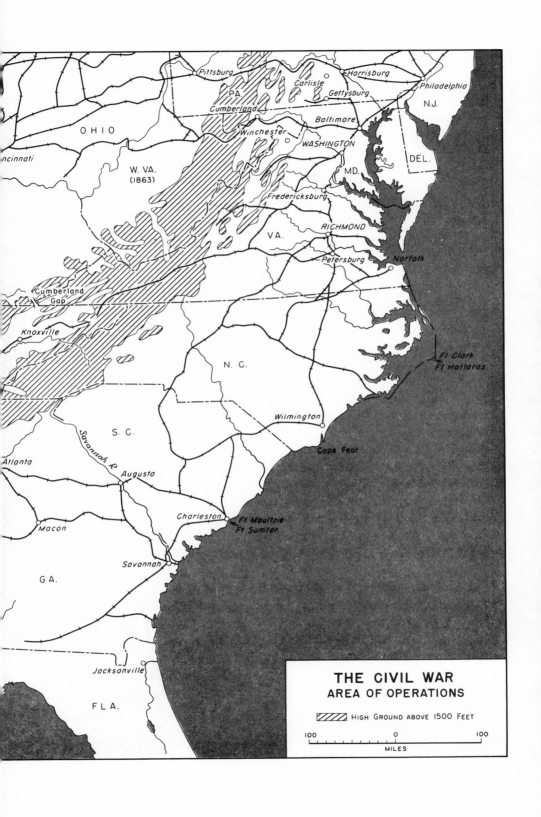

Pittsburg Harrisburg
Carlisle
PA. Gettysburg Philadelphia
Cumberland N.J.
OHIO Baltimore
Winchester WASHINGTON DEL.
MD.
Cincinnati
W. VA.
(1863)
Fredericksburg
RICHMOND
VA.
Petersburg Norfolk

Cumberland
Gap
Ft Clark
Knoxville Ft Hatteras

N. C.

Wilmington

S. C. Cape Fear
Savannah R.
Atlanta Augusta
Charleston Ft Moultrie
Macon Ft Sumter

Savannah
GA.

Jacksonville

FLA.

THE CIVIL WAR
AREA OF OPERATIONS

////// HIGH GROUND ABOVE 1500 FEET

100   0   100
MILES

CHAPTER 1

WAR PREPARATIONS AND THE BALANCE OF MILITARY POWER

———— ◆•◆ ————

Politically, the Civil War began in December 1860 when South Carolina reacted to the election of Abraham Lincoln by seceding from the United States. Fearful of the intentions toward slavery of the first Republican administration, six other deep southern slave states followed South Carolina's example and joined with her to form a new government, the Confederate States of America. Although U.S. President James Buchanan denounced the illegality of secession, the United States, having an army of barely 16,000 men, could do nothing to prevent these acts by states having millions of people, hundreds of thousands of square miles of territory, and tens of thousands of armed men enrolled in their untrained state militias.

Military combat occurred, however, when the Confederate States realized that the United States was going to resupply Fort Sumter, the Federal fort in the harbor of Charleston, South Carolina. Regarding this fort as the post of a foreign power on its territory, the Confederate government authorized G. T. Beauregard, a brigadier general in its new army and its commander in Charleston, to secure the surrender of Fort Sumter. This he did after a bombardment of thirty-four hours, which

P.G.T.

1

inflicted no casualties but forced the surrender of a U.S. garrison short of supplies and without hope of replenishment.

This provided the occasion President Lincoln needed to act against the rebels, and he responded to this attack on Federal territory by calling for 75,000 volunteers for three months service to suppress an insurrection. Since this call on the states for men compelled the slave states remaining in the Union to choose sides, half of them, Virginia, North Carolina, Arkansas, and Tennessee, seceded. Thus two countries, both virtually disarmed but with great military potential, found themselves in a conflict which would have the character of both a civil war and a war between sovereign states.

Thus began a costly, four-year struggle, whose military action depended much on the problems of command and strategy which the civilians and soldiers faced and for which they found solutions of varying merit. Only through an understanding of the alternatives available and through an inquiry into how the northern and southern high commands adapted military means to political ends could one appreciate the considerable sophistication and skill each displayed.

At first glance the fighting seemed merely see-saw operations punctuated by bloody battles which decided little. To some European observers, these indecisive campaigns as well as the great length of the war seemed peculiar when compared with the short, decisive wars of the Napoleonic era and the similar quick wars in Europe in mid-century. This accounts for the European neglect of the war, an attitude exemplified by words attributed to General Helmuth von Moltke, the Prussian chief of staff. He characterized the military operations of the American Civil War as merely "two armed mobs chasing each other around the country, from which nothing could be learned."

Implicitly this scholarly and distinguished soldier stressed the unpreparedness of the belligerents who had to use untrained soldiers, the parity in their strength, and the orthodoxy of their warmaking, which offered no novel lessons to the military observer.

The leaders of the Confederacy designed an army and navy on the U.S. model, and pitted their newly created, amateur force against a similarly nonprofessional Union Army. To raise an army large enough to vanquish a country of the extent and wealth of the Confederacy was the Union's challenge. It could not depend on its tiny regular army, even if it used it as a nucleus and doubled its size by the addition of privates. Instead, the Union used its standing army largely as a reservoir of officers for the volunteer forces, and the Confederates, though they created a regular army, did the same with the pool of regular officers who joined their army. Some of the United States Army's enlisted men followed the region in which they served, manifesting a strong local attachment, and a majority of the officers joined the side of the state of their birth or the one with which they strongly identified.

Both the Union and the Confederacy followed the same procedures in establishing their military commands and recruiting the huge armies they perceived as necessary for attack and defense. Both relied on new volunteer forces, rather than on the ill-trained militia units, to provide the framework for mobilization. Both central governments depended on the individual states to play a crucial part in the creation and mobilization of the armies. This was a natural, and indeed an essential, approach in view of the available machinery of government. In the nineteenth century little other than the post office represented the federal government in any U.S. community, except in the ports where the treasury collected the customs duties that paid for most of the government's expenses.

In their turn the states depended on a good deal of local and individual entrepreneurship. Prominent individuals, for example, received authorization from the governor to raise a regiment which they would command as colonels. Others might raise companies, either as part of an authorized regiment or independently. When ready, the state tendered these regiments to the central government, Union or Confederate. Frequently the state furnished the weapons, sometimes sending their own agents to Europe to obtain them. Many of these new officers were amateurs, but both sides boasted a small cadre of experienced, and sometimes trained and seasoned, men. The Confederacy had the services of 270 regular officers who left the U.S. Army when the war began; most of those remaining from the 1,105 at the beginning of the conflict served with the Union. Graduates of military colleges, particularly the Virginia

3

Military Institute, provided another source of trained men. Militia and Mexican War service also produced men with some military knowledge, able to train and lead the large, hastily improvised armies. Although the state appointed all officers, the men themselves had usually elected them first.

Notwithstanding the military imperative and the issues at stake, politics had much to do with the raising of the armies. This was natural in an era when people took their politics very seriously, reading highly partisan newspapers and finding in political rallies and oratory some of the entertainment which the twentieth century has supplied with motion pictures, radio, and television. The volunteer militia had provided opportunities for increased political visibility and availability, as the prevalence of military titles for civilians illustrates.

Despite the use of democratic methods to choose military leaders, the new soldiers tended to elect people of military experience, if available. Thus they sought to entrust their lives to someone who gave the best promise of competence. When they chose from outside the military, they often put their faith in those with marked ability in another area, hoping this might transfer to the military sphere. Hence many prominent men, lacking any military background, became colonels. Illustrative is the experience of soldiers drilled by a middle-aged colonel who had formerly served in Congress. Sitting on a rail fence and holding an umbrella above himself for protection from the sun, the newly elected officer used his considerable oratorical powers to drill his regiment. Totally unfamiliar with regimental evolutions and commands, he read from the manual until a commotion caused him to look up and see that he had marched his men into a fence. Not disconcerted by this contretemps, he shouted to them to fall out of ranks and reform on the other side of the fence. He went on to receive promotion and display competence as a division commander.

Election of officers did not offer the only example of the appearance of the civilian political culture in the army. Presidents George Washington and Andrew Jackson had shown the potential for the conversion of military fame into civil office. With the election as president in 1848 of popular Mexican War military commander General Zachary Taylor, politicians could see that the Mexican War, like the Revolution and War of 1812,

4

could produce presidential timber. In the presidential race four years later, in 1852, a former senator and possessor of an undistinguished Mexican War record as a volunteer, Brigadier General Franklin Pierce, defeated Major General Winfield Scott, the war's outstanding soldier. These two elections illustrate not only why politicians sought military command during the Civil War but, in the candidacy of the regular army generals, how politically aware were some active-duty military men. Thus many soldiers on both sides would wage war with often strong opinions and sometimes sophisticated understandings about the political objectives underlying the military means which they were applying.

Election of officers reflected a basic assumption in this democratic era that any citizen with common sense could undertake any public employment. Reflected in patronage and militia appointments, this outlook, complemented by the belief that determination itself was sufficient for a soldier, carried over to the volunteer forces raised for the war. In fact, many had a prejudice against regulars, especially graduates of the U.S. Military Academy at West Point. Critics often disparaged these trained men as an overeducated elite, filled with impractical theory and lacking in practical knowledge. Private soldiers electing their lieutenants and captains did not have a monopoly on this point of view and these biases; many of the important civilian and military leaders shared this feeling.

In spite of the prejudice of many volunteers against regular army men and the graduates of the U.S. Military Academy, the guidance and leadership of these experienced and educated soldiers proved essential in organizing and operating the new war machines. The military knowledge and insight of many of the regular officers would have much to do with giving the armies and the war their sophisticated character. That Union and Confederate officers had learned about war in the same army and that the men they led came from such similar backgrounds help explain the equivalence between the opposing forces. The ease with which the rebels as well as the Union could equip their large armies also explains the parity between the belligerents.

At the time of the Civil War, the problem of equipping armies presented particularly little difficulty. Arming the infantry

5

proved fairly simple compared to the more remote past, when some men would have required spears, helmets, shields, and breastplates at least, all requiring the labor of skilled artisans. Others would have needed bows, requiring great skill to use, or the simpler-to-learn but more difficult-to-make crossbows. Both required missiles, the arrow of the bow using the product of two craftsmen, the arrowsmith who made the point and the fletcher the shafts. Even making guns had become easier than in the past, with simple machines supplanting much of the skill of the gunsmith. Thus Civil War soldiers needed only a rifle, and could substitute a smoothbore musket, as many did among both belligerents in the first two years of the war. Because of the comparative simplicity of gunmaking, both countries could manufacture small arms rapidly as well as import them.

Consequently, in the case of many military necessities, the Civil War proved less complicated to supply than earlier or later wars. Initially, some soldiers armed themselves with hunting rifles and other weapons found in the home. Fabricating bullets was far easier than making arrows and, though the ingredients of gunpowder required an organized effort to obtain, neither side suffered a shortage. In theory the soldiers also needed a bayonet but, with little hand-to-hand combat and practically no heavy cavalry charges to repel, few soldiers missed it as a weapon but often found it useful as a tool. Because uniforms served primarily as protective covering and only secondarily to distinguish friend from foe, civilian clothes as well as captured uniforms could substitute. The mounted service could draw upon a plentiful supply of horses and many experienced civilian riders. It took both governments time to find enough of the cavalryman's traditional equipment of pistol and saber, but substitutes abounded, at least one unit arming itself with shotguns and hatchets.

Equipping the artillery proved less difficult than one would have expected because the United States had many cannon distributed across the country in forts, in the hands of militia units, and in arsenals. In addition, existing foundries could make the smoothbore, muzzle-loading guns which soldiers preferred. Both armies had the more complicated rifled cannon, but their drawbacks nullified the benefits of their great range and accuracy. Because their explosive shells tended to bury

6

themselves in the ground before exploding, they did little damage. Shrapnel shells, filled with powder and many small bullets, had a devastating effect when they exploded in the air above hostile troops; but the time fuses needed to make them explode at the correct distance were too inaccurate to make the ammunition dependable. Thus artillerymen preferred the older smoothbore cannon, and governments encountered no difficulty in providing the artillery's guns, wooden carriages and caissons, and horses for traction. Training men in their use presented no problems essentially different from those encountered in preparing the infantry and cavalry.

Like the army, the U.S. Navy, also a small professional force, provided the leadership for the huge naval forces created during the war. Having preformed well in the War of 1812, it continued to improve in the postwar period, when it kept abreast of technological change by adding steam power to its ships. The industrial development of the country adequately supported this change by providing a good machine-building industry and sound metallurgical capabilities. Like other navies, it foresaw the possibility of armoring ships with iron and had conducted experiments with cannon against armor.

Unlike the army, the navy provided the nucleus for the rapid wartime expansion. The United States's huge sail-powered merchant marine made this possible by providing expertise and a large reservoir of seamen and people suitable to become naval officers. These skilled men could make an easy transition to naval service because most of a sailor's knowledge consisted of the special and general tasks involved in operating a ship. Since a warship did not differ very much in its operation from a commercial vessel, prospective naval officers already knew many of their duties when, as masters or mates, they had learned how to sail, maneuver, supply, and navigate a ship. Those sailors and officers on a warship who needed to know how to operate and care for the guns, could learn routines fairly easily taught. The navy was in a position to expand rapidly while maintaining a high level of proficiency.

When naval operations began in the Civil War, the South had no navy to combat the Union's. As a result the U.S. naval forces, having no contest for command of the sea, could commence immediately the blockade of Confederate ports. Yet, of its 42 ships in commission, all but 11 were scattered all over the world, showing the flag and providing security for the United States's equally far-flung commerce. In the era before the international network of underwater telegraph cables, it took a long time to bring all these ships home. Nevertheless, the program of making ready for sea the navy's inactive ships and, particularly, buying and building new vessels brought such prompt expansion that by July 4, 1861, the North had 82 ships in commission.

Although the South had an extensive seacoast, it lacked the North's considerable shipbuilding industry and had no opportunity to establish a navy which could compete with the Union's at sea. It did create a small but active and a skillful force, which played a role in the fighting on the western rivers and in the defense of major ports. In support of these efforts the Confederacy built a number of steam gunboats for river and coast defense work, many of them armored.

The navy was not the only area of power or potential where the scales tipped in the North's favor. The Confederacy was a huge country, the area east of the Mississippi alone being twice the size of France. But the Union was far bigger and had 22,000,000 people to the Confederacy's 9,000,000. Of the 9,000,000 only the 5,500,000 whites could supply recruits. The South also had less industry proportionately than the North, having specialized in agriculture where it had a distinct comparative advantage as the world's dominant supplier of cotton. Still, it did have textile mills, ironmaking and -working establishments, and virtually all of the elements of the industrial revolution. This meant that it had the skills to produce what it needed for a war that had requirements little different from similar conflicts in previous centuries. Keeping the railroads running, particularly in the face of a shortage of iron ore, did prove very challenging, as did clothing the armies. The South needed captured uniforms, home-woven cloth, and home-tailoring to supplement imports and large scale production.

The Quartermaster Department did well in providing for the men, buying from independent contractors and operating its own works. In its Atlanta uniform establishment, for example, 20 tailors cut the cloth for uniforms and 3,000 seamstresses,

8

working under the time-honored putting-out system also used in the North, sewed the uniforms. In the fall of 1862 they produced jackets at the rate of 12,000 per month and pants at 4,500. The issue to the Army of Northern Virginia, July 1864–January 1865, illustrates the success of the Quartermaster Department. That army, numbering just over 70,000 men, received over 100,000 jackets and 140,000 trousers, an adequate provision considering that the soldiers wore out only two uniforms per year. In view of the far greater difficulty in securing shoes, it is remarkable that the Quartermaster Department issued Lee's army 146,000 pairs of shoes in that same seven-month period. Clearly this staff department continued to function well until the end of the war.

Oddly enough for an agricultural country, the troops often lacked sufficient food, in part because farms were slow in converting from cotton to food crops, failures in Confederate finance hampered procurement, and the railways could not always deliver enough on time. Nonetheless, the adequately armed Confederates kept the field.

Inferior in manpower and usually fielding armies only half the size of the North, the Confederacy early adopted conscription, a law that stimulated volunteering by many to avoid the stigma of becoming a conscript. The conscripts as well as the volunteers had a choice of unit, most joining those from their home towns. Later, in resorting to compulsion, the North never had as effective a manpower system and relied much more than the South on raising new regiments rather than keeping the old up to strength. This, together with a high turnover from the discharge of volunteers whose enlistments had expired, meant that Federal armies usually included a higher proportion of inexperienced men.

This was a war in which even the least industrialized of the combatants could supply the essentials to their armies. Since, along with this rough parity in supply, the belligerents enjoyed an equality both in the character and experience of most of their soldiers and the knowledge and competence of their few professional soldiers, the Union's main advantage lay in its naval supremacy and its superior numbers. The U.S. Navy gave invaluable service on the western rivers but failed in its main strategic objective, creating a blockade effective enough to

9

keep the Confederacy from importing most of what it needed. So the Union had to depend on its two-to-one numerical advantage to win.

As the defenders, the South had two major offsetting advantages: the immense size of their country and the traditional supremacy of the defense over the offense. The primitive communications of a country like the South could delay invading armies, and its geographical extent could swallow up a sizable force. The defender could either make use of some of this space to retreat or choose to fight a battle, relying on the dominance of the tactical defense to nullify the Federal force's superiority in numbers.

Although Lincoln made an initial call for only 75,000 men for just three months to suppress the rebellion, both combatants did act rapidly to mobilize their maximum military potential. In spite of a shortage of professional soldiers to train and lead the new armies, the tradition of the citizen soldier, the wide diffusion of literacy, and the enthusiastic response of all segments of the free society helped the quick creation of armies fully representative of the advanced economic and social development of the United States at mid-century. The country's modern regular army had opened its officer ranks to talent, and, through its military academy, subjected most of the candidates to a rigorous process of training and winnowing. From this excellent group came the small cadre of military leaders who provided the belligerents not only with an orthodox art of war but one that, when it matured, would prove sophisticated and innovative. Because of the fairly even match between the antagonists, much would depend on the quality of each's command and strategy.

CHAPTER 2

THE HIGH COMMANDS AND POLITICAL STRATEGY

———————•◦•———————

Kings have fought wars to humble a rival, to revenge an insult, even to bring Helen, the most beautiful woman in Greece, back from Troy. But most wars have a political basis or have needed political judgments and means to attain their ends. They require that military action respond to political objectives. Often, however, soldiers and statesmen have difficulty reconciling military means with political ends. Fortunately, American society facilitated the integration of political and military action.

This made it fairly easy to create a high command which could understand the war's political objectives and the military measures necessary to implement them. The country had much experience of war. Both northern and southern colonists had engaged in some fairly desperate fighting and shrewd diplomacy to wrest from Native Americans a broad foothold on the continent. Survival in the new world had required compulsory military service in the militia and arming virtually every man in the colony. Even when the frontier receded and the seaboard settlers no longer needed such preparedness, war with France and Canada continued to involve the seaboard colonists and their militias, a military tradition that continued through the Revolution, the War of 1812, and the Mexican War.

11

At the same time, the increasingly literate and democratic country had a high level of political interest and participation. In spite of politics having a substantial degree of partisanship and the North and South having distorted views of one another, in the Civil War the citizens and their political leaders had fairly shrewd insights into their adversaries as well as accurate perceptions of their own political cultures. This enabled them to understand the best way to integrate political and military objectives. They understood, for example, the tradition of compromising slavery and other issues between North and South, how the public would respond to military events, and approximately how hard and how long their people would fight for their war aims.

The command structures had the proper organization for combining political and military decisions. By the constitution and the precedent of previous wars, the presidents had the authority and responsibility to make both kinds of decisions. In the War of 1812 with Britain, President James Madison had determined strategy, managed supply, and selected commanders. A decade and a half before the Civil War, President James K. Polk had exercised direct command in the two-year war with Mexico. A former speaker of the House of Representatives and governor of Tennessee, Polk, as militarily ignorant as Madison, nevertheless proved a decisive leader. Though strongly opinionated, he did have the cabinet debate strategy and availed himself of the good advice of the general in chief of the Army, Major General Winfield Scott. Both Madison and Polk had selected civilian secretaries of war who had shown little ability to contribute to the management of the war effort or to the nation's strategy.

Guided by almost identical constitutions and following the same historical precedents, presidents Abraham Lincoln and Jefferson Davis quickly and firmly took command, following in the tradition of Madison and Polk in fully assuming their constitutional responsibilities for the military conduct of the war. Contemporaries and, later, some historians have criticized them for interfering in military operations. Since one can hardly call the exercise of a legitimate command interference, these critics really either disparaged certain of their military decisions or, implicitly endowing military command with a mystique

12

which enabled only the uniformed to exercise it, thought the presidents should have left the war entirely to the generals.

Each participated in military decisions and, had they wished to avoid this, they could have shirked their responsibilities only with difficulty. Both were, of course, well aware of President Polk's management of the Mexican War. Success endorsed this method and both presidents followed it, excepting, for the most part, cabinet participation in strategy, an exclusion that disappointed some in Lincoln's cabinet. Whereas in military command they had an exclusive prerogative, the presidents had the legislatures as partners in making war, depending on Congress for legislation and consent to some appointments as well as for appropriations. Partisanship also affected the behavior of the two congresses as well as their relations with the presidents. Particularly in the North, congressmen held decided views not only on strategy but also on which generals should command.

So, despite the role of Congress, the political and military aspects of the war united in the persons of the presidents. They had the duty not just to measure military means against political ends, but to concern themselves with the politics of the war. This ranged from treating military commands as political, and even patronage, appointments to harnessing public opinion to the war effort. Lincoln, initially faced with more overt dissent about the propriety and the aims of the war, gave greater attention than Davis to the politics of the war. Davis exploited the Confederacy's greater apparent unity and, when he met a conflict, in a promotion, for instance, between military and political needs, used his greater freedom more often to give preference to military considerations.

In appearance and manner the two presidents differed markedly: Lincoln, very tall and ungraceful, strongly contrasted with the trim, erect Davis. Unlike the cool, urbane Confederate, Lincoln had a warm, homespun manner and a habit of illustrating his points with stories, often amusing and always apt, that tended to make him seem rural and uncultured. Together with his relative inexperience in public office, these attributes made it difficult for Lincoln to command deference and ready acknowledgement of his authority and even caused some to patronize him. Davis had the opposite problem. He sometimes had difficulty suffering fools gladly, and when exhausted by

13

bad health and overwork, he alienated people by a brusque manner or a testy reaction.

In background the two chief executives also presented a strong contrast, seeming to have little in common but their Kentucky birth, Davis in 1808 and Lincoln in 1809. The Confederate president, looked after by his wealthy brother, graduated from West Point in 1828 and, after serving in the army for seven years, became a Mississippi planter and congressman. Although missing Davis's educational opportunities, the largely self-educated Lincoln read widely and acquired some of the elements of a classical education, including Euclidian geometry, a valuable background for someone who would later deal with military operations and their representation in two dimensions. Becoming a lawyer and serving in the Illinois legislature and, briefly, in the militia, Lincoln entered Congress just after Davis.

Davis resigned from Congress to fight in the Mexican War, giving a creditable performance commanding a regiment of Mississippi volunteers in the victorious defensive battle at Buena Vista. After the war, he entered the United States Senate and, in 1853, moved to President Pierce's cabinet. Here he did well as secretary of war, making the innovative decision to supply the army with camels in the arid southwest. Yet he also encountered considerable friction with the imposing figure of General in Chief Winfield Scott. Returning to the Senate, where he made a reputation for his emphatic but temperate advocacy of the pro-slavery point of view, Davis put his diverse military experience to good use by serving on the Committee on Military Affairs. The Confederate Provisional Congress chose him president, a choice ratified by a popular vote electing him for a six-year term.

Lincoln also soon left Congress but, after five years of devoting himself to building up his law practice, he returned to politics and by 1858 became the Republican nominee for the Senate. Though the legislature elected his opponent, the short, robust "Little Giant" of the Democratic Party, Stephen A. Douglas, Lincoln became a national figure through his outstanding performance in a series of debates with Douglas. These led to the Republican presidential nomination and to his defeat of Douglas and two other candidates in the election of 1860.

Alike in their success in politics and their other vocations, one as lawyer and the other as planter, Davis and Lincoln also had in common that both had only regional political strength. The issue of slavery and its possible expansion precluded any politician from having universal appeal. Yet they differed in that in gaining his presidency Lincoln had successfully dealt with a complex political situation whereas Davis had attained his without seeking the office. Still, these differences in their political backgrounds are mere nuances when compared with the strong contrast of Davis's military and administrative knowledge and experience with Lincoln's total lack of any background in managing any organization and his unfamiliarity with military affairs. With his service in the regular army, his combat command in the Mexican War, and his administrative and military experience as secretary of war, Davis had equal or superior qualification for high military command than anyone in the country of suitable age.

This military knowledge would be Davis's strength but also his weakness, for it tempted him to focus more on military management and give to finance, supply, diplomacy, and the politics of the war less attention than they deserved. Lincoln's ignorance served him well in that it deterred him from giving military operations too much of his time and energy but served him badly in that he had so much to learn, not just about the art of war but about how such a large and complex organization as an army ought to work. In his first two years in office, Lincoln devoted his strong intelligence and the problem-solving talents gained in his law practice to studying and acquiring the essence of the art of war of his day. Thus, in spite of their different backgrounds, as military commanders in chief Lincoln and Davis ultimately had far more similarities than differences.

They also shared a traditional approach to the appointment of their secretaries of war. Both used the position, as they did other cabinet posts, to recognize or propitiate important political interest groups or states. To meet a political commitment, Lincoln appointed Simon Cameron, the wealthy and powerful boss of the Pennsylvania Republican party. Although Cameron

15

had administrative experience from his banking and railway interests, it did not suffice to counterbalance his military ignorance and his absorption with the political aspects of his job, particularly the awarding of contracts. Lincoln soon had to seek his resignation and send him far away as minister to Russia. On the other hand, Lincoln was fortunate in having the counsel of General in Chief Winfield Scott, one of the ablest soldiers in the nation's history.

Although he had fewer political obligations to meet, Davis proved no more successful in his initial appointment of a secretary of war. He chose the prominent Alabama political leader and strong proponent of secession, Leroy Pope Walker. Experienced in the legislature and as a judge and regarded as the most popular man in Alabama, Walker lacked both the administrative experience and the military knowledge to manage the creation of a huge, modern war machine. Davis soon found it necessary to shunt Walker aside with an appointment as a brigadier general with a minor command. Unlike Lincoln, Davis had inherited no general in chief from a previous administration and initially appointed none. His friction with General in Chief Scott when he was secretary of war may have contributed to this decision as did his appointment of Samuel Cooper to the potentially important position of adjutant and inspector general of the Confederate Army. Cooper had been adjutant general of the U.S. Army and Davis's ally in his disputes with Scott. But, if Davis expected to gain from Cooper valuable advice and strategic vision, he met with disappointment, as Cooper proved little more than a clerk and an adequate shuffler of paper, wise only in the ways of the old army.

Despite these faulty initial appointments, both North and South were fortunate in their choice of commanders in chief. Each man possessed the necessary ability and character to make and adhere to the difficult decisions the war would require. And few leaders would face such daunting tasks. Although the slave states of Missouri and Kentucky had not seceded, factions favoring the Union and Confederacy contested for control of each. Political and potential military conflicts marked these areas and would not wait for the governments or the armies to decide they were ready to begin the contest.

In Missouri secessionists threatened St. Louis, but vigorous political leadership by Francis Preston Blair, Jr., brother of Lincoln's postmaster general, and military knowledge and energy from Captain Nathaniel Lyon of the regular army thwarted their efforts. After securing St. Louis, Lyon advanced westward along the Missouri River, taking the state capital of Jefferson City and, on June 1, defeating the pro-Confederate forces in the Battle of Boonville. Having first retreated into Arkansas, the Confederates returned with reinforcements to conquer Missouri, again meeting Lyon in battle. Although Lyon died in August in his losing battle on Wilson's Creek in the southwest part of the state, the aggressive action of his outnumbered force had halted the Confederate advance.

In the summer Lincoln appointed the nationally prominent Republican John C. Frémont to the military command in Missouri and the adjacent areas east of the Mississippi. Before he was 35, Frémont displayed leadership in extensive and important explorations in the West that had earned him the sobriquet "Pathfinder of the West." An important role in the conquest of California during the Mexican War had added to his fame. His renown, together with his well-known opposition to slavery, earned him the Republican party's first presidential nomination in 1856. With Democratic ties from his marriage to the daughter of the late Thomas Hart Benton, for thirty years Democratic senator from Missouri, Frémont seemed especially well suited for the appointment to command in a state where military action took place amidst a confused and delicate political situation. Instead, Frémont proved a serious disappointment.

Although he had held a commission as second lieutenant in the engineers and had briefly held a command in California, Frémont lacked useful military training or background and was devoid of administrative experience. Even in politics he had little seasoning, having held office only once, as senator from California for a few months. Now he quickly assembled an immense and largely ornamental headquarters staff and mismanaged government contracts at a time when many people, dishonest as well as inept, sought to supply the government's wants.

Soon he naively subverted Lincoln's policy of conciliating slaveholders when he issued a proclamation confiscating the property of all Missourians in rebellion and freeing their slaves, giving credence to one critic's view that Frémont had "all of the qualities of genius except ability." This blunder prompted Lincoln to send a political-military investigating committee composed of Postmaster General Montgomery Blair and the Army's quartermaster general, Montgomery C. Meigs. When their investigation revealed Frémont's military as well as political unsuitability, Lincoln transferred the politically important general to a command in western Virginia and replaced him with a newly appointed major general in the regular army, H. W. Halleck.

The antithesis of Frémont, General Halleck lacked the "Pathfinder's" personal appeal and glamour but possessed ability in abundance, so much so that he had earned the nickname "Old Brains." A West Point graduate who had served in California in the Mexican War, he remained in California when the war ended. There he became secretary of state, studied law, and left the army, after fifteen years of service, just as he received promotion to captain. By 1861 he had made a fortune as a lawyer and in land and railway investments. Still he found time to serve as a major general in the California militia, make a translation of Spanish and Mexican land law, and write a valuable book on international law. Earlier he had shown his scholarly interests when he authored a book on the art of war and a study of bitumin, which doubtless prompted Harvard to offer him the professorship of engineering.

Halleck's time spent as California's secretary of state and in the presidency of a small railroad gave him administrative experience which augmented his knowledge of army procedures. He applied his keen intelligence and relentless energy to bring order and system to the St. Louis headquarters. At the same time he concentrated his forces to consolidate Union dominance in Missouri, a task facilitated by his control of the Mississippi and Missouri rivers and by the use of the three railroads which radiated south and west from St. Louis.

Another border state, Kentucky, divided between a governor favoring secession and a legislature opposed, was seeking to maintain its neutrality. This had resulted in the accumulation of Union and Confederate military forces on its borders and their movement into the state when, without Davis's approval, the Confederate commander in West Tennessee precipitated military action in August by taking control of Columbus, Kentucky, a defensible town and railway terminus on the Mississippi. This had the effect of destroying Kentucky's neutrality and removing the state as a valuable military buffer for the Confederacy. Responding immediately, Union forces moved in and, as a consequence, the Confederates occupied the southern part of the central and western sections of the state and the Federals the northern, with neither doing much to control the rugged and thinly populated east.

Meanwhile, the western counties of Virginia fought to stay with the Union, fending off small numbers of Confederates who sought to control this mountainous area of few slaves. Federal troops from Ohio intervened to help save this region for the Union. The virtually bloodless first conflict earned the title the Philippi Races, owing to the promptness and speed of the Confederate retreat. A month later in July 1861 at Rich Mountain, both combatants fought well. The Union won, but, despite their victory, a strategic stalemate ensued, the mountainous country with few people and poor roads making supply exceptionally difficult and the defense very strong.

These operations brought to the attention of the Union government the young commander who had led his troops from Ohio to victory in battle. George B. McClellan, Mac to his friends, had much in common with Halleck in that both had left the Army as captains and returned as major generals after successful business careers. McClellan differed markedly from Halleck in that he did not share Halleck's unprepossessing appearance and demeanor. In his mid-30s, a decade younger than Halleck, his trim five-feet eight-inch figure and his forty-five-inch chest gave him an imposing appearance, especially when mounted on a horse. His attractive manner appealed to the soldiers' imagination and he readily gained their loyalty.

Although Maryland, another border state with slaves, had southern sympathizers and provided a few volunteers for the Confederate Army, no struggle for the state occurred. The only violence in that state took place when some citizens of Baltimore stoned a militia unit from the North as it marched through the city's streets on its way to Washington. Even if Marylanders had possessed a more active sympathy for the South, the presence of large forces in the District of Columbia would have discouraged any overt support of the Confederacy, just as they cut off easy contact with Virginia.

Besides waging the struggles for the border states, the high commands had to give some thought to their overall strategy. For the Confederates the goal was simply to keep what they had. By establishing its independence, the South had started the war victorious and need only hold onto what secession had given it and, if possible, add Missouri and Kentucky which the Confederacy claimed. Lincoln faced a more complex situation.

Military strategy aims to deplete the hostile military force. Military and political leaders have long had the ideal of doing this quickly through an annihilating victory in a big battle, but this depletion usually comes gradually through attrition. The wear and tear of marches as well as skirmishes, sieges, and battles accumulate losses due to attrition, the by-product of almost any military operation.

The close relationship between politics, on the one hand, and military strategy and the actions of armies, on the other, has meant that strategy and politics have traditionally gone hand in hand, a point emphasized by the renowned German military scholar Karl von Clausewitz. Through most of history countries usually had good coordination because kings often also commanded armies or at least experienced close supervision of military operations. Presidents Madison and Polk both had civil and military power, but they lacked the military expertise so often characteristic of kings; Lincoln's situation did not differ from theirs.

General in Chief Winfield Scott had the combination of qualities, both military and political knowledge, so often associated with kings. But the vastly overweight Scott, who would reach 75 in June 1861, lacked the physical vigor to match his still unimpaired mental faculties. Subject to vertigo and too infirm to mount a horse, he could not give Lincoln as much help as he needed. Still, since he had a thorough understanding of strategy and the capabilities and limitations of military force, he could provide valuable strategic guidance.

Having begun his military service as a captain of artillery in 1808, he suffered two wounds in the War of 1812 and reached the rank of brigadier general before the age of 30. Thus he had ample military experience before becoming general in chief and conducting his brilliant command in the Mexican War. General Scott amplified his broad and outstandingly successful military experience with diplomatic missions, and his Whig presidential candidacy in 1852 deepened his knowledge of domestic politics. Since a civil war demanded familiarity with the political situation, Scott had a good preparation for formulating strategy. As one would expect, the plan he proposed in the spring of 1861 clearly reconciled military realities with what he saw as a political opportunity.

Instead of a military strategy directed at depleting rebel armed forces, Scott proposed a political strategy, one which aimed at securing political results directly. Realizing the difficulty of subduing so large a country as the Confederacy, he thought in terms of military measures that would have a political effect and so help bring the rebels to terms.

Consistent with his concept of the integration of political and military measures, Scott proposed to blockade the coasts of the rebelling states while at the same time sending an expedition down the Mississippi River to control and open it to Union navigation. Holding the river, an important issue and symbol in the early history of the republic, would also sever the Confederacy into two parts, separating Arkansas, Texas, and most of Louisiana from the remaining states east of the river. His strategy to "clear out and keep open this great line of communication in connection with the strict blockade of the seaboard" sought "to envelop the insurgent states and bring them to terms with less bloodshed than any other plan." This proposal failed to capture the imagination of political leaders or public, the newspapers finding little appeal in such a deliberate and undramatic approach and dubbing it the anaconda strategy, after the snake that squeezes its prey to death.

Scott realized that such a strategy would not defeat a determined opponent, self-sufficient in most necessary products. But, since the South derived much income from exports, particularly cotton and tobacco, the blockade would impose economic hardship. Moreover, when combined with Union control of the Mississippi, it would show that the Confederacy had not truly made good its independence. Scott doubtless saw that the

21

best prospect that his strategy offered was that it could lead to negotiation and reunion through a political settlement of the secession crisis, just as the Missouri Compromise and the Compromise of 1850 had reconciled sectional differences. To his mind, the political situation suggested that neither side had an unalterable determination to fight it out.

In the North those who had favored the immediate abolition of slavery saw the war as an opportunity to accomplish this goal. Most had supported Lincoln for president in 1860, but, though he opposed slavery, he did not agree with the abolitionists. They wished to add their goal to the stated aim of the war, the preservation of the Union. Many in the North opposed their radical view as too extreme, and some felt that making the manumission of slaves a war aim would create an insuperable barrier to a quick and easy restoration of the Union. Not only did the dissonance between these groups undermine the coherence of the Union's war effort, but there were others who would have preferred to let the seceding states go rather than use force to keep them in the Union.

The Confederacy also faced a fissure among its citizens, one more divisive but less serious because there were comparatively few who, after secession, continued to oppose the establishment of the Confederacy. The sentiment of adherence to the Union had dominance only among the citizens of the mountainous regions, being strongest in northwestern Virginia and East Tennessee, and, to a lesser degree, western North Carolina. Yet a considerable number of Southerners, most often without slaves, had opposed secession and, presumably, lacked zeal for the war for independence, one precipitated by the threat to slavery which many in the South saw in Lincoln's election. Thus, though the outbreak of war created in the South a more impressive façade of unity than in the North, this may have obscured only tepid support by many.

Southerners differed also in the expectation of what secession would bring. Many anticipated a short war. Only a few predicted the arduous, four-year struggle that ensued, and some foresaw a compromise with little or no fighting. Scott's plan catered to the conflicting opinions on both sides. These divisions opened the possibility that a concession from the North could combine with Scott's anaconda pressure to rally to the Union those in the South who lacked much zeal for a separate nation. Whether or not Scott was optimistic, he believed that political strategy should have a chance first when compared with his vision of what military strategy would require for a victory. He forecast 300,000 trained Union soldiers fighting for two or three years, and over a third of the number dead as a result of combat and disease. His projection turned out to be an underestimate but quite a contrast to Lincoln's call for 75,000 men for three months.

The political situation seemed also to suggest fighting the war with care for the sensibilities of the enemy civilians to avoid alienating latent support for peace. In view of the political objective of the war, reunion rather than conquest, Scott's policy of conciliation appealed to many in 1861. In his July 4, 1861, message to Congress Lincoln asked "whether there is, today, a majority of legally qualified voters of any State, except perhaps South Carolina, in favor of disunion." To avoid estranging these pro-Union voters, he followed a conciliatory policy like Scott's proposal, promising that the armies would shun "any devastation, any destruction of, or interference with, property, or any disturbance of peaceful citizens."

Not all Northerners agreed with the conciliatory approach. Some, especially those most adamant against slavery, wanted to do something more positive about civilians in rebellion. The issue revolved around the fact that when armies operate in the enemy's country, the soldiers, even if pursuing a military strategy of depleting the hostile army, are often faced with deciding the political question of how to treat the civilians. The behavior of the soldiers toward enemy civilians would have important political consequences. They could attempt to intimidate them; but to do so would run the risk of intensifying armed civilian resistance. On the other hand, the soldiers could adopt a political policy of conciliation, seeking to placate opposition and by this behavior offer an apparent reduction of the cost of defeat. But this gentle approach could create the impression of infirmity of purpose and could foster in the enemy civilians a contemptuous recalcitrance.

Soldiers tended to see the merit of propitiating civilians, as did William T. Sherman, brother of an Ohio congressman who moved to the Senate in 1861. This politically acute soldier feared

23

that the newly enlisted volunteer soldiers, quite undisciplined, would, by their "petty thieving and pillaging," do the Union cause "infinite harm" by engendering more antipathy to the Union and its forces. Earlier, when campaigning in Virginia, he worried that the volunteers would have no "respect for the lives and property of friends and foes," and so "henceforth we should never hope for any friends in Virginia." The less politically attuned regular engineer officer, George G. Meade, who became an important Union general, expressed another version of the same outlook when he declared that the Union should wage the war "like the afflicted parent who is compelled to chastise this erring child, and who performs the duty with a sad heart."

Many of the officers understood the political issues of the war and the rationale for a policy of conciliation. Moreover, they found this an easy course to follow because military practice for nearly two centuries had aimed at avoiding the hostility of civilians, and international law offered protection to civilians in wars between nations as long as they did not resist the invader. So military practice and the outlook of many officers harmonized with Scott's political approach. Yet soldiers had little immediate opportunity to practice such restraint because no major conquest of rebel territory directly followed secession.

Both commanders in chief saw the wisdom of waiting for major operations until completing the organization and training of the armies. Alike in this decision, they also shared the fundamental attributes of high ability, dedication to their cause, and the capacity to make difficult decisions without flinching. With more military knowledge, Davis had the easier task, the defense, while Lincoln had the advice of the venerable Scott. Wise in politics as well as war, Scott recommended a political strategy which sought to avoid the costly and divisive search for a military victory. Although Lincoln did not formally adopt Scott's anaconda plan, he proclaimed a blockade and applied part of it by default because the army was unready to attempt a military strategy, and, in any case, the navy would have applied its traditional strategy of blockade.

The soldiers fighting in the highly political environment of western Virginia and Missouri did apply military strategy, the Union troops defeating and driving back the rebels, thus keeping Missouri and much of the future state of West Virginia in the Union. But the biggest battle of the year occurred near Washington in July 1861. It had a political rather than a military inspiration in that it occurred in response to the impatience felt by many in the North for the army to begin suppressing the rebellion and the need to drive the rebel army away from the vicinity of Washington.

CHAPTER 3

MANASSAS, A REPRESENTATIVE BATTLE

The Battle of Manassas involved more soldiers than any battle in American history up to that time. The war's first large-scale combat, in its maneuvers and the dominance of the tactical defense, it embodied the characteristics of all of the succeeding battles. It had this representative character in part because of the determining influence of tactics, that branch of the art of war having to do with the conduct of combat. The tactics of the time centered primarily on infantry fighting. The formations and drill had the purpose of enabling commanders to maneuver groups of men who, in turn, worked together and adopted the best array for marching or using their rifles.

In 1861 the Union and Confederate armies employed the same tactics, taken from French Army manuals. Organized in infantry regiments of about 500 men divided into ten companies, armies formed brigades of two to five regiments, divisions of two to five brigades, and, sometimes, corps of two or more divisions. Regiments marched on roads in long columns and, when going to battle, often marched across country in compact formations from which they could deploy into one or more lines of two rows each. The line constituted the fighting formation because from it the largest number of soldiers could fire their smoothbore or rifled muskets, a powerful, slow-firing muzzle-loader. Inaccurate shooting combined with the hilly and wooded terrain of most combat meant that soldiers engaged in little long-range fire. Soldiers stood or knelt to shoot because of the difficulties of reloading a muzzle-loader in the prone position. The defender enjoyed a considerable advantage over the attacker.

The infantry's preparation for battle consisted of drill, the constant repetition of such maneuvers as forming a line of battle, changing the direction of the line of battle by 90 degrees, and forming a square to offer all-around defense. Thorough practice in these movements enabled the companies, regiments, and brigades to maneuver quickly on the battlefield. Even after combat began and it became difficult or impossible to maneuver, the spirit of the unity of the group, instilled by the constant drill, remained and helped the men to fight together and to stay an organized body even in retreat. In addition to drill, a knowledge of field fortifications would become important during the war. Most of the West Point graduates knew the defensive value of creating breastworks or other types of entrenchments, and the soldiers learned to do this, to improvise by using fence rails to make a rampart, and to gain protection by standing behind a tree when reloading.

In the Civil War cavalry rarely fought infantry unless it dismounted. The armies, following the tradition of the U.S. Army, had little cavalry trained to make a mounted charge against infantry, and the forests of the eastern United States made it difficult to use such cavalry. So cavalry played little part in battles, making its significant contribution in reconnaissance and raiding enemy communications.

The infantry had powerful help from the field artillery, which used smooth-bore, muzzle-loading cannon firing balls weighing four to twelve pounds. In addition to a single ball, the cannon could, by analogy with a shotgun, fire grape or cannister, groups of smaller shot. These shot were particularly effective on the defense and could carry as far as 400 yards. Artillery helped the attackers very little in comparison to the great power it conferred on the already dominant defense.

The new soldiers' tactical skill received a trial in the first big engagement of the war when two armies, equally matched at about 30,000 men, faced one another near Manassas, Virginia, on July 21, 1861. Essentially infantry forces, the men consisted largely of volunteers with two or three months' service. Their generals, though regulars, faced tasks almost as unfamiliar and for which nothing comparable to drill had prepared them. Brigadier General Irvin McDowell, recently a major in the regular army, commanded the Union force. A West Point graduate, McDowell had studied in France, taught at the Military Academy, fought with distinction in a Mexican War battle, but had practically no experience in command.

In their unfitness for their difficult responsibilities the Confederate generals differed little from their northern counterparts. The South's commander, Brigadier General Beauregard, also a former major in the U.S. Army, had served on Scott's informal staff in Mexico but had little more relevant experience than his opponent. Before the battle started, Brigadier General Joseph E. Johnston, who had arrived with the Confederate reinforcements, assumed command on account of his seniority. A decade older than Beauregard and formerly one of the most respected officers in the U.S. Army, Johnston had fought the Seminole Indians and the Mexicans with Scott. Having served in the artillery, engineers, cavalry, and in combat with infantry, in 1860 he had become quartermaster general with the rank of brigadier general. But he, too, lacked experience directing a force even a tenth as large as his and Beauregard's army.

When he had proposed his slow-acting, politically attuned anaconda strategy, General Scott rightly feared that "the impatience of our patriotic and loyal Union friends" would demand quicker and more combative action by the untrained armies. When the administration responded to the popular demand for an offensive against the Confederate army insolently stationed just a few miles from Washington, General Scott sent his forces forward under McDowell's command to execute a plan which he had approved. By the evening of 20 July, McDowell had his men in place with rations prepared and everything ready for an attack the next day. The armies faced each other on opposite sides of Bull Run.

Beauregard, now under Johnston's direction, had not received the last of Johnston's brigades nor had he completed his plan for an attack with his right. In fact, his staff would not finish writing the orders until it was almost time for the attack to begin. McDowell, who, like Beauregard, had adhered to his West Point instruction and entrenched, was ready to begin his attack at daylight the next morning. His plan followed the model established by Scott in the Mexican War. Using what Civil War soldiers called a turning movement, he would send part of his army on a march around the Confederate flank and attack in the rear. McDowell ordered 12,000 men, 40 percent of his force, to march around the Confederates' weak left flank into their rear while 8,000 men distracted the defenders with a frontal assault on the bridge at the extremity of the rebel left.

In spite of the difficulties of moving so many inexperienced men, the turning column, the real attackers, had crossed Bull Run by 9:30 A.M. But the assault on the bridge, already begun by this time, showed such a lack of earnestness that it failed to hold the attention of the Confederate commander, Colonel N. G. Evans, a West Point graduate and former regular army officer. Instead of heeding only the bridge in his front, the vigilant Colonel Evans, alerted by an observation post, detected the Union turning movement and moved half of his brigade to resist it. Thus McDowell lost the opportunity to surprise his antagonist and assail a weak flank in the rear. Reluctant to abandon his plan to assail the Union left, Beauregard at first ordered the attack but also moved two of Johnston's brigades from the right to the left, forming them with Evans's men at right angles to his main line and directly before the advancing Union turning force (see diagram of Battle of Manassas 1). This brought the antagonists into frontal combat, virtually the only kind known to war because soldiers who cannot face their enemy usually flee or surrender.

Although the turning movement had deprived the Confederate defenders of the benefit of Bull Run and of their entrenchments, they still had the defenders' powerful advantage when using a missile weapon against those similarly armed and any who expected to engage in hand-to-hand combat. General Helmuth von Moltke, the Prussian chief of staff at this time, explained the defenders' superiority thus: "It is absolutely beyond doubt that the man who shoots without stirring has the advantage of him who fires while advancing, that the one finds

29

protection in the ground, whereas in it the other finds obstacles, and that, if to the most spirited dash one opposes a quiet steadiness, it is fire effect, nowadays so powerful, which will determine the issue."

To carry out an assault, regiments formed into two lines and advanced, often beside the other regiments in the brigade, and followed at a 200- or 300-yard interval by regiments of another brigade. Two months' experience of soldiering had prepared Union troops to go from march to battle formation and carry out an attack on the outnumbered Confederate defenders.

With regular officers, generals David Hunter and Samuel Heintzelman, in command, the Union forces began to use their superior numbers to outflank the Confederate left. At the same time Colonel William T. Sherman's brigade, part of the division which had ineffectually tried to distract Evans, succeeded in carrying out McDowell's new order to cross Bull Run and assail the right flank of the new Confederate line facing Hunter and Heintzelman. Union frontal pressure and the menace to both flanks caused the defending Southerners to conduct a panicky retreat to a hill almost a mile in the rear. The arrival of both their generals instilled courage and life into the Confederate soldiers, and reinforcements in the form of Brigadier General Thomas J. Jackson with another of Johnston's brigades provided tangible assistance. Jackson earned his nickname "Stonewall" here at Manassas by his stout defense, as Beauregard commanded on the hill and Johnston attended to rushing up reinforcements.

The men's practice at drill enabled them to move into position, but, when the firing started, the situation changed. Failed assaults, and most did fail, often resulted in the men on the offensive taking cover at a distance and firing at the defenders, thus acting much in the traditional manner of skirmishers. Thus for most of the battle the assailants and defenders behaved in much the same way. As a defending South Carolina participant explained, "A battle is entered into mostly in as good order and with as close a drill front as the nature of the ground will permit, but at the first 'pop! pop!' of the rifles there comes a sudden loosening of the ranks, a freeing of selves from the impediment of contact, and every man goes to fighting on his own hook; firing as, and when he likes, and reloading as fast as he fires." As in skirmishing, each soldier "takes shelter wherever he can find it, so he does not get too far away from his company, and his officers will call his attention to this should he move too far. He may stand up, he may kneel down, he may lie down, and it is all right—though mostly the men keep standing, except when silent under fire, then they lie down."

Individual rather than group fire almost always characterized battles. Yet, though the troops have quite properly abandoned their formations, the unit spirit, aided by the experience of drill, continued. That the soldiers at Manassas displayed this is revealed by the South Carolinian's remarks that a "battle is too busy a time, and too absorbing, to admit of a good deal of talk. Still you will hear such remarks and questions as: 'How many cartridges you got?' 'My gun's getting mighty dirty.' 'What's become of Jones?' 'Looky here, Butler, mind how you shoot; that ball didn't miss my head two inches'—'Just keep cool will you; I've got better sense than to shoot anybody'—'Well, I don't like you standing so close behind me nohow.' " Sometimes the soldiers were fortunate to see each other, or the enemy, for the black powder smoke of the rifles and cannon often obscured much of the battlefield, further handicapping accurate shooting.

As the South Carolinian's account shows, the soldiers, volunteers on both sides, displayed courage and fortitude, with their officers setting a good example. McDowell himself led units in attacks. The advantage of the defense offset the Union's superior numbers until, at about four in the afternoon, the Confederates, having added three more brigades, including another of Johnston's just off the train, could then extend their line to menace the Union right flank. As they began thus to turn the turning movement, McDowell's men began to fall back, signalling the end of the battle (see diagram of Battle of Manassas 2).

In its character this battle did not differ from those of the French Revolution and Napoleon. In all of these, survivors of failed charges frequently joined skirmishers to maintain a fire against the defenders; efforts to rally survivors and inspire them to make another assault more often succeeded when fresh troops had joined for the attack.

The events and duration of battle depleted the physical and

31

moral energies of those involved, but fresh troops, formed and responsive to orders, could hearten the defenders or give new impetus to assailants. Experienced commanders called this "feeding" the fight. Some said the technique of winning depended on feeding in just enough resources so as to avoid defeat until one had outlasted the enemy and could commit the final and winning increment of reserves. That the Confederates' last reinforcements enabled them to begin a counterattacking movement illustrated this concept and the validity of the adage that he who uses the final reserve of fresh troops last will win the battle.

The pattern of the action also exhibited the reason for the misgiving some commanders felt about dividing an army to carry out a turning movement. In compelling the enemy to form its line in a right angle, the Union turning movement had given the Confederates a shorter route between their flanks. They exploited this situation by moving troops easily to redress the balance of forces on their left, so that by the end of the day they had committed 8 of their 11 brigades against 7 of McDowell's 11. Thus the rebels thwarted a turning movement that could well have driven them from the field. But even without the surprise needed to attain that level of success, the maneuver had given the Union army the opportunity to attack without facing either the obstacle of Bull Run or the strength of the Confederate entrenchments.

Quicker than Beauregard to grasp the menace of the Federal turning movement, Johnston had commanded well, dividing responsibilities by having Beauregard direct the battle and devoting his own energies to moving men to the fighting. Though much too reluctant to admit that the enemy's initiative had precluded his planned attack, Beauregard carried out his duties competently and probably learned more from his battle experience than either Johnston or McDowell. The Union commander had performed quite effectively in making and executing his excellent plan, the failure of an attack against equal numbers in no way disparaging the general or his men. Had McDowell's subordinates more earnestly assaulted the bridge, they could well have so distracted Colonel Evans as to have given victory to the well-conceived Union plan.

The battle also showed the power of the counterattack, the

32

most effective form of the offensive. Likely to attain surprise, it strikes an opponent engaged in attacking who is psychologically as well as in his dispositions unready to receive an assault. So the Union forces began retreating when faced more with the threat than the actuality of their antagonist's move. Because the attacker is unready to defend, this is also the form of attack which can best disorganize the enemy and so inflict serious casualties on the defeated. In this instance, the early Federal withdrawal and the victor's own disorganization precluded the actual execution of the counterattack.

Manassas differed from those a half century earlier in that cavalry took little part. J. E. B. Stuart's regiment arrived in time to charge the enemy, but did not significantly affect the course of the conflict. Nor did artillery effect the battle's course decisively, even though some Union guns supported the attackers until Confederate infantry captured them. In future engagements, artillery would have more importance, especially in defending the entrenchments which would increasingly characterize Civil War combat. Although at the Battle of Bull Run the turning movement precluded the use of the entrenchments Beauregard had dug along his front, in later confrontations soldiers would learn how to improvise their own breastworks.

The pattern of the battle seemed little influenced by the fact that many men on each side had rifles. As Europeans discovered in the 1850s, the muzzle-loading rifle seems to have made a difference of degree in tactics rather than a difference in kind. Certainly, if cavalry had charged between the lines, the longer range and more accurate weapons would have markedly diminished the horsemen's chances of success, just as the rifles could have made gunners more vulnerable if they had sought to fire their grape and cannister shot at defending infantry. In future battles the artillery would rarely try to help the attack, because of the artillerymen's vulnerability to rifle fire and because trees and rolling terrain obstructed the fire of the cannon. Further, artillerymen knew that their fire would have less effect on entrenched defenders, even those in hastily dug rifle pits or behind piled-up fence rails.

The immediate effect of the Battle of Manassas was to cool the ardor for combat until each belligerent had the opportunity to raise more men and train them more thoroughly. And this battle can also tell us much about the role of battles in the war, of the significance of victory and defeat, and of their possible strategic importance.

McDowell's use of a turning movement would characterize most other Civil War battles, as would its failure. The same facility for movement, given to attackers by maneuvers the soldiers had learned, the defenders could use to change direction in order to face their adversary. The dominance of the defender, even without the aid of entrenchments, constituted the other representative characteristic of this major combat. But the primacy of the tactical defense has typified all combat between soldiers armed alike. And no two adversaries could have been more alike than the Union and Confederate armies. In other respects also the battle would resemble the others in the war and those which had occurred in the past.

After the battle of Union army made a confused and disorganized withdrawal to the vicinity of Washington, intermingling with some ladies and gentlemen who had driven out from Washington in carriages to picnic and see the victory. Considering their lack of training and experience and the demoralizing effect of defeat, the Union forces conducted their retirement as creditably as their battle. Traditionally retreat has signified defeat in battle. In this instance the retreat returned the armies to the situation which existed before the battle and confirmed the failure to attain the brief campaign's simple strategic aim: to drive the rebels from the vicinity of Washington.

But there are other ways to measure the outcome of a battle, and one of these is its tactical effect. The Union army had also suffered defeat when measured by the chief tactical index, casualties in terms of killed, wounded, and missing. McDowell's army, almost evenly matched in numbers with its antagonist, suffered 2,706 casualties, 9 percent of its force, the Confederates 1,981, 6.5 percent of their number available. Thus attrition favored the South, unless one considered that the South had less than half of the North's population. The ratio of losses between the victor and the vanquished followed that usual for the eighteenth century and Napoleonic wars, but the total losses amounted to less than the average. Lightness of casualties would not distinguish the Civil War, its overall percentages

34

closely paralleling the European average. Perhaps the green units lacked the cohesion and morale to attack with enough vigor to suffer and inflict greater losses.

Often a battle will have another means of determining victor and vanquished, an index available by comparing the effect of the symbolism of victory or defeat on the morale, outlook, and attitudes of soldiers and civilians on both sides. By analogy with combat losses of soldiers and equipment, one may speak of battle's political attrition. A defeat would dishearten civilians and soldiers, making them see victory as less certain, more distant in the future, and likely to involve greater costs and sacrifices. A victory would have a reverse effect, engendering optimism and a belief in winning in a reasonable time at a moderate cost. This result of success is, of course, not attrition at all in the sense of battle casualties, and it is doubtful whether the analogy will work in reverse. Morale and expectations are too fickle to enable us to have confidence in making a parallel of storing excess confidence for use in sustaining resolution in a time of adversity.

Most speculation about the Battle of Manassas holds that this defeat stimulated the Union war effort by making many believe that the country faced a difficult war, one requiring increased exertions. On the other hand, some think that the defeat reduced the future effectiveness of the Federal army in Virginia by making it feel inferior to its adversary. Similar conjectures about the effect of this victory on the Confederates suggest that it engendered a temporary complacency which made mobilization seem less urgent. But others think it also instilled a victory-fostering confidence in the Confederate army in Virginia. Yet commentators have typically given more attention to the question of the Confederate use of their victory and failure to pursue their defeated foe.

By the nineteenth century, soldiers had come to take pursuit for granted and many subscribed to what was almost a myth: A destructive pursuit was a natural concomitant of victory in battle. This seems to have resulted from generalizing a few instances into the usual and proper norm, then treating the majority of cases as aberrations from the normal, and attributing the lack of pursuit to lethargic commanders, a faulty theory of military operations, or even sympathy for the enemy.

35

Still, pursuit has not always seemed the obvious move after a victory. Belisarius, the renowned Byzantine general of the sixth century, thus warned of the danger of pursuit and the hazard of overtaking and fighting the enemy again: "So if we compel them against their will to abandon their purpose of withdrawing and come to battle with us, we shall win no advantage whatsoever if we are victorious—for why should one rout a fugitive?—while if we are unfortunate, as may happen, we shall both be deprived of the victory we now have, . . . and also we shall abandon the land of the Emperor to lie open to the attacks of the enemy without defenders." And, like Belisarius, many commanders have not always seen it as the obvious sequel to a victory. Some have viewed it as an opportunity to give the victorious army a well-deserved rest while the defeated endured the arduousness of retreat, losing men through straggling and horses and equipment to the hazards of the march. King Henry IV, the aggressive French battle leader, acted in this spirit when he used the respite earned by a victory to pay a visit to his mistress.

Although victory disorganized the Confederates as much as defeat did their opponent, the southern forces did attempt to follow the retreating Federals. But, with units thoroughly intermingled and even the unengaged troops tired from marching and countermarching as plans changed, they lacked the means to make an effective pursuit. Traditionally cavalry had had a major role in tactical pursuit because it had mobility superior to the infantry; but the Confederates had little cavalry. Further, the horsemen had lost much of their efficacy in executing this mission because they were weaker than infantry in a frontal fight.

The substitution of infantry for cavalry in pursuit meant that, in spite of the same marching speed, retreat moved faster than pursuit. The withdrawing force could do such things as burn bridges, sink boats, obstruct roads with fallen trees, remove road signs, even dig out fords to make them too deep for use. The army in flight could also leave a small force as a rear guard. This detachment, by forming for combat, could force those following to do the same. While the pursuers deployed their men to attack or to turn the rear guard's line of battle, the rear guard would resume its march formation and continue its retreat, leaving their adversary the time-consuming task of re-forming for march.

The decline in the combat effectiveness of cavalry against infantry does not provide the whole explanation for the inef-fectiveness of pursuit. The excellent system of drill and maneu-verability and the subdivision of armies into divisions, brigades, and regiments made them highly articulated and able to resist disorganization and continue to maneuver in the ad-versity of defeat. The Confederates at the Battle of Manassas clearly demonstrated the efficacy of this articulation when they found themselves assailed by two divisions in the rear of their weak flank and were fortunate in being able to redeploy and defend, even with only half of a brigade. Their performance of then facing two-thirds of their army in a new direction in time to win clearly exhibits this superb articulation in action even with ill-trained troops. The armies of veterans which the war quickly produced had far more of that toughness, suppleness, and maneuverability displayed at Manassas, attributes that made the armies virtually indestructible in battle as well as in retreat.

So the Confederates made only a brief and ineffectual tactical pursuit and no effort to make a strategic exploitation of the enemy's retreat to Washington. Some critics at the time and others since have faulted Johnston, Beauregard, and President Davis, who soon joined them on the scene, for not capitalizing on their victory by seeking to capture Washington. In fact, some have spilt much ink in a war of words over such an offensive's chances of success. Inferior in numbers and facing the barrier of the Potomac and the dominance of the tactical defensive, not surprisingly the three decided not to undertake a campaign against Washington and a defense directed by Gen-eral Scott himself. It is possible, however, that they might have taken and fortified a position close to the Potomac and from which artillery could have fired on Washington. Yet the com-mander of such a position could not but have felt acute anxiety in having the Potomac and Union warships on his flank, offer-ing Scott a fine opportunity to dispatch a force into his rear.

Even though the possibility of threatening Washington gave this battle a distinctiveness, its otherwise representative char-acter means that its story can substitute for much of the recounting of the events of subsequent battles. The most notable exception to this generalization is that the use of field fortifications steadily grew until, by the last year of the war, prospective attackers as well as defenders dug themselves in when near an adversary. But this only strengthened that power of the defense exhibited in the first big combat and in no way diminished either the desire to turn the enemy or that exemplary articulation which had made possible the quick move to turn and provided the celerity in redeployment needed to thwart it.

Although most battles share these tactical characteristics, they differ markedly in their tactical effect, the incidence of casualties, and the symbolic significance attached to defeat as manifested by retreat. Some had important strategic results, and almost all had a strategic context as generals tried to use battles to implement their strategy and exercised their knowledge of strategy to fight under the most advantageous circumstances. And just as the Battle of Manassas is representative of the war's tactics, so also does the strategy of the campaign exemplify one of the war's strategic constants.

CHAPTER 4

STRATEGIC CONCENTRATION IN SPACE

---◆---

Manassas, Fort Donelson, and Shiloh Campaigns

Confronted with the dominance of the tactical defense, Union and Confederate commanders naturally saw superior numbers as the way to overcome it. Coming to the war with larger armies offered one path to greater numbers, but concentration of more men at a single point presented another route, able either to multiply the force of bigger or equal armies or to compensate for inferior numbers—a capability valuable to the defense as well. But how could a commander concentrate more men without his adversary doing the same? Early in the war the situation in northern Virginia offered an opportunity for one kind of such concentration, a maneuver facilitated by the railroad and by another important fruit of the industrial revolution.

In the 1840s the electric telegraph came into widespread use, offering speed and reliability at so low a cost that its wires could reach medium-size and even small towns. Thus the high commands could have immediate contact with their armies in the field, and the armies in turn had communication with their sources of supply, with other armies in the theater, and, when they acquired portable systems, even with their own dispersed divisions.

When Virginia's capital, Richmond, also became the Confederacy's, the capitals of two huge countries lay only a hundred miles apart. These cities acted almost as magnet for troops, as the units raised in the more densely populated eastern seaboard flowed to Washington and to the Confederate armies in northern Virginia. These forces remained inactive as their commanders gave attention to training, seeking to convert civilians into soldiers. But the campaign of the Battle of Manassas involved more than pitting McDowell's army against Beauregard's. In addition to Holmes's small rebel force nearby at Acquia, 40 and more miles westward, beyond the low ridges of the Blue Ridge Mountains, two armies faced each other, J. E. Johnston's 12,000 Confederates at Winchester watching Robert Patterson's 18,000 Union soldiers 20 miles to the north. Unlike Beauregard and McDowell, who seemed cast in the same mold, Johnston and Patterson differed markedly. Patterson, unlike regular officer Johnston, had distinguished himself in banking and manufacturing in Pennsylvania as well as in a long affiliation with the militia, having had duty in the War of 1812 and the Mexican War. While Patterson would have great difficulty understanding what Scott wanted of him, Johnston would easily comprehend Davis's orders and act promptly.

The disposition of the four armies offered the Confederates an opportunity to exploit their interior lines of operation. To illustrate this situation, imagine an army of 100,000 men between two hostile armies of 50,000 each, separated from each other by 100 miles and from their adversary between them by 50 miles. This offers the army in between the strategic use of interior lines. To make the most of its position, the middle army must concentrate against first one antagonist and then the other, using its numerical superiority to beat each successively. The general would not usually fight with his whole army but would leave a small part of it to delay one of the hostile armies while he concentrated most of his men against the other. Thus the commander using interior lines would, with force equal to his enemy, outnumber him on each of the battlefields. Generals could use interior lines on the defense as well as the offense, as the Confederates showed when they maneuvered in order to give themselves the best opportunity to win the Battle of Manassas.

To counter the greater facility for concentration which their better rail communications gave the Confederates, Scott planned to employ the accepted antidote to interior lines: simultaneous advances. When McDowell carried out his movement against Beauregard, Scott planned for Patterson to "engage" Johnston or, if Johnston moved eastward, Patterson was to be "on his heels." On July 16, 1861, McDowell began his march toward Beauregard's position. The Confederates made the orthodox response when President Davis, notified by telegraph of McDowell's movement, wired Holmes and Johnston to reinforce Beauregard. Johnston moved promptly, marching his men to the railroad and then dispatching them the remainder of the distance by rail. Meanwhile he sent young Colonel J. E. B. Stuart with his cavalry regiment northward to distract Patterson. Johnston hardly needed to do this, for the confused Patterson was already retreating. So, though McDowell's offensive had given him the strategic initiative, the prompt Confederate response, made possible by the railroad and telegraph, seemed about to wrest it from him (see diagram of Manassas campaign).

Johnston, the senior of the two generals, overruled as too ambitious Beauregard's suggestion that Johnston's men meet his on the field of battle to take the enemy in the flank. Johnston contented himself with joining Beauregard with the bulk of his force on the day before McDowell planned to attack. In spite of the difficulty of moving green troops, the railroad enabled Johnston's army to reach the scene of the battle in time. McDowell had more trouble marching his 30,000 men 20 miles. Most were infantry, but cavalry, artillery, and wagons complicated a difficult task. Staffs had grown to accommodate the complexity of planning and executing just such movements, and McDowell, who at one time acted as his own staff officer when he rode in search of a missing artillery unit, now had a quite small and inexperienced staff, as did subordinates commanding the five divisions into which he had organized his army. Thus it required two and a half days to move 20 miles; seasoned troops normally marched 12 miles per day and could do more when the situation warranted the exertion.

In the Confederates' effective use of the telegraph and railroad to carry out a strategic defensive concentration, the cam-

41

paign of the impending Battle of Manassas established a pattern which would repeat itself more than once during the course of the war. It became such a cornerstone of Confederate strategic planning that generals often kept troops near railroads, poised to move should the telegraph bring the call.

The Confederate victory of Manassas had the strategic result of thwarting the Union's objective of pushing the rebel army farther away from Washington. Many Southerners criticized this as an inadequate strategic return for so fine a victory and thought the Confederates should have captured Washington. But even if this had been militarily possible, it might have offered only a debatable advantage. Since political objectives seemed to dictate the capture of Washington, many have conjectured about the effect in the North of the city's fall. Some have felt that it would have reinforced the numbers of those who favored letting the South secede and would have caused a disheartened North not to wage a war for the Union. Others have thought that it would only have weakened the Lincoln administration by causing many to assail it for incompetence. Others have disagreed, thinking that the loss of the capital to an aggressive Confederate move might have stimulated a war fever in the North and created more unity and greater exertions in the war effort. And some have speculated on the effect on the attitude and actions of Britain and France.

Besides the temptation to try to add Maryland to the Confederacy, what reasoning would have motivated the Confederate leaders to attempt to capitalize on the defeat of McDowell's army to take Washington? Doubtless some would have viewed it as an opportunity to cow the pusillanimous Yankees; but others, in the political climate of July 1861, might have seen the city's capture as a hindrance to the short war or compromise that some expected and more hoped for. Others would have viewed it as a means to secure recognition or other support from Europe, but how desirable would this have seemed to anyone who had reunion as a goal? So, to speculations as to whether the Confederates could have taken Washington, one should properly add those about whether and why the political leaders would have considered it a good idea and what political result would success have produced in the North.

With the northern public perhaps somewhat chastened by

the unexpected outcome of the advance to Manassas, Lincoln and Scott abandoned any idea of immediately trying to drive the rebel army away. The creation of armies had to come first, and to this task the Union applied itself. Immediately after the defeat at Manassas, the president called George B. McClellan to command the Army of the Potomac near Washington. The young general had the respect of his fellow regulars and, according to General in Chief Scott, the president and cabinet had found themselves "charmed by your activity, valor, and consequent success" in his brief campaign with small forces in western Virginia. McClellan, a former railroad executive, set to work with energy to organize and train an army that soon grew to more than 100,000 men. He performed brilliantly in the task of converting civilians into soldiers and a huge mob into an army organized and articulated to respond to the commands of its chief. Upon Scott's retirement in the early fall, Lincoln gave McClellan the additional duty of general in chief. "I can do it all," the young general assured the president.

But McClellan's concentration on thorough preparation meant that he allowed the balmy weather of the fall, the season of the lowest rainfall, to slip away without taking the offensive against his old army friend, J. E. Johnston. That this rebel army, almost disdainfully close to the capital, remained unmolested created a serious political problem for President Lincoln. While many people saw McClellan as the man of the hour and most of his soldiers idolized him, his failure to act exasperated others and some even thought him sympathetic to the rebels. McClellan seemed oblivious to these political pressures for action and even kept his plans secret from his commander in chief. Having known Lincoln from their days in Illinois, the urbane professional soldier apparently had little respect for the country lawyer's ability to discharge his duties as commander in chief.

In the fall and early winter Lincoln's frustration with inactivity included the West as well as Virginia. In Kentucky, Major General Don Carlos Buell, who also gave an outstanding performance in organizing and training his army, seemed poised on the railroad between Louisville and Nashville. But, though a West Point graduate who had suffered a wound and attained promotion while fighting with Scott and Taylor, Buell proved reluctant to interrupt organizing his army and found baffling

43

the problems of supplying an army away from the railroad. In western Kentucky and Missouri the energetic Halleck also trained and organized forces while cleaning up the debris of Frémont's term and at the same time consolidating his control of Missouri. Meanwhile the Confederates directed their energy not only into organizing and training their forces but also to erecting fortifications along the rivers.

Hearing nothing from his commanders except reasons why they could not advance, Lincoln impatiently issued an order for all armies to advance on the same day, February 22, 1862, the patriotic holiday of Washington's birthday. Although Lincoln's reading and his conversations with Scott and McClellan had given him a grasp of the elements of strategy, he had yet to master logistics. The armies were bogged down, unable to move over winter's muddy roads. Lincoln did not realize that the high rainfall of the southeastern United States continued through the winter when plantlife required less moisture and sunshine evaporated less. The resulting mud, rarely frozen, and the absence of paved roads virtually precluded winter campaigning. Consequently all commanders ignored Lincoln's order, with one happy exception.

General Halleck advanced even before Washington's birthday, not in response to Lincoln's order but to anticipate the arrival of large enemy reinforcements rumored to be coming west under General Beauregard. He could move when others could not because he acted on the Mississippi, Ohio, Cumberland, and Tennessee rivers; with steamers to carry his men and supplies, he campaigned in spite of the mud. Further, he had the assistance of the navy's flotilla of seven gunboats, four of them with iron armor, to guard the fleet from the rebel navy and to cope with guns mounted on shore. But the Confederates had sited their river forts to block a hostile advance by river.

Whereas the Union forces had two commands, Halleck's and Buell's, the Confederates had one for the whole military frontier from the Appalachian Mountains to western Arkansas. Albert Sidney Johnston, a distinguished soldier in the army of the Texas Republic as well as the United States and the ranking general in the Confederate Army after Adjutant and Inspector General Cooper, commanded this huge department. He had his headquarters with the main army, facing Buell near Bowling Green, Kentucky. A West Point graduate, he had left the army to fight for the independence of Texas, had risen from private to brigadier general in its army, and then served as its secretary of war. He too had combat service in the Mexican War and enjoyed the respect of all the senior officers of the old army as well as former Secretary of War Jefferson Davis.

Johnston had inherited a defensive arrangement organized in the summer by Tennessee's governor and his inept military adviser, Mexican War veteran Gideon J. Pillow. Johnston continued their cordon approach, stationing detachments of his 43,000 men to block the four routes of advance into Tennessee. Twelve thousand men held Columbus, where formidable batteries dominated the Mississippi. Fort Henry on the Tennessee and, 11 miles to the east, Fort Donelson on the Cumberland had batteries to command the rivers and shared a garrison of 5,000 men. At Bowling Green, astride the railroad from Louisville to Nashville and facing over half of Buell's 45,000 men, Johnston had 22,000. If Johnston wished to emulate Jefferson Davis in the Manassas campaign, he could concentrate by using the railroad interconnections between all four of his forces. General Halleck in St. Louis had accurate intelligence of these defenses and the dispositions of the forces opposing him.

By the end of December 1861 Halleck had the situation in Missouri well enough in hand and felt sufficiently prepared to give thought to a major move. William T. Sherman, his friend from Mexican War service, recalled a meeting with Halleck and his chief of staff, George W. Cullum. "General Halleck had a map on his table with a large pencil in his hand, and asked, 'where is the rebel line?' Cullum drew the pencil through Bowling Green, forts Donelson and Henry, and Columbus, Kentucky. 'That is their line,' said Halleck, 'Now where is the proper place to break it?' And either Cullum or I said, *'Naturally* the center.' Halleck drew a line perpendicular to the other near its middle, and it coincided with the general course of the Tennessee River; and he said, 'that is the true line of operations.' "

Halleck saw not only that the Tennessee provided a line of advance deep into the Confederacy but that an advance along it would have put Columbus in the position of being "turned, paralyzed and forced to surrender." Thus Halleck saw the strategy for an advance down the Mississippi River much as had

General Scott in his anaconda plan: a small force on the river and a large one moving parallel, the two to "turn and capture" the strong points on the river. Further, he had noted that, if he were to strike along the Mississippi and if Buell moved against Bowling Green, the two Union armies would "occupy precisely the same position in relation to each other and to the enemy as did the armies of McDowell and Patterson before the Battle of" Manassas. So, concerned about the enemy's interior lines and wishing to take control of the Tennessee before the arrival of Beauregard and the rumored reinforcements, Halleck ordered his forces into action at the end of January.

The fleet was ready and its able flag officer, Andrew H. Foote, began the first of many major joint riverine operations with the army, all characterized by harmonious cooperation effected without a formally unified command. Halleck was wise and fortunate in choosing Brigadier General U. S. Grant to command the 15,000 troops sent up the Tennessee to take Fort Henry. Enthusiastic enough about the project to have proposed it to Halleck and having experience moving his men and engaging them in a small combat, Grant, like Foote, proved to be the perfect executor of the plan.

Grant had not always been able to inspire such confidence. Like Halleck, a West Point graduate who had served in the Mexican War and resigned from the army as a captain, Grant had left with a reputation for drinking heavily and, unlike Halleck, had met with little success in business. Volunteering early, he had received command of a regiment, and his influential congressman soon secured him appointment as brigadier general.

Halleck directed Grant to land his troops and quickly move them into the rear of Fort Henry so as to capture its garrison. Grant failed in this part of his mission because, even before the fleet came into view, the enemy evacuated most of the garrison from the fort, which was flooded by high water. The deep mud so delayed Grant's turning force that it had no chance of intercepting the retreating rebels.

The few men remaining surrendered to the fleet, and Grant began an arduous march through the 11 miles of mud to reach Fort Donelson, whither the Confederates had retreated. Meanwhile, he followed Halleck's directions to send a force up the river to disable, but not destroy, the railway bridge. This plan reflected Halleck's determination to nullify Johnston's interior lines by breaking his railroad network so as to protect Grant's force from the rebels at Columbus.

Halleck promptly dispatched supplies and rushed reinforcements up the Cumberland River to meet Grant below Fort Donelson and called on Buell to send men to Grant's aid. These almost doubled his force to 27,000 men, enabling him to hold his own against the Confederate army at Bowling Green. Halleck feared an attack because he saw that Johnston could bring troops by rail to Nashville, embark them on boats, come down the river to Fort Donelson in a day, "attack Grant in the rear," and return to Nashville before Buell could reach Nashville. But the Confederates were not thinking like Halleck, the translator of a biography of Napoleon.

Rather than planning a concentration against Grant to recover control of the Tennessee River or, at least, to protect Fort Donelson, Sidney Johnston, believing that the fort was doomed to fall to the fleet that had so easily subdued Fort Henry, evacuated Bowling Green and fell back on Nashville. Yet he reinforced Fort Donelson, sending more than 10,000 men. Instead of entrusting this command to his principal subordinate, the competent regular officer William J. Hardee, Johnston sent Brigadier General John B. Floyd to command the force. Floyd, a former governor of Virginia, had served as U.S. secretary of war, but this, his only military experience, provided little guidance for his important command. Nevertheless, Floyd saw that the best place for his small army was outside the fort on the flank of Grant's advance. But Johnston, still clearly failing to grasp the situation, ordered him to the fort, a position in which his infantry could contribute nothing to the powerful batteries' defense against Foote's gunboats but would find itself well placed for Grant to trap it.

And this Grant did. As soon as he arrived, he made contact with the fleet and his supplies and reinforcements and spread his army around the fort, thus catching the force which rebel bungling had placed within his grasp. The gunboats had then attacked but withdrew when they found Fort Donelson as formidable as Fort Henry was feeble. Meanwhile, contrary to his West Point instruction and the established practice in sieges for

47

thousands of years, the inexperienced Grant had not entrenched his army. This gave the Confederates, trapped against the river, a chance to escape when they attacked southward and opened a gap between the river and the Union lines. But Floyd then vacillated, while Grant, who had been absent meeting Foote, returned and ordered a counterattack which closed the escape route. Floyd then commandeered the available steamers for his Virginia brigade and left, turning over the command to General Pillow who gave it to General Buckner and departed with Floyd. On February 16, the next day, Buckner, in a hopeless position and with inadequate supplies surrendered his 11,500 men to his friend Grant. A strategic debacle for the Confederacy, the loss of so many men along with the fort made the defeat also a catastrophe of military attrition, and the two aspects together caused serious political attrition in the Confederacy. Many discouraged Confederates for the first time began to fear a long and costly war (see diagram of Confederate expectations of victory at the end of the diagram section; consult this in connection with other major campaigns).

Halleck, whom his friend Sherman described as impetuous when he had started an offensive, was making the most of his success by sending steamers and men far south on the Tennessee, almost to the Mississippi border. Meanwhile Johnston fell back farther, abandoning Nashville to Buell's slow advance down the railroad and to the menace of Union men and boats on the Cumberland. The Confederates evacuated Columbus by early March 1862, and Halleck ordered a force under General John Pope to move methodically down the Mississippi capturing forts. Water communications, controlled by the navy, made this tremendous advance possible. Instead of offering barriers to thwart them, the rivers had given the Yankees avenues of advance. Further, unlike a railroad, the retreating Confederates could not destroy them, thus assuring the invader of adequate supply lines.

The Confederates had also contributed to the Union success by seeing their defense as a cordon, a system of strong points with troops attached to them rather than as an army waiting to use a network of rail and water communications to concentrate against a Union threat. The Federals had exploited this weakness by concentrating against the rebel position on the Tennessee and Cumberland. Success here, insured by the warships and transports on the river and by the two-to-one numerical superiority at Fort Donelson, placed Grant's forces between Bowling Green and Columbus. The Confederates retreated, not waiting to see what Halleck would do with his central position or his ability to cut his adversary's communications.

Not only in conceiving the strategy, but by directing Grant and Foote to advance suddenly, pushing them ahead boldly, and aggressively reinforcing success, Halleck demonstrated that he had imbibed some of Napoleon's spirit from his immersion in the emperor's campaigns. And Grant and Foote could properly take pride in their fine cooperation, their energetic action, and their skill in command. In a difficult position and outnumbered two to one, Sidney Johnston had failed to understand the strategic situation. Instead of concentrating the bulk of his Bowling Green force to drive Grant back, he decided on the half measure of sending some men to Fort Donelson under an inexperienced civilian rather than a soldier. Moreover, despite believing Fort Donelson doomed, Johnston had reinforced it and thereby increased its value to the Union by including a huge bag of prisoners.

The Fort Donelson disaster and the collapse of the whole Confederate position in Tennessee galvanized the Confederate command into dramatic and purposeful action. First undertaking to strengthen the menaced line, the Confederates then moved more men to launch a counterattack with a strategic concentration resembling the Manassas campaign but unprecedented in scope. They acted to strike at Union weakness and as a counterattack to recover territory lost in the enemy winter offensive. The Yankee forces gave the Confederates the opportunity to strike at their weakness when Grant's army took up a position on the Tennessee at Pittsburg Landing, Tennessee, near the Mississippi line, far away from Buell's separate army, which began an advance southward along the railroad from Nashville.

President Davis noted the favorable circumstance and mentioned it to Sidney Johnston. He saw that the Confederates could attack the "division of the enemy moving from the Tennessee before it can make a junction with that advancing from Nashville." Seeing the situation in the same way as his opponents, General Halleck urged Buell to make haste to join Grant. He cautioned Grant "not to advance so as to bring on an engagement" until he had received the strong reinforcements that would "concentrate everything possible at Pittsburg Landing." The Confederate concentration had the initiative given by the offensive, but it lacked strategic surprise.

While Halleck acted on his strategic assessment to strengthen Grant, the Confederates prepared to attack before Buell could join him. As in the Manassas campaign, Beauregard and Davis played the major roles, with Beauregard doing more because he had more authority. He had proved a prickly, complaining subordinate in the difficult position of supernumerary general in Joe Johnston's northern Virginia department. The president had sought to soothe him but, finally, vexed also by Beauregard's propensity for corresponding with congressmen, the president gave him an assignment far from Richmond, to help General Albert Sidney Johnston with his huge department. He arrived just as Fort Henry fell, an opportune time for him to have an assignment of adequate scope and for Sidney Johnston to gain an energetic subordinate with a clear and emphatic strategic vision. With Johnston's retreat from Nashville toward Chattanooga in progress and the department divided by the loss of control of much of the Tennessee River, Beauregard assumed command west of the Tennessee.

Promptly taking charge, the general asked permission to evacuate Columbus, arguing that, since the enemy had turned it, the fort "must meet the fate of Fort Donelson." In evacuating Columbus, Beauregard also had the positive aim of concentrating an army at Corinth, a key railroad junction in northern Mississippi. He also ordered to Corinth Major General Earl Van Dorn, a cavalryman, West Pointer, and Mexican War veteran who commanded the Western Department's troops in Arkansas. Over 300 miles away and without a railroad, Van Dorn would have required a long time to reach Corinth in any case, but he encountered additional delay by fighting and losing the Battle of Pea Ridge. Here he failed in an attempt to reproduce Winfield Scott's maneuver in the Mexican War Battle of Cerro Gordo, a movement similar to that attempted by McDowell at Manassas. Urged by Beauregard to join the concentration at Corinth, Johnston arrived with 17,000 men by the third week of

March. With Van Dorn en route, all men in the department would soon be there except some small garrisons left to hold the Mississippi River strong points and four small detachments retained far away in East Tennessee.

In step with Beauregard and Johnston's moves President Davis and his War Department ordered an equally drastic concentration, the president admitting: "I acknowledge the error of my attempt to defend all the frontier, seaboard and inland." As soon as Fort Henry fell, Davis had ordered reinforcements from the Gulf Coast to Tennessee and, after the Fort Donelson disaster, recognized the "necessity of abandoning the seaboard in order to defend the Tennessee line." Major General Braxton Bragg, commanding in Alabama and West Florida, also saw the enemy "weakened by dispersion," and welcomed a chance to concentrate and "beat him in detail." But, despite his zeal for a concentration in Tennessee, Bragg felt the War Department's order to abandon both Mobile and Pensacola too drastic and left behind a small force to hold the valuable port of Mobile. Nonetheless, at Beauregard's urging, he came in person commanding 10,000 men, most of the strength of his department.

In concentrating men from the Gulf Coast, Davis could use interior lines. Bragg arrived promptly because, unlike Van Dorn, he could move his men all the way by railroad. The troops moving from Columbus and Johnston's large force coming from the east rode the rails too. Steam power also expedited the movement of the 5,000 men the War Department ordered from New Orleans, who were transported by steamers on the Mississippi to Memphis and the railway thence to Corinth. Like Van Dorn's men, the two regiments ordered from South Carolina, though coming by rail, did not arrive in time to take part in the campaign. When Johnston and the contingent from Columbus arrived by March 24, the Confederates had 40,000 men with which to assail Grant's 42,000 twenty miles away at Pittsburg Landing (see diagram of Shiloh concentration).

But the Federals, too, concentrated. Halleck had at last gotten the deliberate Buell to move rapidly. Leaving his railroad south of Nashville with 20,000 men, he marched 80 miles across country at 15 miles a day and began reaching his new line of communications on the Tennessee River on April 3. The contrast of this march with McDowell's to the Manassas battlefield exhibited the benefits of the period of training and the effects of Buell's good organization and staff work. Steamers easily supplied Buell's army, which camped beside the river a few miles north of Grant, preparing to join him when all men had come up.

Johnston's army would have 20 miles to march to assail Grant's camp beside the Tennessee. With the Union army on the river bank, it had no vulnerable rear but, since it camped rather than entrenched or deployed for battle, it also had no front or flank, being equally unprotected everywhere. Counting on surprise for success, Beauregard became dismayed when the army marched so slowly that it did not reach its point to begin the early morning attack until four in the afternoon. Convinced that the Yankees must be aware of an army of 40,000 men only two miles away, Beauregard believed "there is no chance for surprise," and "they will be entrenched to the teeth." But Sidney Johnston vetoed his recommendation to cancel the attack now rescheduled for dawn on the next day, April 6.

Beauregard need not have worried. The Union army had no idea that the enemy was nearby and was not looking because Grant had "scarcely the faintest idea of an attack." Grant had refused to believe in the possibility of an attack in spite of Halleck's warnings and expressed conviction that the "great battle of the war" would occur there. As at Fort Donelson, Grant had squandered one of the defense's advantages by not entrenching and would also parallel the earlier battle by being absent the next morning when the enemy attacked. It hardly surprises one that Grant's failings irritated Halleck, who thought him careless of his army. Nonetheless, Halleck recognized Grant's good qualities and retained and advanced him in command.

Early the next morning, as the Confederates attempted to make a surreptitious advance, a deer ran along a line of troops who opened fire on this inviting target; but still the enemy did not stir. Advancing in battle order, Johnston's army met the Union troops camped and at breakfast. This total tactical surprise, with a battle array against unformed men, more than compensated for the superiority of the tactical defense and enabled the southern army to drive back the northern in an all-day battle in which Johnston bled to death from a wound in his leg. Beauregard, who assumed command, reported to Richmond victory in the Battle of Shiloh. But the next day Grant's battered but not beaten army had Buell's three fresh divisions to help it take the offensive against the rebels. Pushed back and with hope of victory gone, Beauregard began his withdrawal toward Corinth in the afternoon.

Union casualties numbered 13,000, Confederate 10,600, but the Confederates lost 27 percent of their men, the Union 21 percent. Thus the tactical result, the loss of men, favored the Federals slightly. But for attrition comparisons to provide a true measure, they should base themselves on the total forces available to each belligerent. Since all the Confederacy's armies numbered only half of the Union's, to keep the attrition even, the southern forces should lose no more than half the northern. By this measure of the outcome of the Battle of Shiloh, the rebels had suffered a substantial defeat of attrition. The Federal armies also won a strategic victory when they repulsed the rebel offensive and retained all of the conquests of the winter campaign.

The battle had only an ambiguous political effect; since Beauregard never changed the impression of victory given in his first report, the South temporarily enjoyed the exhilaration of winning. Moreover, criticism of Grant, because he had allowed the Confederates to surprise him, alloyed the political benefits of the Union victory. So, despite the victory, the battle did not significantly raise northern confidence in an early end to the war or diminish southern expectations of success.

The loss at Shiloh does not diminish the merit of the Confederate execution or the brilliance of the strategic concept of utilizing the telegraph, the railroad, and the steamboat to carry out a Napoleonic concentration (some readers may wish to compare the Shiloh concentration diagram with those on the Defense of Mantua siege). Rather than viewing forces separated by the 800 miles between Charleston and northwestern Arkansas as part of a cordon with a mission of regional or local defense, Beauregard and Davis saw them as parts of the same army and used the products of the industrial revolution to direct them to the same battlefield. That all failed to arrive in time to fight does not reduce the quality of the conception, and the timely appearance of those able to use steam and exploit the interior line between Tennessee and the Gulf shows its practicality.

If Buell had not arrived in time to reinforce Grant, and the Confederates could have driven Grant from the field on the second day of the battle, Beauregard could then have moved his army against the outnumbered Buell. The careful General Buell would have declined to fight and his hypothetical retreat could have taken him north along the Tennessee or to his own railroad to Nashville. But the latter presupposes a long retreat by Grant.

Yet, after this hypothetical defeat at Shiloh, Grant would have had no motive to move more than a few miles north along the Tennessee River, and, well-supplied by the river, would have continued his threat to Corinth while receiving reinforcements sent by Halleck. The Confederates would have found that the Union Navy gave him the river for a supply line but denied it to the rebels. In fact, in the face of the navy, the rebels could not cross the river without building and arming batteries powerful enough to block the river and so protect the army's crossing from the gunboats. So, with the still-dangerous Grant based on the river, the Confederates could not have threatened and pursued Buell.

Thus, if one compares the outcome of the battle on the supposition of a Confederate victory with the actual result, the strategic situation remains the same. This is not an unrepresentative result for other famous Civil War battles nor for some of equal renown in other wars in other times.

Partly as a result of the Fort Donelson and Shiloh campaigns, the Union had made great territorial gains in the West, consolidating control of Missouri and securing virtually all of West Tennessee and over half of Middle Tennessee. Yet, in spite of the loss of those loyal, populous, and productive areas and the industrial output of the Nashville area, the South had still not suffered any serious impairment of its ability to wage war.

Davis, Beauregard, and Halleck had identical understandings of the strategic situation and all responded with a display of excellent strategic discernment and prompt and appropriate action. Their performances harmonize with the command and strategy of the Manassas and the Union conduct of the Fort

Donelson campaign. The commanders on both sides had shown their ability to apply Napoleonic concepts to the age of the electric telegraph and steam power, with Davis primarily relying on the railroad in the Manassas and Shiloh campaigns and Halleck the steamboat in the West. But just as concentration in space had inspired coordinated movements from South Carolina to Arkansas, another motif in Civil War strategy was providing the dominant theme in operations in Virginia.

CHAPTER 5

THE STRATEGIC TURNING
MOVEMENT

Corinth, Peninsula, Shenandoah Valley, Seven
Days' Battles, and Second Manassas Campaigns

After the Battle of Shiloh, Halleck moved south, coming from
St. Louis to take command of the armies of Grant and Buell and
the additional reinforcements he had directed to the Pittsburg
Landing base on the Tennessee. He had already shown his
qualities as a general—decisiveness and the ability to assume
responsibility—by controlling the situation in Missouri, by directing and reinforcing the Henry and Donelson campaign,
and by ordering Buell to reinforce Grant. Still, without experience in field command, Halleck made the battle-seasoned Grant
his second in command. But, since his high administrative capacity, military knowledge, and engineer's eye for the ground
enabled him to manage well on his own, Grant, who had been
"truly glad of it" when Halleck arrived, found himself in the
frustrating position of a supernumerary.

In his opponent, Beauregard, Halleck faced his schoolmate
from West Point who had also graduated high in his class and
entered the elite Corps of Engineers. But the flamboyant, mag-
netic Beauregard contrasted with the careful, unprepossessing
Halleck, the former given to extravagant statements of his ex-
pansive strategic visions, the latter to concise, lucid analyses of
the situation and objectives.

The arrival of Van Dorn and other reinforcements brought the Confederate army up to 70,000 men while Halleck added enough to have 120,000. Beauregard had his base at the fortified railway junction of Corinth, Halleck's objective. According to Grant, Halleck faced a "big job" in getting his "large Army over country roads where it has been raining for the last five months." Further, supply problems were almost insuperable, for, as Grant pointed out: "If we could go strung out along the road where there was not an enemy it would be different. Here, however, the front must be kept compact." Though a compact army ordinarily required more foraging wagons, these had little utility in advancing over a country already thoroughly gleaned by the rebels. So Halleck had to use wagons to supply his army from the Tennessee River, corduroying the muddy roads as he advanced.

Building roads as he marched would have made for a slow advance in any case but, in Grant's words, Halleck "moved slowly but in a way to insure success." He entrenched at the end of each day, a practice older than the Romans that he had learned at West Point and from Grant's experience of being caught in unentrenched positions during the unexpected attacks at Fort Donelson and Shiloh. Beauregard deployed his army to resist Halleck's advance and watched for a chance to overwhelm an isolated detachment; but he never caught Halleck at a disadvantage. Finding his antagonist using his superior numbers to lap around his flanks, the Confederate commander had to steadily fall back to avoid being turned. Realizing that Halleck would connect with rail communication outside of Corinth and would likely surround the small town, Beauregard decided to abandon the city. He retreated very artfully, however. Instructing his troops to greet with cheers the empty trains arriving to take them away, he thus simulated the arrival of reinforcements. On May 29, 1862, after fending off Halleck for a month and leaving him wary about the bogus reinforcements, he departed unexpectedly, further complicating the task of pursuit by taking every road sign with him.

Since Corinth had considerable strategic significance, its fall deprived the rebels and gave the Union control of the junction of railroads from Columbus and Memphis as well as those running south into Mississippi and eastward to connect with

Nashville and Chattanooga. Grant, who regarded Halleck as "one of the greatest men of the age," thought that the slow progress would occasion "much unjust criticism" of Halleck's Corinth campaign, but he thought that "future effects will prove it a great victory."

Though never regarded as a great victory, the unspectacular fall of Corinth and the contemporaneous capture of the Mississippi River city of Memphis did consolidate Union control of West Tennessee and provide a base for an advance into Mississippi.

From the hindsight of his memoirs, written with the operational sophistication he and other Civil War generals had gained in four years, Grant had a different view of the Corinth campaign. He began by reporting that many officers had "believed that a well-directed attack would have partially destroyed the army defending Corinth." Having earlier expressed a desire to have as few "terrible battles" as possible, Grant took exception to the views of the officers, few of whom had a regular army background. Having favored Halleck's earlier method in the Fort Donelson campaign of advancing "as rapidly as possible to save hard fighting," he advocated something similar in his memoir. Criticizing Halleck's methodical advance as well as disparaging the amateur officers desire to run up casualties for no strategic result by trying partially to destroy Beauregard's army, he advocated yet another approach: "For myself, I am satisfied that Corinth could have been captured in a two days' campaign commenced promptly on the arrival of re-enforcements after the battle of Shiloh."

Though Grant does not explain how one would have conducted this quick campaign, he could have had little else in mind than the strategic turning movement. Instead of the tactical turning movement, the threat of which kept Beauregard in retreat, a strategic turning movement could reach into his rear, block his retreat, and capture his whole army. This maneuver would become the dominant motif in Civil War operational strategy because it offered a means of coping with the primacy of the tactical defense. Like the tactical turning movement used by General McDowell at Manassas, the strategic version tried to avoid assailing the enemy in front; but, instead of attempting this through the tactics of a battle, a general tried to move his whole army into the enemy's rear.

To carry this out in the Corinth campaign, the larger Union army, or a major part of it, would have marched around Beauregard's flank. Grant did not assume that the strategic turning movement could actually reach Beauregard's rear, but he knew that the threat of it would send the Confederate army into a precipitate retreat back the 20 miles to Corinth, and, by threatening to reach the railroad south of the city, cause Beauregard quickly to evacuate it.

As Grant's contemporary remarks indicate, the did not then know how to conduct such a two-days' operation, then unprecedented in the war. But the maneuver became one of the war's most often attempted, and in fact, the Union Army of the Potomac in Virginia was employing the war's first strategic turning movement at the same time Halleck advanced on Corinth.

Although this appealing maneuver offered a means of overcoming one of the difficulties of the strategic offensive, others remained. Whereas fighting occurred only occasionally, the mundane activity of logistics concerned commanders and men every day. General William T. Sherman, said to have coined the aphorism that "War is hell," singled out an equally essential truth when he wrote that war was "grub and mules." And, in the Civil War, the immense task of furnishing grub for men, and also for the mules and horses that drew wagons and artillery and mounted the cavalrymen, often shaped strategy and always influenced it.

Compared with the Revolutionary War, the Civil War used enormous armies, many being larger than most American cities. Supplying such armies presented the same problems as feeding a city, but in a place where local food production and stocks on hand were totally inadequate to feed an influx of so many men and horses. Rarely would local supplies last an army more than a few days and, if it were before harvest or a hay crop, the soldiers had trouble finding enough to last a single day. Still, as long as the armies kept marching, each day they could find fresh sources of food for the men and fodder for the animals. Yet most Civil War armies had to spend long periods in one place, those on the defensive watching for the hostile movement and those on the offensive awaiting reinforcements, the movement of other armies, suitable weather, or any of many other causes of delay. So, with armies typically immobile, transportation for their supplies assumed paramount importance.

When General McClellan planned his own movement from Washington into Virginia, he faced the same choices as Halleck moving to Corinth. He could attempt the daunting task of fighting and winning an offensive battle to drive the enemy back 30 miles or he could try to emulate Halleck's slow advance on Corinth. In either case, he would have to repair the railroad as he advanced in order to keep his army supplied. Instead, General McClellan decided to use a strategic turning movement, a congenial concept to someone familiar with the campaigns of Napoleon and a veteran of the Mexican War who had already attempted to copy Winfield Scott's tactical turning movement of the Mexican War Battle of Cerro Gordo.

When, in January 1862, the president finally pressured McClellan into revealing his plans for driving the rebel army away from Washington, the general argued against a direct advance against Johnston's army near Manassas, the obvious approach to civilians. He pointed out that, even if he won a battle, the Confederates "could fall back upon other positions" and "fight us again and again," in successive battles, between which the retreating adversary would "destroy his railroad bridges and otherwise impede our progress." To avoid the power of the tactical defense and the relative indecisiveness of frontal battles, McClellan saw the perfect route to turn Johnston's army: The Chesapeake Bay and its tributary rivers formed a natural avenue into the enemy's rear, a route whose water communications would also assure an ample and secure flow of supplies. Thus he could use water transport, a resource Halleck had exploited in Tennessee but denied him in his Corinth campaign.

In his originally envisioned landing near the mouth of the Rappahannock, McClellan had no plans to distract the enemy and so none for attaining surprise. Without surprise, he could not expect to trap the rebel army and could only aim at the more limited but more realistic objective of forcing it back. Yet the general did expect to have a defensive battle, because, by menacing the Confederate capital, he could force "the enemy to come out and attack us" and so try to "beat us in a position selected by ourselves." He seemed to assume that a victory in this battle in a position which threatened Richmond's communications would result in the fall of the capital.

In a sense McClellan had abstracted from the turning movement two concepts, forcing the adversary back and shifting to him the burden of the attack, thus combining the strategic offensive with the tactical defensive. This made a strategy not just for attaining the political objective of freeing the Washington area of the presence of the rebel army but of coping with the stalemate in Virginia. Instead of menacing the hostile army's communications, he would threaten its capital to bring on a battle in a selected defensive position. Although McClellan had a fairly good understanding of his premises and reasoning, he did not make them completely clear to the president, who, despite this, acquiesced in the plan. Just as McClellan prepared to depart, Johnston, concerned about how easily McClellan could turn his advanced position, fell back 40 miles closer to Richmond, causing McClellan to change his objective to landing in Union-held territory at the tip of that body of land between the York and James rivers called the Peninsula (see diagram of McClellan's move to the Peninsula).

Debarking troops on the Peninsula in late March and early April, McClellan, as he expected, drew Johnston's army after him to protect Richmond from this threat. Yet the main Confederate army did not immediately confront the huge Union force. Instead of facing Johnston's whole army, McClellan had only to cope with a smaller number, but behind a fortified line across the Peninsula. McClellan could not immediately turn this position by landing troops behind it because the Navy feared to try to pass the Confederate batteries at the mouth of the York River or risk the intervention of the powerful rebel ironclad, *Virginia*, originally the U.S.S. *Merrimac*, posted at the entrance to the James River. McClellan saw that he would have to breach the line by the slow process of a siege, thus opening the mouth of the York to the navy and troop transports which could then force the enemy back by the threat of a turning movement by landing men behind. But J. E. Johnston, knowing McClellan and being aware that the young engineers in charge had laid out a poor defensive line, revealed much about the character of his old friend when he wrote that "no one but McClellan would have hesitated to attack."

McClellan had readied his siege and planned to open a prodigious bombardment on May 5, 1862. At the same time he had ships ready to take a division of troops up the York River when he cleared the route. Johnston avoided the bombardment of his weak defenses by retreating northwest. Nor did he tarry long, Lee having warned him of what he already knew, that the Federals could land a force "to intercept your retreat, and will have turned the line of your land defenses." Using his entrenchments at Williamsburg to fight a delaying battle, he earned time for his army to get away toward Richmond without undue haste. James Longstreet, West Pointer and veteran of Mexico and Manassas, performed well in command of the rear guard at Williamsburg, stopping the pursuers until a Union brigade got around his flank and forced his retreat at the end of the day. As Johnston continued his withdrawal, the Union division that landed at the head of the York, meeting a Confederate division sent to intercept it, presented no threat.

Reaching the vicinity of Richmond by the fourth week of May, McClellan drew his supplies from the York River along a railroad which connected the river with Richmond. Now he could begin siege operations and test the validity of his strategy's key assumption: that the menace of his army to Richmond would compel the rebels to attack, giving him the advantage of fighting on the entrenched defensive.

Only seven years earlier the French, British, and their allies had besieged the Russian city of Sevastopol during the Crimean War. Unable to surround it to starve it out, the siege operations lasted 322 days and involved immense amounts of artillery and prolonged bombardments. The Confederates feared that the Union's army, with the same advantage in matériel as the French and British, could employ Crimean War methods to capture Richmond. With the recent Sevastopol example fresh in their minds, they felt an especial urgency to drive the Yankees back.

The disposition of McClellan's army, with a part of it south of the Chickahominy River where high waters threatened the bridges, invited a Confederate attack on that almost isolated detachment. Johnston accepted the invitation with a well-conceived offensive which aimed to overwhelm McClellan's detached force with assaults on front and flank. Longstreet had charge of the attack but, despite his good performance at Williamsburg, lacked sufficient experience in managing large numbers. Without proper maps, a situation usual throughout the war, he so bungled the operation that only half of the men got into action and those half a day late. Toward the end of the day reinforcements reached the Union corps, using a bridge over the swollen Chickahominy that only the weight of the marching men kept from washing away. Not feeling well, McClellan did not reach the front until the close of the battle, but his subordinates displayed competence and initiative in conducting the defense in his absence.

The Union won the Battle of Fair Oaks because it repelled the Confederate attack. It also won tactically, losing about 5,000 men to the Confederate's little over 6,000 with the percentage of losses of total available forces even more favorable to the North. The failure of the battle to result in a rebel retreat meant that it had little impact on the public. McClellan then improved his position but did little to begin a siege; instead, he told Washington that the enemy outnumbered him and called for reinforcements.

At Fair Oaks Johnston had received a severe wound, depriving President Davis of the "valuable service" of this "good soldier." Davis promptly handed the command of Johnston's army to General R. E. Lee, his chief of staff. Davis and Lee collaborated to prepare for a second and more effective counteroffensive to drive back McClellan.

One of the senior and most respected officers in the U.S. Army, Lee had attended West Point with Jefferson Davis and J. E. Johnston and given General Scott distinguished service in the Mexican War. After duty as superintendent of the Military Academy, he transferred from the engineers to the cavalry. On the secession of Virginia he had assumed command of the Virginia state forces and then entered the Confederate Army with a rank junior only to Adjutant General Cooper and Sidney Johnston. Lee and Davis's similar background, mutual respect, and long acquaintance aided but did not guarantee the particularly smooth-working relationship that characterized their collaboration throughout the war. Prepossessing in appearance, exceptionally intelligent, and liberally endowed with the spatial visualization aptitude so essential to engineers and field commanders, Lee also had ample administrative ability and an excellent faculty of working with people. Self-confident and capable of making difficult decisions, he had all of the attributes needed to give an outstanding performance. That he did not distinguish himself in command in western Virginia had not diminished Davis's confidence in him when, three months before, he had called him from the coastal command in South Carolina to Richmond to become his chief of staff.

Lee settled easily into his new command and he and Davis deliberated about how to cope with the threat presented by McClellan and his army of at least 90,000 men. Meanwhile, northwest in the valley of the Shenandoah River the Confederates were causing the Union to weaken McClellan's army by means of the operations by Major General Thomas J. Jackson, a campaign worthy of Napoleon himself in the quality of its command and strategy.

Jackson, a penniless orphan whose hard work and good intelligence enabled him to overcome his poor preparation for West Point, graduated in time to give an outstanding performance as a lieutenant with Scott's army in the Mexican War. Soon after, Jackson, earnest and deeply religious with eccentric ideas about his health, left the army to join the faculty of the Virginia Military Institute. Receiving a colonelcy at the opening of the Civil War, he distinguished himself commanding a brigade at the Battle of Manassas. His reading of Napoleon's campaigns helped prepare him for higher command, knowledge he soon exploited brilliantly. By the late winter of 1862 J. E. Johnston had given Major General Jackson a small command, barely 4,000 men, and large responsibility not just to guard the Shenandoah Valley but to distract the Union's General Banks enough that he could spare no reinforcements for McClellan.

Nathaniel P. Banks had as his main qualifications to command an army his political experience as a former speaker of the House of Representatives and governor of Massachusetts. But his lack of capacity for military command prevented him from attaining his ambition of furthering his political career by gaining military glory. Further, his performance deprived the Union of an adequate general on a number of important occasions. As McClellan moved to the Peninsula, Banks marched south from the Potomac River to carry out his own instructions to drive Jackson from the valley before reinforcing McClellan. Since he advanced with a superior force of 16,000 men, Jackson fell back, evacuating Winchester and retreating more than 30 miles farther south. Believing that he had thus cleared the valley, Banks began to send men to McClellan, leaving General James Shields with 9,000 men holding Winchester. Jackson responded with an immediate advance against Shields in order to attack him and thus hold all of Banks's men in the valley. Meeting Shields at Kernstown, south of Winchester, Jackson sent one of his brigades forward while using his other two to turn the Federal position. In Shields he faced a man of political importance and military experience. Shields had served as senator from both Illinois and Minnesota, and he had also fought well under Scott as a brigadier general, suffering two wounds. Like Jackson, he had been at Cerro Gordo and, with his two-to-one numerical superiority over Jackson, found it easy to defend against the Confederate general's turning movement by halting it with two brigades of his own. Jackson's offensive gave him the initiative, but the lack of surprise in Jackson's attack enabled Shields to seize the initiative when he moved to counter the turning movement. Driven from the field, Jackson retreated southward. But tactical defeat proved as useful as victory by giving him strategic success: Banks returned all of his men to the valley after Jackson's attack had so emphatically advertised his presence.

Jackson soon began a campaign in which he coordinated the movements of his force, now increased to 6,000, and two others. Both of these forces had as commanders able and resourceful West Point graduates and veterans of the Mexican War and long service in the U.S. Army. General Edward Johnson, southwest at Westview with 3,000 men, watched the mountains while Richard S. Ewell, with 8,000 at Gordonsville in central Virginia, awaited orders. Small in numbers, the armies that maneuvered in the Shenandoah Valley found ample food and fodder in this productive farming area, freeing them from dependence on a railroad.

The hostile armies disposed themselves so that Banks, with 15,000 men to the north, opposed Jackson, and General John C. Frémont, recently transferred to Virginia from Missouri and reinforced to 15,000, had some of his men facing Edward Johnson. In addition, General Irvin McDowell, with 30,000 at Fredricksburg, stood by to act against Jackson if needed. Displaying superior energy and ability, Jackson so exploited interior lines or gained strategic surprise that he outnumbered the Union armies in three of the next four battles they fought, his average strength in all four being 8,500 men and theirs only 4,850. Ironically, the Union generals had far more men available, an average of 32,250 to his 14,875. Although stronger overall in the theater of operations, the Federal generals had fewer men in battle because Jackson had conceived and managed his strategy so well.

Resolving to join Edward Johnson and overwhelm the force opposing him, Jackson placed the dependable Ewell at a gap in the Blue Ridge Mountains to stymie or at least delay an advance by Banks while Jackson led his men southeast toward Richmond, a move calculated to confuse the enemy. But this march offered the advantage of an interior line because it led to the railroad where Jackson boarded westbound trains and joined Johnson to attack their locally outnumbered foe. Before they could attack, the Federals obligingly assailed them. Repulsing the attack, Jackson then attempted to pursue his beaten antagonists, but the Union forces made this even more difficult by setting forest fires in his path (see diagram of Jackson's concentration against Frémont).

When Jackson next moved north to join Ewell to operate against Banks, he found the Yankee forces weakened by having had Shields's division withdrawn to reinforce McDowell. Having fallen back and blocked the valley, Banks entrenched 7,000 men at Strasburg and posted only 1,000 at Front Royal. With the valley divided by the ridge of the Massanutten Mountains, Ewell moved north on the east of the mountains while Jackson advanced on the west until he joined Ewell by marching through a gap in the Massanuttens. Together they overwhelmed the tiny Federal force at Front Royal, taking most of it prisoner (see diagram of Jackson's concentration against Banks).

Seeing that Jackson could now turn him, Banks retreated north toward Winchester. Jackson's turning force reached the Winchester road only after the fleeing Federals had passed, while Ewell's division, which aimed to intercept them farther north, did not move promptly enough to block Banks's retreat there either (see diagram of Jackson's effort to turn Banks). Jackson's failure illustrates the difficulty of reaching the enemy's rear and blocking his retreat, even when a general as brilliant as Jackson led a turning force twice as strong as that with which Banks made his escape. On the other hand, this small operation, which deprived the Union force of the advantage of its entrenchments, illustrates the power of the turning movement to compel an adversary to retreat.

The next day Banks attempted a stand at Winchester, but Jackson, with a three-to-one numerical superiority, easily outflanked the defenders and pursued them relentlessly for 25 miles until they crossed the Potomac. But he went too far. Jackson's pursuit so far north gave the Union forces a chance to capture his army by reaching his rear, an opportunity Lincoln insisted his generals take. With Frémont moving northeast to close the valley at Strasburg and 20,000 men under Shields marching west to block Jackson's retreat at Front Royal, the Confederate general faced a serious peril. He responded by retreating as rapidly as possible, travelling by night and day, and, though Shields took Front Royal, all of Jackson's men marched by before Frémont reached Strasburg. Jackson's narrow escape from a hazard brought on by his futile chase of the defeated illustrated the basis for Belisarius's skepticism about the value of pursuing a beaten foe. On the other hand, by advancing to the Potomac and thus inadvertently offering himself as bait, Jackson helped accomplish his objective of distracting the enemy and keeping forces away from supporting McClellan's offensive (see diagram of Jackson's pursuit of Banks).

Jackson's escape ushered in the final phase of the Valley campaign as the two Union armies, led by Frémont and Shields, pursued Jackson south in the valley, with Frémont on the west side of the Massanutten Mountains and Shields on the east. Keeping ahead of Frémont, Jackson destroyed not only the bridges across his route of retreat but those over the Shenandoah River, which would enable Frémont and Shields to communicate with one another. When he reached Cross Keys, he controlled the only bridge over the Shenandoah, with Frémont near and Shields's men at a distance and spread out along the road.

Just when Jackson had resolved to use his interior lines to strike Frémont first, the Union commander obliged by attacking him. Having repulsed Frémont, Jackson turned against Shields's advance guard of only 3,000, which, after a stout resistance at Port Republic, he outflanked, drove back, and then pursued until the fleeing foe met Shields himself with his main force and gained enough support to halt the rebel pursuit (see diagram of Cross Keys and Port Republic; readers may wish to compare this with the Defense of Mantua diagrams).

The Federal forces ended their operations, withdrawing northward while Jackson stayed near Cross Keys, where he had good access to the railroad leading to eastern Virginia. The pattern of the movements in this Valley campaign may well have reflected Jackson's reading of Napoleon, the roots of its successes and failures fitting the Napoleonic model well. The marches had also proven the difficulty of pursuit under Civil War conditions: Jackson's chase of Banks had exposed his army to extreme hazard, and both Frémont and Shields's pursuit of Jackson south in the valley had led to their rebuffs at Cross Keys and Port Republic. But the Valley campaign had a major part in a larger strategic drama.

Jackson's campaign and his troops had the central role in Lee and Davis's planning of a campaign to drive McClellan away from his threatening position near Richmond. At first the Confederate leaders considered reinforcing Jackson sufficiently to enable him to advance north and cross the Potomac River, expecting that this apparent menace would draw Union troops from McClellan. Instead, they decided to concentrate against McClellan, bringing reinforcements to Richmond from the Carolinas and Georgia and, only at the last moment, utilizing the railroad and the Confederacy's interior lines to bring Jackson from the valley.

Lee's plan called for concentrating two thirds of his men on his north flank against one third of McClellan's army, the 30,000 men north of the Chickahominy. Still, Jackson's movement to participate provided the essence of the offensive. Jackson's mission was to turn the enemy position, reach his rear, block the railroad from the York River, and thus "cut up McClellan's communications and rear." Following the same reasoning as McClellan had used for his campaign, Lee believed that this threat to his adversary's communications would compel him "to retreat or give battle." Although Jackson's 18,000 men would bring Lee's force up to parity with McClellan's, this number would hardly suffice to drive back the well-trained, entrenched Federal force without Jackson's turning movement.

When the main effort began on June 26, 1862, McClellan, though expecting an attack, did not prepare for Jackson's turning movement. Fortunately for McClellan, Jackson was a day late, making the first of the Seven Days' Battles a frontal attack and an easy Union victory (see diagram of Battle of Mechanicsville). The next day Jackson struck from the north but, with the Union flank withdrawn and facing north, he did not even threaten its flank seriously until late in the day, when the Union force retreated across the Chickahominy (see diagram of Battle of Gaines's Mill). Although the turning movement failed to reach the Yankee rear, it did inspire McClellan to change his base from the York to the James River and then to retreat south to the James. While Lee planned a pursuit, McClellan's outlook underwent a transformation. His early assessment that, "assailed by double my numbers, I should have no fear as to the result" gave way, by the beginning of his retreat, to the gloomy recrimination: "I have lost this battle because my force was too small." His subsequent panicky telegrams to Washington frightened and demoralized the president and the secretary of war and indicated that McClellan had lost his nerve when confronted with his first really big engagement.

Lee's pursuit resulted in three battles, in two of which the Confederates encountered repulses in their assaults against rear guards. In the last, at Malvern Hill, Lee mistakenly believed he assailed a retreating foe. Instead, he met a bloody defeat when the whole Union army hurled him back from its strong position, its powerful artillery displaying its virtuosity in the defense. The battle and the campaign of the Seven Days' exhibited that nothing had altered either the dominance of the tactical defensive or the virtual indestructability of trained

69

armies organized on the modern model. Lee's effort at pursuit, costly in casualties, had even less chance of success than usual because he did not pursue a beaten foe; McClellan retreated with two thirds of his men fresh and the remainder withdrawing in good order, veterans of mostly successful defenses.

The Seven Days' Battles also showed that, though the small units performed well, the generals and their staffs had not yet mastered the techniques of maneuvering their forces. Jackson's failure to appear when ordered and his lethargic performance in the whole campaign showed that his tactical skill did not match his strategic prowess. Lee and his staff, in their first campaign together, showed their inexperience. The lack of, or reliance on, erroneous maps plagued both sides. The "Confederate commanders," according to one of their generals, knew "no more about the topography of the country than they did about Central Africa." Yet Lee's concentration and use of the turning movement displayed his mastery of strategy, and his firm conduct of the operation showed that he possessed the qualities of a careful, confident, and decisive commander, though also one rather pugnacious and a believer in the myth of pursuit. McClellan, on the other hand became demoralized and unable to function properly when his strategy produced the expected result of an enemy attack. Successful as a strategist, he failed in command.

The Confederates, on the offensive, lost 20,000 men, about 22 percent of their force, and the Union, about 16,000, or 18 percent of their men. Compared to the total manpower resources of the belligerents, the percentages were even more unfavorable to the South. So, though retreat usually signifies defeat, in terms of the tactical results—the attrition—the Union had won. But the Confederates had achieved their strategic objective; McClellan's new position on the James was too far away to threaten Richmond with a siege. Remaining inert, McClellan declared himself outnumbered and in need of reinforcements in order to take the offensive.

In addition to fulfilling the Confederacy's strategic aims, the Seven Days' Battles gave a political victory in that they raised the expectation of Southerners for an early end of the war. They had the opposite effect in the North, causing many to forecast a long, costly, and doubtful war. The gloomy response

in the North impressed on Lincoln the wide divergence between symbolism and substance in military events. Realizing
the North's tactical victory in the Seven Days' Battles, the president noted that, "in men and material, the enemy suffered
more than we, in that series of conflicts; while it is certain that
he is less able to bear it." Yet the retreat of the Union army, its
"half-defeat," had such an adverse "moral effect," that, for the
public, it completely overshadowed Halleck's victories in the
West, "a series of successes extending through half-a-year, and
clearing a hundred thousand square miles of country."

With McClellan on the defensive, Lincoln organized all the
forces in northern Virginia into a substantial army under General John Pope, brought from successful independent command under Halleck. Eager to exploit their interior lines
between McClellan and Pope, Lee and Davis saw Pope's
weaker army as the obvious objective. Further, they perceived
that significant strategic benefits would accrue from driving
him back: the recovery of lost territory and supplies in northern
Virginia and the provision of more security for the logistically
valuable area north of Richmond and the capital's railroad to
the valley. But they wished to avoid more wasteful battles such
as Fair Oaks and Seven Days. Lee stated the new doctrine as
"not attacking them in their strong and chosen positions. They
ought always to be turned." Later he would restate this to
Jackson, saying that it was "to save you the abundance of hard
fighting that I ventured to suggest for your consideration not to
attack the enemy's strong points, but to turn his position. . . .
I would rather you have easy fighting and heavy victories."

None of this was new to Lee or Jackson but, in spite of better
intentions, the recent battles had all involved frontal attacks;
thus the leaders took pains to reaffirm their commitment to the
practice of Scott's doctrine of turning the enemy. Lee's ideas
went beyond this operational level to embrace also the concept
of the strategic raid, but his immediate goal was to force Pope
back and, with logistic considerations always in mind and often
paramount, "consume provisions and forage now being used
in supporting the enemy."

After first sending Jackson northward toward Pope, which
led to a clash with a Federal detachment, Lee moved up with
the remainder of his army, now organized in two corps, one

71

under Jackson and the other under Longstreet, both seasoned in battle command. These corps commanders would make it possible for Lee to carry out the brilliant campaign of the Second Battle of Manassas.

After first trying without success to turn Pope's left with his whole army, Lee returned to Scott's formula of dividing his forces. Leaving Longstreet to distract Pope, Lee sent Jackson on a rapid two-day march, gaining the initiative by going around the enemy army and reaching a point near Manassas on Pope's rail line of communications. Although Pope knew when Jackson marched away, Lee attained surprise because the Union commander did not understand his direction or purpose. Longstreet followed in Jackson's track as Pope, learning of Jackson's position behind him, prepared to take advantage of his interior lines between Jackson and Longstreet (see diagram of Second Manassas Campaign 1). Though Lee planned only to compel Pope's retreat and so avoid battle, he must have anticipated that Pope might try to take advantage of this division of the army to exploit his interior lines in order to have a battle with a two-to-one numerical superiority. Nevertheless Lee's experience in having assailed McClellan's army must have convinced him that he need not worry if Pope should attack Jackson or Longstreet. This showed him confident that the southern commanders could receive any assault in front, conduct a skillful defense, and repulse the Yankees.

After destroying the depot at Manassas, Jackson withdrew a few miles west, giving Pope a clear route for a retreat to Washington and himself a good defensive position on a ridge closer to Longstreet's route of approach. Choosing to fight rather than retreat, Pope turned toward Manassas to attack Jackson's 25,000 troops with his 60,000. But, unable to find him immediately, the Federal general did not fight until another day had passed and Longstreet had taken a position near at hand. Pope's all-day frontal attack on the unentrenched Jackson failed; Jackson's men had defensive help from the excavations of an unfinished railroad. The next day, when Pope renewed his assaults, Lee sent Longstreet to attack Pope's flank. This failed to inflict a disastrous defeat because Pope, exploiting the excellent articulation and responsiveness of his now-veteran troops, succeeded in bending his line into an arc. That night he withdrew (see diagram of Second Manassas Campaign 2).

The next day, after the end of the Second Battle of Manassas, Lee pursued, but having learned his lesson, not in a way that would risk a frontal confrontation such as occurred during the Seven Days' Battles. Instead, he repeated his maneuver of having Jackson turn while Longstreet remained in front to distract Pope's force, now halted five miles from the battlefield. But Pope, often confused in the previous days and obtuse in neglecting to provide for Longstreet's appearance on his flank, this time anticipated Lee's movement and, while he resumed his retreat, sent two divisions to prevent Jackson from reaching his rear. When these forces repulsed Jackson's attack at Chantilly and Pope's army moved into the Washington defenses, the operations ended.

McClellan had used a turning movement to reach Richmond, but his had not involved surprise nor had it interrupted the enemy's communications. Lee's well-conducted maneuver had all the classic elements and would provide an inspiration for other generals, both North and South.

The campaign attained Lee's main objective of forcing the enemy back to Washington and giving him the "beef, flour, & forage" of the Rappahannock area. Although Jackson had deliberately withdrawn from Pope's line of communications and route of withdrawal to Washington, Pope had attacked him. This thwarted Lee's goal "to avoid a general engagement" and simply drive the enemy back "by maneuvering." Thus the battle had as its strategic significance the recovery of logistically valuable country. Its attrition slightly favored the rebels, who lost about 9,500 men, approximately 19 percent of their force, while the Yankees lost 14,500, about 24 percent of theirs. But the southern casualties, increased by the assault at Chantilly and by an attack by Jackson the day before the battle, did amount to a somewhat higher percentage of all their armies than the Union's. Still, the Confederates had a fine political victory in winning so decisively so near Washington. It sustained their morale and gave them heroes in Lee and Jackson, while correspondingly discouraging the North.

For this defeat Lincoln removed the unfortunate Pope from

command and sent him to Minnesota where he immediately had to cope with an Indian war. There he proved himself as an excellent departmental administrator.

Six months of campaigning in Virginia had forced the rebel army back from the vicinity of Washington to defend its own capital, only to return to its old position by driving the invading Federal army into Washington's defenses. This was the sort of warfare that caused the Prussian von Moltke to remark that the Americans seemed little more than "two armed mobs chasing each other around the country." Still, in the process the soldiers became veterans of combat, the staffs learned how to perform their duties, and the commanders and their subordinates developed some operational skill.

Though so conventional in their strategy that von Moltke could see them as campaigns "from which nothing could be learned," the Seven Days' Battles and Second Manassas campaigns gave rise to a Confederate strategy for Virginia, one based on avoiding battle, especially on the offensive, and making an innovative use of the strategic turning movement as the defensive device to implement this doctrine. For Union strategy these campaigns signaled a failure of McClellan's version of the turning movement and his use of Chesapeake Bay and its rivers as an efficient and secure line of communications. In fact, the Peninsula campaign caused much controversy over the strategy and the ultimate withdrawal of the army from the Peninsula. Further, this, and controversy over McClellan's merits as a general, became involved in partisan politics, with Democrats siding with McClellan and his strategy and Republicans rejecting both. This meant that it became politically impossible for any general to repeat the movement to the Peninsula, even if Lincoln had permitted it. Thus this made one more strategic complexity for the Union high command.

CHAPTER 6

THE EVOLUTION OF THE HIGH COMMANDS

———————•◆•———————

The high commands consisted of the presidents, the secretaries of war and navy, and others involved in making key decisions. They formulated strategy, directed some operations themselves, and placed the execution of most of it in the hands of the principal commanders. Thus the presidents could direct concentrations such as the Shiloh campaign but, of necessity, left to a commander the decision on whether and how to employ a strategic turning movement with his army. In addition to directing major concentrations, deciding the most fundamental questions of military and political strategy, and seeing to the maintenance of the armies and navies, both presidents devoted their attention to designing effective headquarters and field organizations and to making difficult decisions about appointments and dismissals.

In view of the hurried and sometimes haphazard method of selecting the first Civil War generals, it is surprising that as many worked out as well as they did. Among the first military figures to go was not a general but Confederate Secretary of War Walker. A civilian chosen for political rather than military reasons, he dissatisfied many. One critic commented that, if Bonaparte, himself, had applied, Walker would not have given him a commission. Davis soon replaced him with Attorney

General Judah P. Benjamin, the astute former senator from Louisiana. But, in spite of Benjamin's high intelligence, his lack of military knowledge or administrative experience prevented him from performing well. His limited effectiveness and the bad military news, especially the disasters in Tennessee, made a change in the War Department politically important. In March of 1862, the president replaced Benjamin with George W. Randolph. A former naval officer and a militia artilleryman who had shown enough promise to gain promotion to brigadier general, Randolph also gave Virginia representation in the cabinet.

A lawyer with some interest in politics, Randolph brought some military knowledge and brief experience to the War Department and staffed its executive positions with people known to him. This contributed significantly to making the tiny Richmond bureaucracy more effective in managing the complexities of the war effort. Randolph also recognized an impending crisis: When the soldiers who volunteered in the spring of 1861 for one year of service would leave the army the Confederate land forces would disintegrate. The president and the Congress accepted his remedy, legislation which held the one-year volunteers in the army and made all others eligible for conscription. This national law, without precedent in the United States, also gave an impulse to volunteering. Men joined both to avoid the stigma of being conscripted and to be sure of being able to choose service with a unit originally raised in their home neighborhood, a right the law had wisely granted.

With amendments, this law governed Confederate manpower policy throughout the war. Toward the end it also brought state militia forces completely within the Confederate military system by classifying them as reserves and placing a Confederate general in each state to command them. Composed of those exempt from service as too young or old or on account of their occupations, the reserves entered active duty only to repel a threat to their region. Especially valuable for coast defense and replacing or augmenting Confederate regular forces, they allowed greater concentration against the principal Union threats.

The states of the Confederacy made other contributions as significant as furnishing their own forces. So much did the states do that each governor functioned in part as a commander in chief and partly as a subordinate of his presidential commander in chief. His principal operational role occurred when an invasion by land or sea threatened his state. This consisted in working closely with the secretary of war in deciding when to call out the militia or reserves and in what strength.

In addition to this important operational role, the states made a major contribution to logistics and soldier and civilian morale. Having raised most of the troops, the states did not abandon them when they entered the Confederate service. They provided a continuing flow of clothing and blankets to their soldiers in Confederate service. Of particular importance, because it supplemented the soldiers' meager and inflation-eroded pay, was state and county aid to soldier families. Often faced with destitution because of the loss of the soldiers' crucial labor on the farm and their inability to provide support from their pay, the families turned to the governments, which, acting generously and decisively, did much to meet their needs. In 1864 Georgia, probably most outstanding in this respect, spent 43 percent of its budget on military expenses. This outlay brought many things, including ships chartered to run the blockade to take out state-owned cotton and bring back needed supplies. Further, the state spent 51 percent of its budget on welfare, and the counties even more. Thus, through an unplanned division of labor, the state and Confederate governments made an effective team in prosecuting war.

Although they had no invasions to repel, northern governors and their states still remained active partners in the war effort but exercised less initiative than those in the South. They continued to play a critical part in raising the men for the U.S. Army because, in the absence of conscription and even after the draft law of 1863, the Federal government levied the states to supply men. The states offered bounties and other inducements to volunteers but also resorted to compulsion to fill their quotas. Because northern states could recruit southern blacks to fill their quotas, this encouraged their enlistment in the Army. Many blacks volunteered with enthusiasm for a war which had become one against slavery as well as for the Union.

Beginning the war as the essential element in creating the armies, the states continued to have a fundamental role in the war's logistics. Never mere agents of the central governments, the states both exercised sufficient autonomy and displayed such a high degree of responsiveness to national needs as to be an integral part of the command structure of each belligerent.

In spite of the success of the northern states in raising troops, Randolph's conscription act gave the Confederacy a more effective and responsive manpower system than the Union possessed. His act also made a most timely contribution by keeping the veterans with the armies in 1862. But Randolph had much less to do with operations than with logistics. His stamina already sapped by tuberculosis, he ultimately failed to work well with Davis. He found quite frustrating Davis's way of reaching decisions, especially the frequent and sometimes protracted discussion of military problems, often conducted without any urgency about coming to an immediate decision. Davis's reorganization of the high command, though only briefly fully effective, also contributed to limiting Randolph's role in operations. At the same time that he selected Randolph secretary, Davis had appointed a de facto general in chief. He made it a powerful and clearly defined position when he gave General Lee charge of military operations under his supervision, a position which today one would describe as chief of staff.

In addition to bringing Lee to Richmond as chief of staff, Davis reorganized the military departments, a system of regional commands which embraced the whole South. Each with its own army and a geographical area which provided a source of supplies, the department, which the United States and other armies traditionally used, became the basic command organization for both combatants. Originally the Confederacy had had a multitude of miniature departments centered on the coasts and a huge one facing north, Department Number Two or the Western Department, which stretched from the Appalachian Mountains westward. Consolidating the small departments, Davis also cut down the Western Department by separating East Tennessee and placing it under the command of the promising veteran of the Battle of Manassas, General Edmund Kirby Smith.

In the previous summer of 1861 Davis had received an incredibly long and quite abrasive letter of complaint from J. E. Johnston, protesting the president's decision to base his Confederate Army seniority on his line rank as a lieutenant colonel rather than his quartermaster rank of brigadier general, thus depriving Johnston the position of senior Confederate general. Probably Davis had not thought he should outrank A. S. Johnston and Lee, whom Davis esteemed more, simply because Secretary of War John B. Floyd, Johnston's cousin, had chosen him rather than Lee or Sidney Johnston as quartermaster general. His reduced seniority never ceased to rankle Johnston; but Davis, whose administrative experience had taught him the need to work with prickly subordinates and who at that time tolerated Beauregard and other difficult people more readily than later in the war, seems not to have held it against Johnston.

Having Lee and Randolph in Richmond, Johnston in field command in Virginia, and Beauregard, the supposed victor of Shiloh, in the West must have made Davis feel comfortable about his command situation in April as McClellan began his Peninsula campaign. President Lincoln doubtless felt otherwise about his command.

In March 1862 Lincoln also reorganized his command when he relieved McClellan of his duties as general in chief as he began his active field command in the Peninsula campaign. Rather than replacing him, Lincoln carried out an innovative experiment by creating the War Board, composed of the chiefs of the staff departments. These, principally the adjutant general who dealt with orders and personnel, the commissary general who provided food for the men, the quartermaster general who supplied and moved the armies, the chief engineer, and the chief of ordnance, were what today we call special staff. But Lincoln tried to use them as a general staff, which traditionally would advise commanders not on specifics but on the broad areas of operations, intelligence of the enemy, and logistics, including personnel. Few people understood a general staff, the need for it, or its functions of making recommendations to a commander and supervising the execution of his orders. Typically each staff department supervised its own specialty and had nothing to do with the command of troops, which was the task of the line officers. The system had functioned well since the time of its establishment early in the century.

To head his War Board and act as adviser to the secretary of war, Lincoln called back from retirement General Ethan Allen Hitchcock, a highly respected soldier who, having already seen forty years of service, returned to active duty with reluctance. The appointment of a leader formalized the informal links of collaboration which necessarily existed between the quite separate staff bureaus. The War Board experiment also reflected Lincoln's confidence in Edwin M. Stanton, his new secretary of war, who had to make the board work and on whom some of the duties of the former general in chief would naturally fall.

An Ohio Democrat who had briefly served as President Buchanan's attorney general, Stanton was a brilliant lawyer and proved a capable and relentlessly energetic administrator. He served the president well by making friends with some of his Republican critics, by the excellence of his direction, and by the quality of the appointments he made, particularly in bringing in businessmen to give their talent and vigor to the management of the war effort. On the other hand, Stanton was abrasive, arbitrary, and devious, with a talent for intrigue and naive ideas about warfare.

Lincoln, Stanton, and the War Board took over operations in Virginia, controlling two separate departments in northern and western Virginia as well as McClellan's huge force. In the West, however, the president at last eliminated the anomaly of two separate departments fighting the same enemy when he put Halleck in charge of Buell's department as well as his own. Confidence in Halleck must have helped counterbalance the misgivings he surely felt about McClellan and his strategy.

Many political leaders and their constituents had far stronger misgivings, not only about McClellan and his strategy but about the whole conduct of the war. Secretary Stanton, who held the very concept of strategy in contempt, believed that "patriotic spirit, with resolute courage in officers and men, is a military combination that never failed." Seeing war as battles and these in terms of victorious charges, he believed that the capture of forts Henry and Donelson showed that "battles are to be won now and by use in the same and only manner they were ever won by any people, or in any age since Joshua, by boldly surprising and striking the foe." Stanton represented a widely held civilian view, one echoed in the South by Governor Joseph E. Brown of Georgia who, having faith in a spear called a pike, believed that, if at Fort Donelson the Confederates had had these, they could have, "with a shout of victory" rushed "with terrible impetuosity into the lines of the enemy" and won the battle because "hand to hand the pike has vastly the advantage of the bayonet."

Lincoln and his generals came under particularly severe criticism from those who, ignorant of logistical constraints or tactical realities and disapproving of a conciliatory policy, wanted an end to "sickly inoffensive war" and a beginning of action "suited to remorseless revolutionary violence." Many blamed West Point and the professional soldiers for the lack of a quick victory and yearned for generals "whose intellect has not been narrowed down to the rules of your military school." They believed that "common sense" and a "stout heart" sufficed to make good generals.

Others feared that the cause of the lack of decisive offensive action lay in "lukewarm, half secession officers in command who cannot bear to strike a blow lest it hurt their rebel friends or jeopardize the precious protectors of slavery." Thus, discounting military factors, many saw inaction and the conciliatory policy as evidence of sympathy with rebellion and slavery. McClellan's delays and his slow progress had played into the hands of the censorious and dismayed many others. Lincoln, who shared the critics' impatience, had a daunting task in standing between those skeptical of the professional soldiers and the generals, whose problems he increasingly came to comprehend.

In July 1862 President Lincoln again reorganized his command system just as Lee and Davis initiated another move to make the most of the strategic situation in Virginia. After journeying to West Point to seek the advice of the retired General Scott, Lincoln appointed Halleck to the office of general in chief. This decision reflected both his confidence in the country's most successful general, and the failure of the War Board to supply the kind of strategic advice the president needed. In part the board failed because General Hitchcock's poor health prevented him from providing much leadership.

Upon his departure from the West, Halleck left two separate armies behind, Buell on the offensive in Middle Tennessee and Grant guarding northern Mississippi, his advance southward

81

temporarily stymied by drought and other supply difficulties. Halleck had divided the big army he had concentrated to match the Confederates at Shiloh and Corinth in part because of the obstacles to an immediate advance south from Corinth. Thus Halleck had returned to the original two lines of operations, the Mississippi and Middle Tennessee, again placed under separate command by his departure for Washington.

When Halleck arrived in Washington he found that Lincoln and Stanton had combined the forces in the Shenandoah Valley and near Washington into an army of 50,000 in northern Virginia under General John Pope. But Halleck fixed his attention on McClellan and his army, both inert beside the James River a few miles east of Richmond. Taking with him the intelligent and versatile engineer officer, Quartermaster General Meigs, Halleck promptly visited McClellan, who was asking for reinforcements to resume his advance against Lee's superior numbers. He found that McClellan failed to realize that, since he had ceased actively to threaten Richmond, he now merely awaited the rebels on an exterior line, a situation quite obvious to Halleck. Returning to Washington, the new general in chief concluded that McClellan did "not understand strategy and should never plan a campaign." He ordered him and his army to Washington.

The situation of the armies of McClellan and Pope with Lee between, facing the "daily risk of being attacked and defeated in detail," made Halleck "so uneasy" that he "could hardly sleep." Anxious about the vain and pompous Pope facing seasoned and well-led Confederates, Halleck warned him to be careful, cautioning him that Lee might "turn your right." Just as before Shiloh, Halleck made the same strategic assessment as the rebels, and, as Lee's Second Manassas campaign demonstrated, he was correct about the danger to Pope's right and in his belief that the enemy would concentrate against Pope's forces and move forward to the Potomac.

Union and Confederate high commands had displayed a certain symmetry as each attempted to do without a general in chief. Davis had hoped to substitute the experienced Adjutant and Inspector General Cooper and Lincoln his innovative War Board led by the equally seasoned General Hitchcock. Both experiments failed, largely because of the inadequacies of the two generals. Each president then returned to the system of general in chief, Davis's order defining Lee's powerful position exactly. Although, in appointing Halleck, Lincoln did not eliminate the vagueness associated with the powers of the general in chief, in practice he gave him as much power as Lee exercised. The presidents had both chosen men of exceptional ability whose talents well matched their positions. Each general had to form a working partnership with the secretaries of war, something Halleck did with success and Lee had too little time in office to accomplish. But the Union drew ahead of the Confederacy when Davis, wisely, met the emergency of Johnston's wounding by appointing Lee to succeed him but unwisely leaving the position of chief of staff unfilled.

In spite of having a better headquarters organization, events of the late summer and early fall of 1862 would overwhelm Halleck and his evolving staff. Halleck had hardly settled and coped with the Second Manassas campaign when the Confederates unleashed two menacing raids.

CHAPTER 7
THE EMERGENCE OF RAIDS

———•————

Kentucky and Antietam Campaigns

Raids proved one of the Civil War's most effective strategies. Probably the oldest form of warfare, by the end of 1862 the Confederates had made it a full strategic partner with the Napoleonic operation strategy of concentration and the turning movement. Essentially an offensive strategy, the raid could succeed because it avoided the enemy, or at least any of his main forces. An incident in West Tennessee illustrates the characteristic approach of this strategy.

After a long record of consistent Union failure to control Confederate guerrillas and raiders in West Tennessee, in 1864 Major General Cadwallader C. Washburn superseded General Hurlbut as Union commander in the region. The capable and energetic Washburn fared little better than Hurlbut. One reason for the general's failure was that his area received the virtually undivided attention of General Nathan Bedford Forrest, the most redoubtable of the rebel raiders in the West. Frequently raiding West Tennessee, sometimes remaining long enough to recruit men there but always wrecking railroads and burning supplies, General Forrest, a former Memphis merchant, finally made a night raid on the city of Memphis, Washburn's headquarters. Briefly controlling the center of town, he would have captured the sleeping general had Washburn not escaped from his bedroom clad only in his nightshirt. This gave Hurlbut the delicious opportunity to remark: "They removed me from command because I couldn't keep Forrest out of West Tennessee, and now Washburn can't keep him out of his own bedroom."

Forrest's brief foray into Memphis well illustrates the nature of a raid. The Confederate general had neither the goal nor the ability to capture and hold Memphis, a town with strong Union forces nearby. The raid's essence is to injure the enemy with a quick strike, to burn a railway bridge, or execute the propaganda coup of capturing an enemy general in his own headquarters. The strength of raiders lies in the elusiveness of their transitory presence; they exploit on the offensive the superiority of retreat over pursuit. Further, the variety of their possible objectives creates an unpredictability which makes it very easy for raiders to surprise their foe. Since surprise is almost synonymous with finding the defender weak and unprepared, the raid is usually stronger than the defense.

Raids had a far larger role in the Civil War than in wars fought in western Europe during the previous two centuries. Raids against logistic objectives like bridges, typical of those carried out by Forrest, played a significant part in defeating the next Union offensive in the West.

After the fall of Corinth and a token pursuit to push Beauregard away from the vicinity of the city, Halleck immediately chose a new line of operations, one eastward along the Memphis and Charleston Railroad, over a hundred miles of which the Union already controlled. Rather than attempt to follow Beauregard southward, rebuilding a destroyed railroad in the heat and possible disease of the Mississippi summer, Halleck wanted to take advantage of the enterprise of General O. M. Mitchel, who had led 8,000 men south from Nashville to gain control of the Memphis and Charleston Railroad almost as far east as Chattanooga. So, on June 10, 1862, he sent Buell east with 30,000 men, with orders to move rapidly along the captured railway. Two days later he reported to Secretary Stanton that he expected Buell soon to be near Chattanooga and, "if the enemy should have evacuated East Tennessee and Cumberland Gap, as reported, Buell will probably move on to Atlanta."

Two factors prevented the realization of Halleck's vision of taking Chattanooga and placing Buell's army on the direct rail line between Atlanta and Richmond and between Beauregard and East Tennessee; and neither had anything to do with the enemy. Mitchel had not, as Halleck supposed, captured an intact railroad. Rather, broken bridges and trestles divided the line into segments and destruction on the railroad from Nashville interrupted service from the North as well as from Corinth. Nor could the Tennessee River make up the transportation deficiency, because low water in the summer and shoals, an obstacle to navigation, restricted the movement of boats. The other factor was General Buell. When Lincoln had expressed admiration for his "cautious vigor," he understood him well. Buell could not ignore the defects in his communications and make the daring dash that Halleck's strategy required. Instead, and in spite of the high agricultural productivity of Middle Tennessee, the cautious Buell halted and established a communication link by repairing the railroad to Nashville.

While sending Buell east and dispatching men to reinforce Kansas, Halleck expected the navy to continue the southward advance along the Mississippi which had brought the capture of Memphis in early June 1862. This city and Corinth belonged in Grant's department, and he found it difficult to keep his railroads running. Raiders did the damage, the raiders being rebels who showed their hostility to the invaders by, according to Halleck, "giving much annoyance in burning bridges, houses, and cotton." Quite knowledgeable of the countryside, these hostile inhabitants easily carried out raids and, with almost equal facility, avoided pursuit, as Grant found when his troops failed in their effort to "clean out the guerrilla parties in West Tennessee and North Mississippi."

In Middle Tennessee the guerrillas had a significant strategic effect when they played a major part in defeating Buell's advance on Chattanooga. A largely spontaneous opposition, guerrillas had started their activities soon after Mitchel moved south from Nashville, when he reported: "Guerrilla warfare has been inaugurated along my entire line, and we are attacked nightly at bridges and outposts." Railroads were terribly vulnerable. Merely loosening a rail would cause a train to leave the tracks, and the burning of a bridge or a trestle would interrupt service until the completion of repairs or rebuilding. Thus the elusive guerrilla raiders nearly paralyzed rail traffic.

Two raids by regular Confederate cavalry forces completed the work of halting Buell's railroad-dependent, summer advance. Brigadier General Nathan Bedford Forrest led one of these. One of the ablest soldiers of the war, Forrest had left his prosperous business interests to volunteer as a private. Soon becoming a colonel, he had displayed what became his typical enterprise when he led his unit through enemy lines just before the capitulation of Fort Donelson. Using substantial force, he cut the railroad south of Nashville, defeating a Union brigade and capturing nearly $1,000,000 worth of supplies. His destruction of bridges kept the railway from running for two weeks. Farther to the north in Kentucky, Colonel John Hunt Morgan, also a merchant turned soldier, raided for three weeks, destroying depots, taking prisoners, and disrupting the railroad between Louisville and Nashville (see diagram of raiders and guerrillas).

Buell withdrew two divisions from his advance against Chattanooga in order to "guard against the recurrence of such raids." Thus the vulnerability of Buell's supply lines not only caused a shortage of supplies but also reduced the number of men committed to the advance. As a result, he halted his offensive, apprehensive about trying to lengthen his already disrupted communications and because his weakened advance met apparently strong resistance from East Tennessee's energetic defender, General Kirby Smith.

It is not, however, surprising that a few guerrillas and two cavalry raids halted more than 40,000 men. They succeeded because their strategy aimed not at hostile soldiers but at their supplies. Aided by the fragility of the railroad and the invaders' dependence on outside food and forage, raiders found Buell's logistics very vulnerable. The other strategic element which favored the guerrillas and the cavalry was the raid. Individual guerrillas setting out to move a rail, or a band aiming to overcome a few guards and burn a trestle, depended on their mobility to shun stronger opponents and to pounce on the weaker, an unguarded section of track or an inadequately defended bridge. Cavalry raiders had the same advantage as the guerrillas. They both avoided predictability in their routes of march or their objective and rarely retreated by the same route by which they had come.

With guerrillas and cavalry raids complementing each other, the Confederates' logistic raiding strategy stopped Buell and gave them the opportunity to plan another campaign. This operation came at the initiative of the new commander of the Western Department, General Braxton Bragg.

When the president had relieved Beauregard in June, Bragg had replaced him. After the first day of the Battle of Shiloh, Beauregard had prematurely announced a victory and had never told the government the real outcome. Lee had written him, just before the evacuation of Corinth, that the government had hopes that, after "the victory of Shiloh," Beauregard would advance. With the loss of Corinth and the immediate fall of Memphis, the president learned the truth. After sending an aide to question Beauregard, Davis took the opportunity to relieve him when Beauregard went on sick leave. Davis returned him to duty as commander of the Department of South Carolina, Georgia, and Florida, an appointment welcomed in those states. Bragg had done an outstanding job in organizing his department, training and disciplining its army, and willingly and promptly responding to the crisis in Tennessee by going north with virtually his whole force. Already promoted to full general, he then received the command of the department and army upon the relief of Beauregard.

At West Point with Beauregard, Bragg had graduated in time to fight in the Seminole War. An artilleryman, Bragg's name became a household word as a result of General Taylor's oft-quoted, quaint way of ordering him and his guns to fire more grape shot at the Battle of Buena Vista: "A little more grape, Captain Bragg." Having left the army to farm in Louisiana, he received an early appointment as brigadier general and had made an admirable impression on his superiors. Yet in the old army he had earned such a reputation for contentiousness that at least two jokes circulated about him. One had him, when serving as quartermaster and as a unit commander simultaneously, sending written requisitions for supplies to himself; as quartermaster he disapproved them in writing, then protested the disapproval and so had a protracted argument with himself. In the other, which also illustrated his inability to get along with his fellows, he put people under arrest until he had everyone arrested and then placed himself under arrest. The abrasive quality illustrated by these stories would prove a serious handicap for this accomplished officer.

Bragg's army had two corps, one of them under William J. Hardee, who had been at West Point with Bragg. Hardee had shown his ability at Shiloh and had distinguished himself in the U.S. Army, fighting under Taylor and Scott, authoring the army's version of the French infantry regulations, and serving as commandant at West Point. The other corps commander, Major General Leonidas Polk, had quite a different background. At West Point with President Davis, the imposing and fluent Polk had early left the army to become an Episcopal clergyman. Soon rising to bishop, he became so prominent a figure throughout the South that he received a commission as major general. Handicapped by his lack of military experience, he gave an uneven performance in many commands.

Realizing that a two months' drought and the well-foraged state of the country around Corinth meant that "neither of us could well advance in the absence of rail transportation," Bragg obtained the departed Beauregard's advice on a plan of campaign. Like Halleck a month before, he decided to change his line of operations, proposing to distract the enemy in front by creating the "impression" that he was advancing. Meanwhile he planned to take his army eastward, "where our cavalry is paving the way for me," and arrive in Tennessee before the enemy "can know my movement." Thus he projected a turning movement on a gigantic scale, enabling him to gain "the enemy's rear, cutting off his supplies and dividing his forces so as to encounter them in detail!" Leaving one force to guard the Mississippi and another to distract Grant, he moved by rail to Chattanooga with half of his army.

Organizing his circuitous rail movement via Mobile with typical thoroughness, Bragg made sure that his commissary representatives met rail-borne soldiers at stations along the way with the rations which they had not been able to forage for themselves from a moving train. Moreover, to expedite the movement, Bragg sent the Mobile garrison ahead, confident that "as long a we are passing, Mobile is safe." Since the last units to leave northern Mississippi made up the new garrison of Mobile, Bragg's method had used the railroad as if it were a pipeline: Units flowing into one end pushed the units already in the pipe out. When turned off, the pipe still contained the last units to enter. This pipeline method of reinforcement became a feature of Confederate strategy, permitting more rapid concentrations, particularly along the Atlantic coast.

Beginning his move in July 1862, after less than a month in command, Bragg reached Chattanooga and, in August, marched into Kentucky. He coordinated his advance with Kirby Smith's from Knoxville but, since Kirby Smith headed a separate department, the armies did not have the advantage of unity of command. Absorption with events around Richmond and Davis's predilection for allowing his commanders full discretion made the president and the secretary of war mere spectators of Bragg's gigantic maneuver.

In mid August Kirby Smith had left Knoxville in East Tennessee and marched 10,000 men into central Kentucky, reaching the exceptionally fertile Bluegrass region in two weeks. Here, at Richmond, Kentucky, he met 6,000 Union troops who, though most had just mustered in and knew nothing of drill, made a surprisingly good resistance before suffering annihilation. They lost nearly 90 percent of their force, four fifths of them in prisoners, compared to 4.5 percent for the veteran Confederate force. This victory gave Kirby Smith control of this rich area and of the Kentucky capital.

Meanwhile Bragg, with 30,000 men, moved north from Chattanooga, passing Buell's army dispersed on the railway network south of Nashville. Realizing that Bragg was marching toward his rear and the railroad to Louisville, Buell also understood that, if he fell back too precipitously in order to cover his rear, Bragg could change direction and pounce on Nashville, Tennessee's capital and a valuable commercial and industrial center.

Consequently Buell garrisoned Nashville strongly while concentrating the bulk of his force north of it at Bowling Green in Kentucky. So, though Bragg had turned Buell back, he had not gained Middle Tennessee and had dim prospects of doing so even if he should get astride the railway. Were the rebel general to seize this crucial position, he still could not force Buell to attack him because the thorough and imperturbable Yankee general knew he could march northeast to an alternate depot on the Ohio where he could meet steamers with supplies and have transportation to Louisville. But Buell did not count on needing this expedient for, with the food in his depots, including a month's rations ready at Bowling Green, he could wait until Bragg had to leave the railroad or make his army vulnerable by dispersing it to look for food (see diagram of Bragg turning Buell).

And this is what happened in the middle of September when Bragg reached Buell's rear and dug entrenchments as he prepared to receive Buell's attack. Since Bragg lacked access to a fertile base area, two days in the "barren and destitute" country forced him away from the railroad to join Kirby Smith in the fertile Bluegrass; and Buell promptly marched north to Louisville, retaining control of the railroad all the way to Nashville. By failing to hold the railroad, Bragg had limited himself to the role of raider, in spite of his temporary logistic affluence in the Bluegrass. With only primitive road communication through the rugged mountainous country in the east of Kentucky and Tennessee, he could hardly remain in Kentucky facing a stronger enemy who could supply and move on a parallel track by rail. He could remain for a while, but he could not control the state.

When Buell reached Louisville, he met reinforcements of green troops which he skillfully incorporated into his veteran army and, at the beginning of October, the enlarged force moved out on a broad front to drive Bragg from Kentucky. When the Federal forces approached Frankfort, Bragg, at the inauguration ceremonies for the Confederate governor of Kentucky, ordered an attack on Buell's main army at Perryville, having mistaken it for a detachment. Rebuffed in this battle, discouraged and finally better understanding the situation, he decided that the time had come to withdraw to Tennessee. Though he might have prolonged his raid a little longer, having to concentrate to resist Buell made it difficult for him to supply himself even in the Bluegrass, a problem not so acute for the Union army, which had two railroad links to Louisville. With the enemy before them, Bragg and Kirby Smith followed much the same route by which Kirby Smith had come, until Bragg finally reached Murfreesboro, southwest of Nashville. Buell wisely made no effort to pursue Bragg over the unproductive and already well-foraged eastern Kentucky and East Tennessee route.

Buell's decision not to pursue and his failure to do more harm to Bragg in battle led Lincoln to relieve him of command. Halleck, who recognized Buell's good qualities and the difficulty in finding better commanders, compared this with the guillotining of generals during the French Revolution. Unrealistic civilian expectations in the Kentucky campaign had caused the loss of a capable but often too deliberate general.

The Kentucky campaign showed that Bragg, the brilliant strategist and superb organizer and administrator, did not perform well when operating close to the enemy. He often failed to understand the situation and his judgment became unreliable. Kirby Smith, who believed Bragg had become a different person once he entered Kentucky, would have agreed with the appraisal of one of his brigade commanders that "there was no man in either of the contending armies who was General Bragg's superior as an organizer and a disciplinarian, but when he was in the presence of an enemy he lost his head."

Thus Bragg had much in common with McClellan, excellence in strategy and management, inadequacy in command. But they differed in that McClellan's charisma blinded his subordinates to his deficiency, while Bragg's abrasiveness made his generals particularly aware of and discontented with his special inadequacy.

Bragg's Kentucky raid had enabled him to live at the enemy's expense for two months and Kirby Smith a little longer. That it had also drawn Union forces away from Chattanooga, recovered a part of Middle Tennessee, and removed the immediate threat to East Tennessee made it a moderate strategic success. It had a neutral tactical effect in terms of the losses in the two battles, Richmond and Perryville, during which the Confederates lost 3,800 to the Union's 9,500, favorable as a percentage of the forces engaged and neutral in comparison to population. Yet the raid failed in its quasi-political objective of bringing many Kentucky volunteers into the Confederate ranks, an expectation encouraged by the Kentuckians in uniform and in the

92

Confederate Congress. Many in that slave-owning state had strong southern sympathies, but few wished to fight for the Confederacy.

Because of the expectations raised by Bragg's raid, the retreat caused the symbolism of the campaign to hurt Confederate morale. On the other hand, the exploits of Morgan and Forrest elevated morale because the public understood that they were raiders and would return. Southerners had difficulty seeing the advance and the inevitable retreat of a large raiding army in the same way as they would a small band of cavalry raiders. That the Battle of Perryville immediately preceded the Confederate withdrawal reinforced the image of a defeat and a retreat.

When McClellan and his men returned to northern Virginia from the Peninsula, he assumed command of the consolidation of his and Pope's beaten army. He was to have no respite for rest and reorganization, because Lee again would do what Halleck forecast, this time "cross the Potomac, and make a raid into Maryland or Pennsylvania."

Having regained the same position Johnston had held for over a half year, Lee could well have victoriously concluded his three months in command by going on the defensive. Instead, he took his weary army on another turning movement, this time into western Maryland. It differed from the Second Manassas campaign in that, by attempting no distraction and moving around the enemy's flank with his whole army, he lacked surprise and had neither the ability nor the purpose of reaching the enemy's rear and intercepting his retreat. Moreover, unlike the operation just completed, this would be a raid, a transitory rather than a permanent occupation. This campaign shared the logistic aim of its predecessor, in this case to live for a while at the enemy's expense on the "supplies of the rich and productive districts" of Maryland. Meanwhile Lee's commissaries and quartermasters would scour Virginia and lay in all of its produce for the army's winter needs.

Lee understood the political aspects of a movement into Union territory and knew that one of them was not "any general rising of the people on our behalf," even though Maryland had slavery and some volunteers in the Confederate Army. He did, however, realize that his presence in Maryland during the

Congressional elections had political implications and might even present an auspicious occasion for a southern "proposal of peace."

Crossing the Potomac west of Washington, he sent Jackson to capture Harper's Ferry and so open a line of rail communication to Winchester, spreading his other troops out to forage. Here, in addition to its logistic merits and political effect, the army's position enabled it to defend Confederate territory. As long as it continued there, Lee believed that it could so threaten the flank of any Union advance south as to "detain the enemy upon the northern frontier until the approach of winter should render his advance into Virginia difficult, if not impracticable." Consequently this raid would function as a defensive turning movement, driving the enemy back but not involving any battle.

Only his estimate of McClellan explains why Lee expected to remain in Maryland unmolested for two or even three months. The Union general's refusal to move in the fall of 1861, his elaborate preparations to besiege the weak line on the Peninsula, and his failure to begin siege operations against Richmond must have persuaded Lee that McClellan would not attack him before he was ready to go back to Virginia. In any case, Lee contemplated extending his raid into Pennsylvania, a movement which would give the cautious McClellan a reason for still more delays.

But the situation helped change McClellan's behavior. Lee's entry into Maryland presented the Lincoln administration with a political crisis which McClellan realized he could not ignore. Further, although General in Chief Halleck had been friendly to McClellan since his recall from the Peninsula, he also had left him in no doubt as to who was in charge. Though Halleck now had become mystified by Lee's purpose, Lincoln believed that Lee had placed himself in a dangerous position, vulnerable to being cut off. So McClellan moved quickly, leaving Washington on September 6, 1862, the same day Lee completed his crossing of the Potomac. As McClellan's 80,000 men advanced with such unaccustomed celerity against Lee's scattered 50,000, Jackson trapped and besieged 12,000 Union troops in the Potomac River town of Harper's Ferry (see diagram of beginning of Antietam campaign). McClellan, the subject of contradictory instructions from his president and from his general in chief, increased his rate of advance when he captured a copy of Lee's order revealing all his dispositions.

Realizing that McClellan's unexpected behavior had defeated his raid, Lee moved to recross the Potomac while delaying McClellan at the passes in the low mountains between the two armies. But, when an incompetent defense gave Jackson the capitulation of Harper's Ferry and its garrison, Lee decided to concentrate his army and offer to fight a defensive battle. This offer McClellan accepted, the political situation giving him no choice. Lee's turning movement had forced McClellan to attack for reasons comparable to those which had compelled Lee to attack McClellan in June in the Seven Days' Battles.

On September 17 McClellan, in his first offensive battle, spent the day conducting poorly coordinated frontal attacks along Antietam Creek. In the all-day battle, Lee, with at least 40,000 men against 70,000, defended himself only with great difficulty by skillfully moving reinforcements to meet successive attacks. The next day McClellan did not resume his assaults, though Lee remained in his position, demonstrating to his army as well as to his adversary that he had won the Battle of Antietam. Lee won because he had achieved his goal, the repulse of the Union attack, and McClellan had lost because he failed to attain his objective, driving the rebels from their position.

Yet Lee then retreated. He did so because, as a raider, he could not remain concentrated and unable readily to forage. On the other hand, McClellan, only 20 miles from the railroad to Baltimore, could draw on his base area and remain concentrated with comparative ease. So, on September 19 Lee recrossed the Potomac and took up a position south of the river in the north end of the Shenandoah Valley.

Because Lee, like Jackson three weeks earlier, had made the mistake of failing to entrench at all, the Confederates lost heavily in their precarious defense. The very bloody Battle of Antietam cost the Confederates 13,700 men, 34 percent of their available force, and the Union 12,350, 18 percent of its. For the entire campaign, the 12,000 prisoners taken at Harper's Ferry raised the Union loss to 30 percent.

With loses so close to even, the tactical result of the campaign had less importance than the strategic, which merely circumscribed Lee's foraging area by forcing him to spend the fall feeding his army south of the Potomac but nonetheless still enabled him to protect Virginia by maintaining his position on the flank of any advance. But the bloody battle, followed by a rebel retreat, gave the Union a major symbolic victory. The pugnacious Lee had made a risky military decision to fight, considering his numerical inferiority, failure to entrench, and position with his back to the Potomac River—which, though it protected his flanks, could impede retreat. Moreover, Lee made a serious political error when he elected to fight a defensive battle against McClellan. Lee's withdrawal, even after his winning defensive battle, made the victory appear a defeat. This was the inevitable outcome, no matter how decisively successful the defense he had made—as long as McClellan avoided making the blunder of retreating. As a raider, without a means of feeding his concentrated army, he could not remain where he was; and McClellan, with his access to the railroad, could outwait him and thereby use Lee's otherwise necessary departure to turn a failed offensive battle into an apparent victory. If Lee had withdrawn without a battle but with the prisoners from Harper's Ferry, it would have been a successful raid, the prisoner trophies proving it. This would have given the Confederacy a modest symbolic victory and a handsome one in attrition, a fine consolation for the strategic failure of not spending the fall dining on Maryland harvests.

The North reaped a fine political harvest from the battle and Lee's retreat. Lincoln used the image of a victorious Union as a springboard for making his preliminary proclamation freeing the slaves in the states in rebellion. The symbolism of Lee's retreat helped Lincoln take a step which did much to harness antislavery sentiment in the North, and, gradually, in the world, to the Union cause.

The battle's role has led to speculation about what would have happened had Lee won. Presuming that winning consisted of McClellan retreating after the first day of battle, he would doubtless have fallen back to a strong position in closer touch with his railroad. Lee likely would have resumed foraging rather than raiding north and leaving McClellan's big army between him and Virginia. If Burnside had then replaced Mc-

Clellan as he did later, one might reasonably expect to have seen earlier the same Federal movement toward Fredericksburg, Virginia, desired by Halleck and Lincoln, thus drawing Lee also toward Fredericksburg. In any case, Lee would have had to withdraw no later than toward the end of autumn. That three northern victories, two by Grant in Mississippi and Buell's at Perryville, came within three weeks of the hypothetical Union defeat at Antietam would certainly have mitigated the effect of Lee's longer time in Maryland, a stay extended by McClellan's retreat. This melioration of the damage to the Lincoln administration's image would probably have limited the Republican loss in the fall Congressional elections to only a few more seats than those actually lost.

Some have seen a Union retreat as potentially decisive because they believe that it would have induced the British and the French to recognize the Confederacy and intervene in some way. This would have made Lee's hypothetical victory, insignificant militarily, decisive in the political dimension. Had the hypothetical Confederate victory at Antietam led to action by Britain and France, it would have made the diplomatic and political situation far murkier than the military. Certainly the British action would have provided the impulse for the Army of the Potomac to march sooner toward Richmond, a move which actually occurred in late October and November of 1862. This drawing of Lee out of Maryland to cover Richmond would have somewhat diminished the éclat of the rebel victory.

Pushed back in the winter and spring of 1862, the Confederates innovatively combined the strategic turning movement and the raid to make a brilliant summer riposte. Of course Bragg had not intended a raid at the outset, but, when he had to withdraw from Buell's rear, he turned his campaign into a raid and joined Kirby Smith, never more than a raider. Unable to reach his adversary's rear or control a railroad, Lee had initiated his campaign as a raid and based it on an optimistic assessment of McClellan's behavior. Although the raids made only temporary logistical gains and perhaps marked up some loss in Confederate morale, they most surely forestalled any Union offensives in the affected areas. And they hardly provided an auspicious beginning for Halleck's service as general in chief. When Lee's army was in Maryland, Halleck's new headquarters functioned poorly and Lee caused such anxiety and activity in Washington that Halleck hardly slept for days.

But the campaigning season had not ended. As Lee and McClellan rested and supplied their men, and as the armies in Kentucky moved back to Tennessee, the fall season, with the year's lightest rainfall, offered the opportunity for the new Union general in chief to make another application of Lincoln's strategy of simultaneous advances.

CHAPTER 8

CONCENTRATION IN TIME

Fredericksburg, Holly Springs, Chickasaw
Bluffs, and Stones River Campaigns

Whereas the turning movement and the raid provided means of evading the defenders' strength, concentration sought only to outnumber the adversary. But a general could readily unite concentration with turning and raiding, augmenting his force for a turning movement or a raid or, as Lee and Bragg had done, combine the two. Thus concentration had a dominant or, at least, a subordinate role in most Civil War operations. There was another means of concentration besides moving men to the same place: moving them in separate places at the same time. And concentration in time could secure an even greater preponderance in numbers than concentration in space but at the cost of a maneuver more difficult to execute.

The Confederate use of interior lines to reinforce Beauregard in time for the First Battle of Manasses made a profound impression on the Union high command. This successful Confederate concentration in space contributed to what at one time was a ridiculous, almost paranoid, Union overestimate of Confederate capacity for strategic troop movements by rail. A glance at the map, which showed a shorter southern rail link in the line running from Richmond through Chattanooga to Memphis, Tennessee, led northern leaders to imagine troops moving along this route to augment the rebel forces in either Virginia or Tennessee. In fact, the rebels never so used this rail link, but the capability and the delusion that it frequently moved men made cutting this strategic railroad a major Federal objective. Other than railroads running inland from the coast, it was the only major example of southern interior railroad lines. The whole northern assumption ignored the speed of train operation, which increasingly favored the northern railroads as they sustained a higher standard of maintenance than those in the South.

This overestimate of Confederate concentrations by rail turned the thoughts of the Union leaders to means to counter what they perceived as this major Confederate strategic advantage. To oppose the enemy's ability to concentrate in space, Lincoln early prescribed the concentration in time of simultaneous advances. This strategy, which Scott had directed for McDowell and Patterson, distinctively belonged to armies on the offensive and would counteract southern defensive concentrations by making the most of the rebels' weakening of one army to strengthen another. Concentration in time thus enabled an undiminished Federal army to assail a reduced Confederate force.

Concentration in time early became a firm principle of Union strategy, but implementation proved difficult, largely because of logistical problems. Armies found it hard to ready themselves to move all at the same time. The first attempt at concentration in time came in the winter of 1862, when Lincoln issued his order for all armies to advance on the same day, February 22, 1862, Washington's birthday. But the muddy winter roads had bogged the armies down.

In spite of the failure of the Washington's birthday order, Halleck moved by water in February and McClellan, also by water, in March, a month after the fall of Fort Donelson. Thereafter operations occurred simultaneously in east and west. Banks advanced in late March just as Buell moved to reinforce Grant at Pittsburg Landing, McClellan's siege of Yorktown began two days before Shiloh, the fall of Corinth occurred two days before the Battle of Fair Oaks, and Buell's advance and Bragg and Kirby Smith's Kentucky campaigns took place simultaneously with the summer operations in Virginia. Illustrative of the Union's overestimate of Confederate capabilities, many Union soldiers and civilians believed that reinforcements from Beauregard in Mississippi had taken part in Lee's concentration for the Seven Days' Battles. But this coordination of Union activity on the eastern and western fronts occurred fortuitously and not as a result of any plan. It was not until December 1862 that the Union planned and successfully executed its first concentration in time.

A comparison of the two forms of concentration in terms of obtaining superiority of force favors concentration in time. If two opponents each had 100,000 men, one force concentrated in an interior position and the other on exterior lines and divided evenly into two armies of 50,000 each, and if the interior force divided itself and sent 75,000 men against one hostile army and used 25,000 to keep the other in check while, at almost the same time, each exterior force responded with simultaneous advances, the interior force would attack with a contingent of 75,000 and defend with 25,000. When each of the exterior armies with 50,000 men, advanced, one army would go on the defensive when it faced 75,000, but the other one, which opposed 25,000, would press its offensive. Therefore this pitting of concentration in space against concentration in time would result in 75,000 men in the interior opposing 50,000, a 3 to 2 superiority, and 50,000 on the exterior opposing 25,000, a 2 to 1 edge, giving the army that concentrated in time a greater advantage in force and better odds for victory, albeit one involving smaller forces.

More effective in securing numerical superiority, concentration in time had the disadvantage of greater complexity in execution. A commander exploiting interior lines had only one force to move, while the one employing concentration in time had to move two armies and, still more difficult, they had to move nearly simultaneously. In view of the multitude of problems armies faced when they attempted to move and that only one of the two armies could have immediate supervision of the commander, the chances were excellent for either delay or a lack of synchronization. Halleck's experience in carrying out the Union's first planned and fully coordinated simultaneous advances faced all of these obstacles. Nonetheless he succeeded in having offensives from three main armies in December plus two diversionary moves and an uncoordinated battle in Arkansas. In readying the northern armies for simultaneous advances, their leaders faced different problems, which in Virginia most directly involved Halleck.

After his victory in Antietam, McClellan delayed to accumulate supplies and replace equipment prior to his projected advance on Lee in the Shenandoah Valley. Neither the delay nor the plan suited Lincoln and Halleck because they believed McClellan took too much time to prepare, and they disagreed with his conviction that he must advance directly against Lee. They placed no credence in McClellan's belief that it would be too hazardous to advance toward Richmond and leave the rebel army to his flank and rear, which was just the view of the strategic situation Lee expected him to take. Halleck and Lincoln saw that McClellan was closer to Richmond than Lee and, to persuade him of their view, even quoted an injunction of the noted military expert Jomini " 'to operate upon the enemy's communications as much as possible without exposing your own.' "

By the time McClellan finally moved in late October 1862, the president was ready to relieve him, replacing him with Ambrose E. Burnside, the conqueror of Roanoke Island, a rebel stronghold on the North Carolina coast. Imposing in appearance and agreeable in manner, Burnside had left the army a few years after graduating from West Point, working first in manufacturing and then for his friend McClellan in railroading. He accepted the command reluctantly, believing correctly that he lacked the requisite ability. Burnside continued the march along the route advocated by Halleck and Lincoln, proving them correct when Lee followed to the Rappahannock River to block his path toward Richmond. But slow arrival of pontoons from Washington delayed his passage until Lee arrived. So Burnside prepared to cross the river and fight on the south bank. To supplement Burnside's offensive, Halleck had arranged simultaneous advances from three small forces: at Fort Monroe, on the North Carolina coast, and from the Potomac west of Washington.

Misjudging the enemy dispositions, Burnside crossed his

army over the Rappahannock at Fredericksburg, facing all rather than only a portion of Lee's army, which occupied the heights somewhat behind the town on the south bank of the river. After devoting December 13 to futile attacks against Lee's strong position, he withdrew his men back across the river. The Confederates had the advantage of the heights and, in one place, a natural trench made by a sunken road with stone walls on each side. In fact, Lee's position had such strength that J. E. Johnston, his envy aroused, wrote a friend: "What luck some people have. Nobody will come to attack me in such a place." But, in an innovation for Lee's army in a field position, Longstreet's men had entrenched. The obvious merit of this traditional practice so appealed to officers and men that belatedly it became standard policy, one enthusiastically pushed by former engineer officer Lee.

The Federals had lost 12,500 men, the Confederates, in spite of their lack of full entrenchments, only 5,300, a clear tactical defeat for Burnside. In halting his advance, the South had achieved a strategic as well as symbolic victory, encouraging rebels and disheartening Yankees. Burnside's troops booed him after the battle, and many of his officers thought that he had made his blundering frontal assault on the orders of that unsophisticated, combative civilian, Secretary of War Stanton.

With Grant already in motion, Halleck telegraphed, without effect, the commander in Middle Tennessee to move or face relief from command. Still, in the December advances, which occurred in a closely spaced sequence rather than simultaneously, Grant's became the next army to act. Since Halleck's departure for Washington, Grant had exercised an independent command, holding Memphis and Corinth against the rebels in north Mississippi while the Navy tried to take the river stronghold of Vicksburg and Buell and Bragg campaigned in Kentucky. During this time Grant showed his mastery of orthodox operational strategy when he took advantage of the division of the Confederate forces of generals Sterling Price and Earl Van Dorn to concentrate against Price near Iuka. Sending part of his force directly against Price to hold his attention, Grant sent the other under the energetic General Rosecrans to take them in the rear, to trap them, and to force them to "conquer their way out." But, heavy rain delaying Rosecrans, the

Confederates escaped. When they later spent a day and a half assaulting the skillful Rosecrans in the fortified city of Corinth, the defenders repulsed the attacks, inflicting fifty percent more casualties than they received. Wary of his opponent and without supplies, Grant attempted only a brief pursuit.

With men and commanders thus seasoned, Grant planned a campaign southward to capture Vicksburg, the more powerful of the last two Confederate strongholds on the Mississippi River. If he could take it, he would control the river all the way to Port Hudson in Louisiana, depriving the rebels of their crossing points between the two cities and dooming Port Hudson to a siege by the navy and Federal forces converging from above and below. Grant's plan called for moving south along the railroad to take Vicksburg in the rear by first capturing Jackson, Mississippi.

But this campaign would have another feature. The West, where the Republicans had lost heavily in the recent Congressional elections, had enough political importance to warrant an additional advance down the Mississippi to be led by a general with a western political affiliation. John A. McClernand, an Illinois Democratic leader and former congressman, who had early become a general, raised the troops for this special expedition. In spite of the conviction of the regular officers, including Grant and Halleck, that he lacked competence as general, political considerations made it important that he command an additional advance on Vicksburg.

In December 1862, the Mississippi became the object of yet another political-military expedition, this one raised in Massachusetts under the leadership of ex-governor Major General Banks, who had failed against Jackson in the Shenandoah Valley. In part reflecting Massachusetts's interest in cotton for its mills, the expedition originally aimed at Texas; but Lincoln, to Halleck's satisfaction, directed it to New Orleans, captured by the navy and army in May 1862. Here General Banks arrived in December to drive northward toward Grant. Halleck sent him instructions, including an explanation that the simultaneous advances of armies driving from the north should make it safe for him to operate on an exterior line. But Banks had such green volunteers, many not having yet held a gun, that he could not join the December movements against Vicksburg.

104

Grant and Halleck managed to circumvent McClernand and give their friend and Grant's subordinate, the highly competent and imaginative strategic thinker William T. Sherman, command of the force on the Mississippi. Sherman's 30,000 men were to coordinate with Grant's along the railroad, with the hope that simultaneous advances would enable one of them to get through. As Grant pushed south against the bulk of the Confederate forces, Forrest began another of his raids, one in Tennessee, far in Grant's rear, which broke the railroads by burning fifty trestles as well as tearing up much track. At the same time, Van Dorn, leading the cavalry of the defending Confederate army, conducted a raid that had a greater and more immediate impact when it captured Grant's depot in Holly Springs on December 20, 1862. Taking 1,500 prisoners, including Mrs. Grant, whom he immediately released, and much booty, Van Dorn destroyed $1,500,000 in property. With his communications in ruins and in a country already well foraged by the retreating Confederates, Grant withdrew. Again, by use of only a few men, the Confederate raiding logistic strategy had defeated the advance of 40,000 men.

Since the navy delivered Sherman's men right to Vicksburg, he encountered no such difficulty about supply, but he faced swamps and bayous north of the high ground of the city. Finally deploying his troops, he could only assault the rebels in front, entrenched on Chickasaw Bluffs. Failing, as he expected, he did not increase his casualties by persevering in a hopeless endeavor (see diagram of first advance on Vicksburg). Sherman withdrew, meeting McClernand coming down the river to take command. As the failed double advance against Vicksburg involved small losses in manpower on each side, it had its main military significance in the Union's strategic defeat. But the symbolism of the destruction of the Holly Springs base on December 20, Sherman's repulse on December 29, and the subsequent retreat of both forces followed the defeat at Fredericksburg on December 13 and so had a depressing effect in the North.

Just as Sherman landed his men before Vicksburg, Major General William S. Rosecrans began moving his 44,000 men from Nashville the 25 miles along the railroad to Murfreesboro to fight Bragg's 38,000. A West Pointer who had missed fighting in the Mexican War and left the army for a business career, Rosecrans had success in western Virginia first under McClellan and then independently. Going west as a major general, he served in the Corinth campaign, succeeded to Pope's command, and earned Grant's recommendation for his performance at Iuka and in the defense of Corinth. A hard-drinking Democrat, popular with his men, and seeming the ideal general to replace Buell, he immediately displayed his predecessor's penchant for thorough preparation, a trait which caused delay because guerrillas and raiders kept his railroad to Louisville broken over half of the time he held this command. But by Christmas he had accumulated enough supplies to advance. Because he was one of the few regular officers in army command who believed in and applied a combat strategy, he had a simple concept for his campaign, to attack Bragg's forces and "crush them in a decisive battle."

With good intelligence of Rosecrans's approach, Bragg deployed his army on both sides of Stones River, near Murfreesboro, and prepared some entrenchments for receiving the assault. But when the Union army did not attack promptly, Bragg decided to do so himself on the morning of December 31, 1862. Determined to overwhelm the enemy's right flank, he transferred troops from his right to his left to carry this out. Rosecrans had the same plan, assail his antagonist's right, but Bragg took the initiative, routed Rosecrans's right-hand division, and threatened to envelop the right side of his army. Rosecrans quickly moved men from his left, deployed them well, and ended the day with most of his army of well-led veterans fighting at right angles to his original line. Expecting to crush the enemy, and just escaping serious defeat himself, he had shown how difficult such a task was unless, as had happened at Richmond, Kentucky, veterans fought men just mustered in.

By the next day, the Union army had entrenched thoroughly and awaited another Confederate attack. Expecting the defeated Yankees to retreat, Bragg had already reported his victory to Richmond and did not attempt a repeat of the previous day. After three days of facing the Union army with only some minor action and apparently disheartened by the failure of his victory to materialize, Bragg withdrew, marching down the road the 20 miles to Tullahoma.

Although the total Confederate forces in the field equaled about half the Union's 500,000, each side brought nearly equal numbers to the battlefield of Stones River. The great number of men Rosecrans had to commit to guard his communications goes far to explain the comparative weakness of his army. That also provides a commentary on the military attrition of the battle, which produced 11,739 Confederate casualties and 12,906 Union, 31 percent of the Confederate and 29 percent of the Union soldiers. Yet, compared to overall numbers available, their nearly equal losses in the battle show the Confederates losing a double percentage. Thus, in this respect, the battle favored the North. For attrition to affect the outcome of the war, one belligerent must consistently deplete a smaller portion of its military resources than its opponent, increasing a preponderance or diminishing an inferiority. Attrition could even give victory by eventually creating enough of an imbalance of forces that one contestant obtained such a superiority as to be able to overwhelm his adversary.

The battle had the essentially inconsequential strategic result of pushing Bragg back 20 miles. But the public could appreciate this symbol of victory but not easily comprehend that the heavy losses, about the same on each side, hurt the South more than the North; further, many would not applaud this kind of victory even if they understood it.

Civilians and soldiers had markedly different worlds but shared their perceptions through the mail. Commanders often had differing views from civilians, and many soldiers viewed Stones River as a severe check for the North because it showed a stalemate in Tennessee. Others knew that the success of raiders and guerrillas in halting Buell in August and Grant in December had more significance than most battles; these constituted important and ominous Confederate strategic victories that civilians and many soldiers would overlook. Thus the political effect of military events would not always harmonize with their military importance.

Not only battles but all military events acted politically to alter attitudes. Further, the cost of the war, the inflation, the losses of soldiers in skirmishes and to accidents and sickness as well as in battles, all worked like attrition to raise in the civilian as well as the soldier doubts about the cost of the war, and so undermine the conviction that victory was worth its apparently ever-escalating price. So political attrition could cause one belligerent to lose its willingness to pay the cost of victory more rapidly than the other, thus potentially leading to a compromise or an abandonment of the struggle. But it is extremely unlikely that, with differing motives and goals, each side would have the same degree of desire for victory. So one must also compare how much each adversary desired to win with how much political attrition each suffered. The belligerent that wanted victory more could withstand more discouragement, hardship, and losses than the other. Therefore one antagonist could sustain a greater depletion of its confidence in winning at a reasonable cost yet outlast its opponent because of a more than proportionate desire for victory.

Winning the Battle of Stones River, coming on the heels of defeat in Mississippi and Virginia, proved very important to the North. Stressing the symbolic importance of the victory, Secretary of War Stanton wrote Rosecrans that "the country is filled with an admiration of the gallantry and heroic achievement of yourself and the officers and troops under your command." Regarding the victory as crucial in stemming a rising tide of the sentiment of defeatism, Lincoln later wrote Rosecrans: "I can never forget, whilst I remember anything, that about the end of last year, and beginning of this, you gave us a hard earned victory which, had there been a defeat instead, the nation could scarcely have lived over. Neither can I forget the check you so opportunely gave to a dangerous sentiment which was spreading in the north." Thus did Lincoln estimate the danger of defeatism and the value of the symbolism of Rosecrans's victory in reviving public hopes for winning in a reasonable time at a bearable cost.

The Battle of Stones River caused little political attrition on the Confederate side because of the initial report that Bragg had won and the earlier southern triumphs in December. But it did arouse the sarcasm of a Richmond newspaper, for which Bragg's initial report of winning doubtless recalled Beauregard's about Shiloh. The paper commented that in first reports from the West the troops have always "exhibited an irresistible and superhuman valor unknown in history this side of Sparta and Rome. As for the generals, they usually get all their clothes shot off and replace them with a suit of glory. The enemy, of course, is simply annihilated." But, in the end, the reports, "make a mist, a muddle, and a fog of the whole affair."

Halleck had orchestrated his simultaneous offensives well, but they still could not assure victories. Yet they had actually worked as intended and gained a bonus when the Confederates had reinforced the army in Mississippi in December 1862 by moving a large infantry division from Bragg's army in Tennessee before the Battle of Stones River; but that division reached Mississippi too late to have much effect in repulsing Sherman (this was actually the work of a few well-entrenched men). In fact, cavalry raids had defeated Grant's thrust, the most menacing of the advances against Vicksburg.

The North's largely futile operations in December seemed merely to reaffirm the dominance of the tactical and strategic defense. Still, the North's month of campaigning offered hope because of the achievement of the difficult task of concentration in time. In May of 1863 the armies in Virginia and Mississippi moved simultaneously, but, for excellent reasons, Rosecrans delayed his advance; and in the late fall the armies in Virginia and Tennessee campaigned at the same time. The major failure to synchronize operations occurred in August and September of 1863, a fault on Halleck's part that had serious consequences.

Success in concentrating in time had resulted in the gloom of defeats and the lack of significant strategic fruit from the single victory at Stones River. The problems and achievements of the high commands would mirror the campaigns' picture of encouraging and disheartening developments.

CHAPTER 9

THE MATURITY OF THE HIGH COMMANDS

By the late fall of 1862 presidents Lincoln and Davis had essentially completed the building of their military high commands. In spite of the similarities of the armies and the organizations, the two high commands differed much in spirit. Whereas Davis's organization kept firmly oriented towards its military objectives, the war direction in Washington responded more readily to a variety of nonmilitary influences. Particularly did the cabinet and Congress have political concerns which found a way to express themselves in ideas about strategy or the choice of generals. But both headquarters faced comparable problems in finding suitable commanders, the Confederacy having most of its difficulties in the West, the Union in the East. And both organizations also displayed the behavioral tendencies which organizations bring out in people and the good and ill effects of these, many of which faced General Halleck in his own headquarters.

Halleck had only reluctantly come to Washington to serve as general in chief, and once there he found Lincoln difficult to work with. Lacking administrative experience and, for several months having done without a general in chief, the president continued to have direct correspondence with commanders and so, without grasping the undesirable consequences, bypassed

Halleck on some important matters. Further, the cabinet continued its participation in operations and appointments, planning and promoting expeditions and pushing commands for favored soldiers and political leaders. All of this led Halleck to exclaim: "There are so many cooks. They destroy the broth." Lincoln also had a particular concern for military appointments, displaying an informed and sophisticated grasp of the political and military import of each. Thus he once stated how he compared the political advantages of a particular appointment with the military liabilities in giving political attractiveness priority over military competence: "In a purely military point of view it may be that none of these things is indispensable, or perhaps, advantageous; but in another aspect [the political], they would give great relief, while, at the worst, I think they could not injure the military service much." And Lincoln never pushed generals with primarily political appeal for command of the major armies that would have to face Confederates in the field.

Nevertheless, the possibility of unsuitable appointments constituted a constant source of worry to Halleck, so much so that he controlled the western departments from Washington, not proposing to fill his old command over them for fear of who might receive the appointment. Halleck, like Lincoln a lawyer, sought to avoid unnecessary friction by keeping out of the president's way. Realizing he could not change the culture of the administration, he, probably wisely, adapted to it. Yet with Grant and Rosecrans in the chief-commands, the Union had a strong team in the West.

After the Battle of Fredericksburg, Lincoln recognized that Burnside's abilities did not equal his assignment. Concerned about the propriety of the distraught Burnside's plans for his next move, Lincoln directed Halleck to go to the general's headquarters, evaluate his plans, and decide what he should do. To Lincoln's intense annoyance, Halleck thereupon resigned, making most emphatically the point that headquarters should not try to control generals as if they were marionettes. The president and Halleck soon agreed that the general would continue and Lincoln, reluctantly at first, learned the lesson his general in chief, more experienced in management, wished to teach. Thereafter, Lincoln realized that he should not try to manage generals from Washington and, if he lacked confidence

111

in them, replace rather than try to direct them. So the president relieved Burnside, returning him to command of his corps and sending them to Kentucky.

The command of the Army of the Potomac seemed the only weakness in the Federal main armies. Rosecrans had given satisfaction and Grant, one of the most seasoned field commanders on either side, though compelled to retreat at Vicksburg, had proved a consistent, sound, and competent performer. But the Virginia theater was about to have its fourth commander. McClellan had come from Western Virginia, Pope from the West, and Burnside from North Carolina, and each had failed. Lincoln now chose from within the Army of the Potomac Joseph Hooker, a corps commander who had lobbied for the job. A West Pointer who, after distinguished Mexican War service, had left the army for farming, he had fought in all the battles of the Army of the Potomac, rising from brigade to corps command. He had the respect of many, earned the devotion of the troops, but was not Halleck's choice. Nor was Halleck alone in thinking him unequal to the task. When William T. Sherman learned of the appointment of Hooker to command the Army of the Potomac, he wrote: "I know Hooker well and tremble to think of him handling 100,000 men in the presence of Lee."

The involvement of the cabinet and Lincoln's unsystematic intervention inevitably created many shoals which Halleck had to avoid in steering his bureaucratic course. But other potential complexities proved assets. Although he and Stanton had opposite ideas about tactics, they worked well together, the secretary giving much of his attention to raising troops and helping the quartermaster and commissary departments in procurement and transportation. Halleck also benefitted immensely from the tradition of collaboration left by the brief functioning of the War Board.

With a staff of only twenty-three officers and men, Halleck faced a huge task controlling far-flung armies and departments as far away as California and the Dakota Territory. But the personnel of the staff departments had already learned much about working together, making it relatively easy for Halleck to coordinate the staff departments to support his operational objectives. In turn, this experience made it easy for them to give him and his little staff informal support in carrying out their duties. The civilian assistant secretaries of war also became part of this informally organized general staff. Immediately his most important collaborator became the brilliant and resourceful executive and perceptive strategist, Quartermaster General Meigs.

Thus the exigencies of war and the abilities and temperaments of a variety of people created an effective general staff in Washington, one that fortuitously resembled the highly proficient Prussian general staff of that time. Something similar, but less effective, happened also in Richmond, where the organization lacked a general in chief, the crucial figure who made possible the high level of Union effectiveness. After Lee assumed command of Johnston's army, he made only a brief attempt to continue discharging his duties with respect to military operations. He did, however, continue his role informally, as Davis's most influential and valued military adviser. But, even though a stream of long letters on many topics flowed to Davis from Lee's headquarters, his habitual absence from Richmond prevented him from doing more than offering advice, sometimes based on inadequate information.

So everything depended on the secretary and the president. When, in the fall of 1862, Randolph realized that he and Davis could not make a good team, he resigned. Davis then appointed a civilian, James A. Seddon, a former congressman from Virginia. Extremely intelligent and dedicated to the job, Seddon quickly learned the fundamentals of logistics and strategy and became one of Davis's most effective collaborators. They rarely disagreed, least of all concerning appointments. To these Davis applied military criteria only, knowingly depleting some political capital by refusing to give recognition to generals whose military ability did not match their political prominence. He even refused promotion to the prominent Robert Toombs, also the first Confederate secretary of state, causing Toombs to resign and go back to Georgia to spend the remainder of the war criticizing the administration and complaining about West Pointers. Further, Seddon gave good leadership to the staff departments and the civilians, but in his absorption with operations he tended to neglect the Confederacy's supply and transportation problems.

Some have seen Davis as his own secretary of war; rather, he was his own general in chief. When Lee held that post, he was

Lee's collaborator. The departmental organization tended to ease Davis and Seddon's task of operational control. The transition from many small to a few large departments eventually evolved into Beauregard's Department of South Carolina, Georgia, and Florida; a separate Department of Trans-Mississippi for Arkansas, Texas, and most of Louisiana; and Lee controlling Virginia and North Carolina.

Randolph's legacy included the plan for the completion of the system of regional commands which would leave to Richmond only the most important strategic decisions. Three departments shared the West between the Mississippi and the Appalachians: the Department of East Tennessee, the Department of Mississippi and East Louisiana, and the remainder, as Department No. 2 or the Western Department. These had emerged from joining Bragg's old Department of Alabama and West Florida to Department No. 2 and the subsequent stripping away of Mississippi and East Tennessee because the department seemed too big for one man to manage. But in Randolph's last months in office western affairs had required more control from Richmond than the War Department could effectively give from such a distance. Randolph saw the need for a new organization.

In addition to their need for strategic direction, the western commanders themselves would have caused a discerning observer some concern. Some of General Bragg's officers had already become restive, a sign of defects of his performance in Kentucky; and adjacent East Tennessee would have a succession of capable generals but none with sufficiently long tenure to affect the situation. When an unsavory personal life caused the rejection of one senior major general and the stigma of having surrendered New Orleans disqualified another, the command over the confused situation in Mississippi had gone by default to the third ranking, the commander of the fortified river city of Vicksburg. Promoted to the newly authorized rank of lieutenant general, John C. Pemberton lacked any experience beyond command of coast defenses in South Carolina, from which Lee and Davis had removed him because he could not get along with the local authorities. Doubtless they saw his new post at Vicksburg as dealing only with fortifications; but the department command involved much more. Davis and

Randolph proved too casual in promoting the untried Pemberton; they should have sent Beauregard or such tested veterans of subordinate field command as Longstreet or Hardee to face the now-seasoned and obviously highly competent U. S. Grant.

Randolph's idea of putting the area between the Mississippi and the Appalachians under a super department to provide strategic coordination combined this need with the availability of a man suitable for the command. Having spent the summer and early fall in Richmond recovering from his wound, J. E. Johnston had reported himself well enough for service. Naturally he wanted to return to the command of his old Virginia army, but its glorious and dramatic career under Lee precluded his replacement in spite of Davis's need for Lee in Richmond and Johnston's desire for the command. So he received the Department of the West, a vast area composed of three departments and their armies. Randolph's idea, implemented by Seddon and Davis, had the added merit of placing the only two departments which faced main Federal armies under the Confederacy's two best generals, Lee and J. E. Johnston. But Johnston saw his new position as a desk job, less desirable than the command of a single army with which he would face an enemy. Yet, glad to be back on active service, he went west to take up his new duties and try to achieve strategic coordination even wider than his own department.

Johnston and Secretary Randolph, having an exaggerated idea of the number of troops in the newly created trans-Mississippi department, entertained the idea of combined action between these and the forces in Mississippi. But, when Van Dorn had brought his command from Arkansas to Mississippi after the Battle of Shiloh, he had left scarcely an armed man in Arkansas. Nevertheless, thanks to the productive and unremitting energy of the colorful and capable Major General Thomas C. Hindman, Arkansas had acquired a considerable number of newly organized troops by the fall of 1862. Still, with most undrilled, many unarmed, and others having only shotguns or hunting rifles, they would not have constituted an army, even if they had had enough suitable officers and generals. Moreover, most Arkansas forces were far from Mississippi, deployed in the northern part of the state to guard against a Union invasion from Missouri. And this was not the only reason that Johnston's idea of joint action proved impractical.

The trans-Mississippi department had some men in less-threatened Louisiana and also included detachments in New Mexico and Arizona as well as Texas. The gigantic size of this thinly populated department presented a problem as did poor communications. Arkansas, for example, had only one railroad, an incomplete line between Memphis, in Union hands, and Little Rock, the capital in the center of the state. The major navigable rivers, the Red, Ouachita, Arkansas, and White, flowing from northwest to southeast into the Mississippi, provided the principal means of efficient transportation but experienced the vagaries of seasonal variations in water levels.

Thus the whole region and its various parts presented immense difficulties for troop movements, concentration, and supply, sometimes handicapping defenders almost as much as invaders. The area, so unpromising for decisive campaigning, absorbed Confederate and Union resources throughout the war. Although the Union had much better means for transferring men to the east, it did not make much use of this until 1864 and 1865. So it is not surprising that the Union forces west of the Mississippi had no formal participation in Halleck's simultaneous advances in the late fall of 1862.

Most Union civilians, and even many soldiers, failed to notice, or at least to appreciate, the significant achievement of the essentially simultaneous advances of the three main Federal armies. But the Confederates noted the concentration in time, because it defeated their concentration in space. In the middle of December 1862, while visiting the West to confer with the generals and make speeches to raise public morale, Davis had transferred Stevenson's division of 9,000 men from Tennessee to Mississippi. In this he overruled Johnston and Bragg, who believed Tennessee the more vital theater. The division, which used the rail route employed by Bragg the previous summer, arrived after Grant had begun is retreat, but in time for some of its components to be on hand for the easy repulse of Sherman at Chickasaw Bluffs. Thus the division added nothing important to the defense of Mississippi but had left Tennessee before Bragg faced Rosecrans in the Battle of Stones River, a clear triumph for concentration in time.

This experience reinforced Johnston's reservations about his command which he believed would not work as the president and Secretary Seddon conceived it. Well read in military history and having a reputation in the U.S. Army for his understanding of strategy, Johnston realized that he was "to operate in Napoleon's manner" in defending Mantua by concentrating "the forces in Mississippi and Tennessee in whichever might be first attacked." But he believed that too much distance separated his troops in Mississippi and Tennessee and he found the rail link too circuitous. Estimating that a movement would take a month whether on the direct route by foot or roundabout by rail, he asked Davis: "Which is the most valuable, Tennessee or the Mississippi?" But, the president, having confidence in the capacity of the new departmental arrangement to save both, gave Johnston no definite guidance.

In spite of his reservations, Johnston worked out a plan for rapid troop movements between the departments. In this he intended to follow the pipeline approach Bragg had used; thus he planned to move the garrison of Mobile first, but he did not adopt the president's suggestion of stationing a brigade at Meridian, Mississippi, so as to put more men in the pipeline between Mississippi and Tennessee. This system received only one test, a partial one from a false alarm in April, when Pemberton reported that Grant seemed to be reinforcing Rosecrans. Before he ordered the reinforcements, Johnston directed the placement of brigades at Jackson and Meridian. The plan worked remarkably well, the Mobile garrison reaching Bragg at Tullahoma, Tennessee, in six days, with troops from Mississippi already beyond Atlanta. At this point, when it became clear that Grant was not moving after all, the reinforcement ended and the men returned. Still, in spite of his protestations, Johnston had men arriving in Tennessee in a week rather than the month he had prophesied and had used the telegraph and railroad to concentrate in Napoleon's manner over a vast distance with a speed that would have amazed the emperor.

Yet Johnston saw the key to victory not in emulating Napoleon but in cavalry raids like those which had halted first Buell and then Grant. Like Davis and Lee, Johnston had served in the cavalry, but former artilleryman Bragg demonstrated the most zeal for the cavalry raids. When, earlier, Johnston thought that a raid on his communications "may delay General Grant,"

Bragg had argued that "Grant's campaign would be broken up by our cavalry expeditions in his rear before Stevenson's command would meet him in front." Johnston, who had first visited Bragg in Tennessee and then come to see Pemberton in Mississippi, doubtless had imbibed some of Bragg's enthusiasm. By the end of the year Johnston had appropriated Van Dorn, the raider of Holly Springs, and most of Pemberton's cavalry, combined it with half of Bragg's, and stationed it in Tennessee where, from this central position, Van Dorn could halt an advance by either Rosecrans or Grant through striking their communications. Thus Johnston sought to foster and obtain the most from the cavalry raid, which had emerged as an innovative and devastating addition to the Confederacy's main defense, reliance on its mastery of Napoleonic strategy.

Yet a significant lobby for using the railroad for Napoleonic concentration in the West already existed and steadily gained adherents from a variety of sources in the Confederacy. Four factions, or informal organizations, shared objectives sufficiently and had enough commonality among their members to constitute an embracing informal organization, the Western Concentration bloc.

One of its constituent organizations, the Abingdon-Columbia bloc, had much of its basis in family ties of the Johnston and Preston families from Abingdon, Virginia, and Columbia, South Carolina. General J. E. Johnston, superintendent of conscription John Smith Preston of South Carolina, Confederate Senator William Ballard Preston of Virginia, General William Preston of Kentucky, General Wade Hampton of South Carolina, and General John B. Floyd of Virginia were all related. They all had an interest in forwarding Johnston's military career and came to support the ideas of their friends, such as former South Carolinian, Texas Senator Louis T. Wigfall, and General Beauregard, both of whom knew each other and Johnston well. Many of these, particularly Beauregard and Wigfall, sought influence over strategy, Wigfall being well placed as a member of the military affairs committee of the Confederate Senate and having attended law school with Secretary Seddon.

The number of high-ranking officers in Bragg's Army of Tennessee who felt hostile enough toward him to work actively to replace him constituted an anti-Bragg bloc. Through such contacts as anti-Bragg General William Preston, they reached out to others with influence, such as members of the Abingdon-Columbia bloc, some of whose members would have liked to see Johnston or Beauregard take over Bragg's command. The anti-Bragg generals tended to favor Beauregard, only briefly their commander but to whom some gave allegiance as an informal leader. Bragg's defects in personality and performance doubtless made Beauregard's magnetism and confidence even more appealing.

The last informal organization, the Kentucky bloc, consisted of Kentuckians in the army and government, including General William Preston, who wished for a Confederate conquest of their state. Although it was they who had prompted the idea that the people would rise and volunteer for Confederate military service when Bragg's army entered the state, they clung to their illusion of a powerful Confederate sentiment in Kentucky, blamed Bragg, and sought help for an offensive into Kentucky.

Having served in South Carolina, Virginia, and the West, General Beauregard had come to influence many people and, by the tirelessness and eloquence of his exposition, convinced many that the essence of Napoleonic strategy lay in the surprise concentration against enemy weakness. This idea, which had animated the Shiloh campaign, helped him accumulate enough followers and admirers to form a bloc. Commanding the Department of South Carolina, Georgia, and Florida, a large department but one which did not face a hostile army, Beauregard had the leisure to think about strategy for the Confederacy as a whole and the detachment to do so without falling into the commander's usual trap of seeing his own department as the most important.

He identified Rosecrans's army in Tennessee as the Union weak point, a perceptive choice since he had barely outnumbered Bragg at Stones River. Beauregard planned another Shiloh concentration with troops to come from Mississippi, Virginia, and South Carolina. Bragg would then have the numbers to win so overwhelming a victory against Rosecrans as to eliminate his army from the military chessboard. Beauregard then envisioned Bragg's army making a gigantic turning movement, marching 200 miles westward to reach Grant's rear and block his retreat. This extension of a sound idea was inspired not only by the strategy of Napoleonic campaigns but by their logistical simplicity. But so easily living off the country was an unrealistic expectation in the South; Bragg's army would have been merely a raider, unable to turn Grant. The extravagance of the plan destroyed some of Beauregard's credibility and diverted attention from his main idea. This lack of logistical realism characterized other plans that Beauregard made during the war and diminished their and his influence.

The formation of informal groups with common interests to influence strategy could have had as much influence as the heritage of Napoleon had Beauregard not harnessed the informal organizations to his efforts to promote a Napoleonic offensive concentration against Rosecrans. His friends and followers added numbers to the Western Concentration bloc, and Beauregard's ideas gave the bloc a doctrine that supported a concentration in the West, something agreeable to virtually every member of the large group's constituent informal organizations.

While Beauregard developed offensive plans for the West, J. E. Johnston completed his preparations for defending his Department of the West. By the middle of January he had concentrated 6,000 cavalry with Bragg's army in order to raid the communications of any force advancing on either Bragg or Pemberton, and he organized the railroad pipeline for reinforcing either of his two major commands. He had misgivings only about what would happen if his department had to face simultaneous advances and doubts about Pemberton. Realizing that Vicksburg's defender visualized his situation largely in terms of his fortifications, Johnston had apprehensions that Pemberton could not understand the need to defend his position by concentrating the largest possible force outside of the fortifications to fight Grant's army; if Pemberton failed to understand this, Johnston knew that he could share the fate of the large force bottled up in and surrendered at Fort Donelson. Yet Johnston faced a more immediate problem in late January, when President Davis ordered him to Bragg's headquarters at Tullahoma to deal with a serious personnel issue.

From the president, Johnston learned that, when the defeat at Stones River exacerbated the dissatisfaction of his officers,

Bragg had reacted by asking his corps commanders to evaluate him. When they had made the most of this opportunity, division commanders also joining in the caustic vote of no confidence, Davis sent Johnston to assess the situation and General Bragg's fitness for command. Having found the army recruited in strength since the battle and the men "healthy and in good spirits," giving "positive evidence of General Bragg's capacity to command," Johnston recommended against Bragg's removal. Johnston added that, should the president decide to replace Bragg, neither he nor any of Bragg's subordinates should receive the vacated command, so no one would benefit from involvement in the affair.

Acutely aware of the seriousness of the situation and perceptive about Bragg's weakness, Davis and Secretary Seddon tried to change Johnston's mind. Seddon wanted to replace Bragg and had certainly learned from Johnston's friend Senator Wigfall that Johnston wanted to command an army. He tried to persuade Johnston to stay with Bragg's army and take command in fact, using Bragg "as organizer and administrator" under him. In spite of receiving a warm letter from the president urging the same thing, Johnston refused to go along with the disguised replacement; but he did remain with Bragg's army rather than returning to Mississippi.

Thus the unsatisfactory Bragg remained in command over a demoralized group of senior officers. Not only did Johnston refuse to take command of Bragg's army, but Davis and Seddon failed to consider anyone but Johnston as a replacement. Beauregard would have provided a perfect solution to the problem. As a former commander of the Army of Tennessee, enough officers would have given him a cordial reception to quiet the personnel difficulties. Further, Beauregard's coast defense department could have provided a suitable shelf upon which to lay Bragg, former artilleryman and admirable organizer. But Beauregard's prickly behavior in 1861 and his blunder in not telling the whole truth about Shiloh, followed by the fall of Memphis and Corinth and his retreat of 50 miles, had destroyed the confidence Davis had in a commander who was not one of the senior officers in the old army. After the Shiloh mistake, Beauregard had gone on to become a model of proper deportment, usually telegraphing a situation report every day. Yet he

121

had great difficulty overcoming the taint of his past performance. On the other hand, Bragg's initial favorable impression, along with his real abilities, had helped blind his superiors to his serious deficiencies.

So with General Kirby Smith's departure from his successful command in East Tennessee to take over the trans-Mississippi department, with Beauregard unusable, and with Bragg and probably Pemberton requiring replacement, the Confederacy faced a shortage of commanding generals unless it could dig deeper into the ranks.

Although the experience of the high commands amply illustrates the difficulty of selecting and promoting good generals, it also showed that it could be even harder to remove those whose performance fell short of expectations. Whereas Lincoln displayed a calculated tenderness toward the politically important in uniform, he removed unsatisfactory soldiers with little compunction. Thus, in four months, he relieved three army commanders: Burnside, Buell, and the politically sensitive McClellan. Davis, on the other hand, avoided this ruthless pruning. When inaction would serve, as when he did not give Floyd a new command or when he declined to promote even the influential Toombs, he did better. He seemed to try to save the individual pain, as, when removing Pemberton from his South Carolina command, he gave him another and when he placed Kirby Smith over Theophilus H. Holmes as commander of the trans-Mississippi rather than simply replacing Holmes with him. This sensitivity may have motivated him in only seeking to supersede Bragg with the distinctly senior Johnston. Since Davis did not avoid dissension in other instances, this behavior seems to have emanated from a too great concern for the individual rather than an aversion to conflict.

Johnston's continuing presence at Bragg's headquarters probably increased his sensitivity to the strategic importance of Middle Tennessee. But when he asked for reinforcements for Bragg, he did not think in terms of Beauregard's concept of an offensive concentration against weakness in Tennessee. Rather, he viewed Middle Tennessee as a place to defend at all costs because he placed such a high strategic value on the area and the railroad route southeastward to Atlanta. Like Beauregard and others, he attached comparatively little importance to control of the Mississippi because few supplies could move east or west and, though he had originally looked to the trans-Mississippi for reinforcements, he had come to see that, without a rail or secure water link, the Confederate armies on either side of the Mississippi could have little strategic coordination. Thus Johnston gave priority to the defense of Tennessee and had convinced Seddon that men should come from the East to reinforce it.

When Secretary Seddon responded by asking Lee whether he could spare men for Tennessee, the secretary had just learned that a Union corps had gone west from Virginia and had heard the false intelligence that Grant was reinforcing Rosecrans. In making this inquiry, Seddon relied on a strategic assumption basic to Confederate strategy from the outset, one congenial to Lee from his practice and one which he had thus already succinctly expounded: Believing that "the enemy cannot attack all points at one time," Lee saw that southern "troops could be concentrated upon that where an assault should be made." Hence "we must move our troops from point to point as required & by close observation and accurate information the true point of attack can generally be ascertained."

But now Lee took an emphatic position against the strategy he had earlier preached and practiced. He seemed to suffer from cognitive dissonance in trying to reconcile his allegiance to his army with his ingrained strategic concepts. Cognitive dissonance, the psychological discomfort resulting from attempting to reconcile knowledge that contains contradictions, required accommodating orthodox strategy, which would result in the weakening of his department, with his need as a commander to keep all of his men.

Lee achieved this by insisting that, in spite of the reduction in enemy strength in Virginia, the main Yankee spring offensive would come in the East. He also showed that reinforcements for Bragg should come from the deep South, Mississippi and South Carolina, because the summer heat precluded an enemy attack and, were the troops to remain so far south, they would "perish of disease." He made this assertion in spite of the experience of the Revolution when his father had campaigned in the South in the summer. Finally, Lee denied much of the essence of his own and Napoleon's strategy when he

123

argued against concentration in space and urged that it is "not so easy for us to change troops from one department to another as it is for the enemy, and if we rely upon that method, we may be always too late." As an alternative, and in spite of his intimate knowledge of the strength of the defensive, he argued that all troops should remain in place and conduct simultaneous counteroffensives, thus causing the enemy to abandon his concentration. So Pemberton should have taken "the aggressive" to induce Grant to call back the men he had sent to Rosecrans; and for Lee's army "to cross into Maryland" would provide "the readiest method of relieving pressure upon General Johnston."

Thus Lee reconciled the dissonance between what he knew to be the proper strategy and his need to keep his army intact. From so brilliant a strategist as Lee, such views are quite bizarre and indicate how nearly impossible it is for army commanders to maintain objectivity. Johnston could have detachment in assessing the needs of the various parts of his department but not as far as his whole command was concerned. Thus, though Rosecrans in battle barely outnumbered Bragg and Beauregard correctly identified that Federal army as the enemy weak point, Johnston asked for reinforcements for the Department of the West from Lee, who was much inferior to his opponent in Virginia. Of the department commanders, Beauregard had the most objectivity because he commanded a coastal department which had the U.S. Navy as its main adversary. But, if Lee was wrong about where the main Union offensive would occur, he was right that he would have to face an enemy attack and not at a convenient time or place.

Rather than use measures such as Johnston's cavalry concentration and arrangements for quick troop movements, Lee, the belated convert to entrenchment, fortified the Rappahannock along 35 miles of its length with entrenchments at the fords and likely crossing places and lookout positions. And on much of the south bank he dug entrenchments on the hills, inviting another assault as at Fredericksburg. Lee's fortified line recalled those popular in the Netherlands and northern France, long an area of military deadlock. In the early eighteenth century, the Duke of Marlborough won fame by using distraction to gain surprise and pierce two defense lines built by the

French, one 90 and the other 150 miles long. Thus similar stalemate conditions of a high ratio of force to space elicited like responses more than 150 years later.

During the winter of 1863 Lee endeavored to alleviate his supply problems by sending Longstreet with half of his corps to southeastern Virginia, a less intensely foraged region where he could also try to push the Yankees back closer to Norfolk. Lee's always paramount concern about supply also made him fear a siege of Richmond on logistic grounds, believing that the contraction of his foraging area would make him too dependent on the War Department's inadequate supply system and the overtaxed railroads. So, whereas Halleck wished to avoid a siege because he saw that it would give Lee a tactical and strategic advantage, Lee wished to avoid it for logistical reasons, not believing that the Confederacy's supply organization could sustain a besieged army. Lee's anxiety about food and fodder dominated his strategy, making him not just anxious to avoid a siege but feel a strong logistical imperative to retain as much of Virginia as possible.

Although it is doubtful that Seddon found Lee's novel strategic ideas persuasive, the general's adamant position against reinforcements for Tennessee proved sufficient to induce the secretary to look elsewhere for men. In May, when Seddon again asked about reinforcements, this time for a crisis in Mississippi, Lee, having just repulsed a formidable Union offensive in Virginia, made similar arguments and again prevailed. The subject of reinforcements for the West then remained dormant until the end of the summer, allowing Lee three months to give his full attention to the problems of his own army.

The give and take between Lee and Seddon was representative of all levels of command in both armies and characteristic of most military and other organizations. This could occur in Richmond, Washington, and other headquarters and by letter and telegraph over great distances. Sometimes an army commander would "talk" to the secretary or the general in chief when each would sit down beside the telegraph operator and immediately respond to each other in a sequence of messages.

Discussions about strategy rarely placed generals in a position as stressful as Lee's, if only because most could not see both sides of the question with sufficient clarity to experience serious cognitive dissonance. Decisions about people, again typical of most organizations, proved the most difficult. Having enough information to make a reasonably valid evaluation of a subordinate's performance almost always presented a problem. But an appointment to new responsibilities also involved guessing whether the prospect could cope with the demands of the new position. Moreover, compared with decisions about strategy, those concerning people were more likely to involve emotions as well as such factors as prejudice, friendship, and obligations. Even scruples, such as concepts of behavior appropriate to gentlemen, could cause difficulty, as in the case of Johnston's unwillingness to serve as Bragg's replacement.

The informal organization, exemplified by the Western Concentration bloc, also had significant influence on all types of decisions. That the Western Concentration bloc could flourish over great distances in a time of difficult travel and no telephones emphasizes the ubiquity of such groupings and alliances throughout the armies.

Just as people naturally create informal organizations, so do they also find informal leaders. McClellan's position with the Army of the Potomac provides a superb example of this. As the creator and first commander of that army, he had claims to loyalty which his charisma and the appeal of his Peninsula campaign's strategy intensified. Even after he had left the command, his position of formal leadership, he continued to exercise great informal influence. This often took the form of the officers of the Army of the Potomac displaying hostility to the secretary of war and an unshakable allegiance to the strategy of the Peninsula campaign. No successor in command could ever displace him as the army's informal leader, a situation which made it difficult for every subsequent commander and limited the ability of the president and the general in chief to enjoy any widespread, deep-rooted support. On the Confederate side, however, Lee's three campaigns in four months immediately eclipsed Johnston's memory and established him as the informal as well as the formal leader of the Army of Northern Virginia.

In the West the situation differed markedly. The Union armies there, briefly commanded by Halleck, never developed a strong loyalty to a formal leader. Halleck, as general in chief, enjoyed unchallenged formal power because he received reinforcement from his successful command in the West. As a consequence, none of the armies in the West had an informal leader like McClellan, thus simplifying the task of the new commanders. On the Confederate side, many in the Army of Tennessee certainly pined for a general other than Bragg and doubtless first thought of Beauregard, its only living former commander and then of Johnston, who had authority over it as commander of the Department of the West.

Although the ability of the commanding general and his principal subordinates had the most to do with an army's performance, the informal command situation doubtless contributed in a small way to the successes and failures of the armies concerned. Thus the Confederate army in the East and the Union armies in the West did better than their opponents, each of which had impaired support for its generals.

CHAPTER 10

THE DEVELOPMENT OF UNION AND CONFEDERATE STRATEGY

In what clearly had become a long war, the North faced a capable adversary who ably exploited the strengths of the defensive. Concentration remained the Union's main operational strategy, and, like all Union strategies, it developed out of a realistic and sophisticated assessment of the difficulties it faced. These difficulties included not only the intrinsic advantage of the defense over the offense but the problems of supplying armies over long distances and the vast extent of the South. The greatest obstacles were more logistic than tactical and the Union based much of its strategy on these logistical concerns.

Without adequate transportation and supply, the armies could not hope to even enter the Confederacy's territory. The movement of supplies depended on wagons in areas of good roads and pack animals on very bad roads or across country. A wagon drawn by a six-mule team on a macadamized road could carry as much as 4,500 pounds at two-and-a-half miles per hour. On the poor roads found in the southern United States wagon loads averaged only 2,500 pounds and at lower speeds. Even this was more efficient than a pack mule carrying 200 pounds, but the wagons themselves constituted a problem. Four or, preferably, six horses or mules drew each wagon; and every animal consumed about eight times as much food and water as a human being. Even though rail transport cost more than traveling by water, a train's ability to move at 30 or more miles per hour meant that rail usually offered more speed than steamers and was much more efficient than wagons on even the best road. Moreover, the railroad offered greater dependability, without interruptions caused by freezing or low water. The proliferation of railroads made it possible for armies to operate from bases at a considerable distance from the action.

Almost all the supply calculations that the U.S. Army had derived from the French assumed campaigning under logistic conditions similar to those of western Europe. But not only was the Confederacy three times the size of France, a major obstacle in itself, but it had less than a third of France's population and, consequently, food production per square mile. Virginia, for example, even without its thinly settled counties which became West Virginia, had one fifth the population density of France and southern Germany and an eighth that of Belgium, the theater of so many European wars. Tennessee, the other state with the most protracted large-scale military operations, had the same density as Virginia, and Georgia and Mississippi had even lower ratios of people to land area. Furthermore, all states devoted some land to the cultivation of the inedible crops, cotton and tobacco.

This meant that armies of the size typical of Europe and common in the Civil War could not long remain motionless in such country unless they could disperse very widely or supply themselves from a base. Even dispersing widely would require far more wagons than the armies had envisioned in order to bring supplies from a wider radius. Except from a nearby base, an army would require water or railroad transportation.

Although the railroads, all built in the three decades before the war, were primitive by modern standards, they enabled armies far from water transport to supply themselves. Yet the slow, short trains, which carried 10 to 15 tons of cargo per car, were less efficient than large river steamers, which could carry 500 tons of cargo. A river could easily carry more steamers than a rail line could trains, a factor counterbalancing the higher speed of locomotives. Sabotage or destruction by raiders could disable railroad tracks far more easily than it could harm steamers in a river.

Dependence on a line of supply hindered the attacker more because the defender could retreat toward his base of supplies, while the army on the offensive moved away from its supplies, often along a destroyed railroad over already well-foraged country. These logistic difficulties were unprecedented in most of the Napoleonic campaigns from which the North took its strategic models. Thus the North needed time to adjust, to realize that armies needed 20 to 30 supply wagons per 1,000 soldiers and not the 12 prescribed by the French army and originally required by Civil War armies.

Still another factor hampered troop and supply movement. The comparatively warm southern climate seemed to offer the aggressive army an opportunity to continue campaigning in the winter rather than, as in Europe, keeping the soldiers under cover to avoid heavy losses in men and horses. But the warm climate was also distinguished by a heavy winter rainfall, which took away the mobility necessary for armies to exploit the mild winters. Without leafy trees or growing grass and crops to consume moisture, the high monthly rainfall of three to four inches soaked into the earth and caused the unpaved roads of the South to become impassable channels filled with mud.

All of the Union armies faced these supply and climate difficulties but an army in Virginia also confronted the obstacle presented by a small theater of war. Eastern Virginia north of the James River and between the Blue Ridge Mountains and Chesapeake Bay had a land area about the size of Belgium, where European armies had struggled in essentially stalemated combat for almost two centuries. Belgium differed from Virginia in that fortified cities studded the country, blocking rivers and roads and containing garrisons too strong for an invading force to leave in its rear. Still, Virginia's rivers offered serious obstacles because, broader and deeper than those of Belgium, they ran from west to east across the theater of war, with the York, the Rappahannock, and their tributaries forming two barriers between the Potomac and the James. If military operations in Belgium offered a valid parallel, the North could easily encounter a stalemate based on too high a ratio of force to space.

Thus stalemate conditions in Virginia as well as particular logistic difficulties trammeled Federal offensive efforts. In addition, the Union forces had to confront the traditional ascendancy of the tactical defensive between similarly armed infantry.

An attack against the rebel armies would have offered a simple path to victory only if the tactical offensive had as much strength as the defense and pursuit was faster than retreat. Had these conditions prevailed, numerically stronger northern armies would have met and defeated southern armies. The Union forces would then have pursued, overtaken, and defeated them again and again until they had destroyed all their foes and occupied the country. But, in reality, the tactical defense dominated the offense and retreat outran pursuit. This operational reality gave the Confederate armies the choice of defending from a strong position against a frontal attack or declining to fight by retreating.

In fact, the likelihood of annihilating a hostile army in battle had so decreased in the preceding two centuries as to make such an event extremely improbable. Changes in weapons, training, and organization from the early seventeenth to the late eighteenth century combined to reduce the average casualties of the defeated from 37 percent of his forces to 22 percent, a figure that did not change during the Napoleonic wars. The casualties of the victor remained at 12.5 percent throughout. Accordingly, with less to lose in the case of defeat, commanders became willing to engage in a battle when they had a lower estimate of the chances of victory than they would have in earlier times.

This change did not mark the end of big battles of annihilation which, because of their drama and occasional importance, had occupied a large place in the narrative histories of wars. But, since they had in fact occurred rarely in the history of warfare, readers would not particularly note their absence.

Thus it is hardly surprising that the eighteenth century witnessed only one battle of annihilation, that at Blenheim in 1704 where the French lost two-thirds of their army, while their adversaries, commanded by the famous generals Marlborough and Eugene, lost less than a quarter of theirs. This weakening of the French enabled the Anglo-Imperial victors to take much territory in southern Germany. In the next most costly major battle of the century, Zorndorf in 1758, the Russians lost 53 percent of their force, but the Prussians almost annihilated themselves in the process of gaining their victory, losing 35 percent. The battle had the result the Prussians sought, the Russian abandonment of their advance. In several of the many battles of the Napoleonic era the casualties of the defeated exceeded 40 percent; but that period did not have any battles comparable to Blenheim either.

Still, in the American Civil War, many civilians failed to understand the virtual impossibility of fighting a single battle that destroyed an enemy army or to grasp the primacy of the defense and retreat. But most of the professional soldiers understood this reality and saw that they could only win through the slow process of conquering southern territory. Implicitly they rejected a combat strategy and chose a logistic strategy. This strategy aimed at weakening and ultimately depleting the hostile armies by taking away their means of supply and thus depriving them of weapons, horses, recruits, food, and fodder.

This logistic strategy is as old as warfare. Julius Caesar said that he preferred "conquering the foe by hunger than by steel," and he almost invariably decided to avoid combat, and instead to attack his antagonist's supplies.

The Union Navy's blockade and capture of ports was one aspect of the logistic strategy that aimed to deprive the rebels of key imports. The army, on the other hand, had to implement logistic strategy more tediously, through conquering the Confederacy's territory by driving back its armies. In this way the rebels' base area, which supplied food, weapons, ammunition, and recruits for their army contracted, thereby weakening their defending forces and accelerating the Union occupation of their land and depletion of their resources. Thus the Union embarked on a long war, seeking victory by military means but not forsaking much of the initial conciliatory political strategy which aimed at facilitating compromise or, at least, not making eventual reunion more difficult.

Although the Union relied on a logistic strategy, it required combat to implement it through conquering southern territory. In spite of the failure of the December 1862 concentration in time to conquer much territory, simultaneous advances remained an integral part of Northern strategy. As the Federal command and its ideas matured, the operational conditions in Virginia helped to shape the overall strategy.

The Battle of Fredericksburg did not resemble the year's four other big combats in the East because no turning movement had motivated Burnside's tactical offensive. McClellan's turning movement and its threat to Richmond precipitated Johnston's tactical offensive at Fair Oaks and Lee's intended turning movement to begin the Seven Days' Battles. So also Lee's turning movements had provoked Pope's attack at Second Manassas and McClellan's at Antietam. Nothing of the sort made Burnside's assaults imperative, but his battle nevertheless shared a characteristic of both Pope's and McClellan's in that, in all three Union offensive engagements, the armies made a series of frontal attacks. They all carried out the straightforward, fighting advance that fit the civilian concept of warfare.

The experience of the Confederates in trying to assail their adversary in the flank or reach his rear showed the difficulty of thus catching the enemy at a disadvantage. Johnston's failed at Fair Oaks and nothing Lee tried ever worked: neither on the first or second day of the Seven Days' Battles nor at Frayser's Farm during the pursuit did an apparently exposed flank prove vulnerable when the Confederate forces arrived to make their assault. Lee's men had the same experience at Second Manassas both in Longstreet's assault and Jackson's turning movement at Chantilly.

Well-drilled Civil War infantry usually failed in flank attacks because it faced men trained in the same way with the same degree of maneuverability. Since soldiers always wish to face their opponent, the defenders either changed direction to confront the would-be flank attackers or avoided combat all together by retreating. Without attacking soldiers with mobility superior to the defenders', most flank attacks failed.

These Civil War battles conformed to the pattern established over thousands of years: Among similarly armed infantry flank attacks rarely succeed. Although during the history of warfare many tacticians had striven to solve the problem, successful flank attacks usually depended on the superior mobility of cavalry. Traditionally formed on both opposing army's flanks, the horsemen charged each other and, when the victorious cavalry had driven the vanquished from the field, they won the battle by defeating the infantry by assailing it in the flank and rear. Hannibal's victory over the Romans at Cannae in 216 B.C. is the most famous example of this technique.

The introduction of the bayonet, the French Revolutionary drill, and the better-articulated infantry each diminished the cavalry's ability to catch the infantry at a disadvantage. The introduction of the rifle continued the process of reducing the chances of a successful cavalry flank attack. The wooded terrain in which the Civil War battles took place further diminished the opportunities for successful cavalry maneuvers and contributed to the decision by both sides not to develop large numbers of heavy cavalry trained to make such charges.

With the possibility of a cavalry flank attack eliminated as the basis for battle tactics, all Civil War soldiers had the same battlefield mobility. Without troops able to maneuver more easily or rapidly than their adversaries, commanders encountered far more difficulty in mounting successful flank attacks or concentrating superior numbers at a given point in the line. With such evenly matched and identically organized opponents in the Civil War, the offensive had even less chance than it had in Europe. This situation of the weakness of infantry armies in the offensive against each other continued, reached its apogee in the First World War, and began to recede with the reintroduction of cavalry in the form of tanks and aircraft.

When Lee and Davis realized the difficulty of making other than frontal attacks, they also adopted the strategic turning movement. This produced the desired result in that it put them on the defensive in the next two battles, with Burnside presenting them with a third defensive battle at Fredericksburg. Yet Lee and Jackson failed to make the most of the defensive by neglecting to entrench, something West Point had emphasized in Jackson's classes and Lee, an engineer, should have thought of doing.

Military history may help explain their behavior for, insofar as they had studied military history, they had probably limited themselves to the Napoleonic wars, where field fortifications had a far smaller role than in most conflicts since the introduction of gunpowder. Perhaps the aggressiveness of both Jackson and Lee helped keep them from thinking of something so obvious as the advantage of entrenchment. But, when Longstreet demonstrated its use at Fredericksburg, they became diligent practitioners of what West Pointers, such as McDowell, Beauregard, and Halleck, had done since the outbreak of hostilities.

With the addition of field fortifications, Lee believed that he had perfected his strategy, one so well served by the power the turning movement had shown on the defense when it pushed back Pope and enabled Lee to raid into Maryland. Although Lee had fought his battles on the defensive, in both campaigns he had failed in his more ambitious objective: to turn the enemy back while avoiding battle altogether. In each his adversary had not reacted as expected: Pope acted more aggressively than Jackson's strong position and Longstreet's presence made wise, and McClellan moved with unusual rapidity and joined battle with little hesitation. Still, if Lee had another opportunity to employ his maneuver defensively, he could still look forward to the possibility of avoiding battle or fighting on a defensive enhanced by entrenchments.

For the North, McClellan had demonstrated the turning movement's power to reach Richmond and begin a siege. But this did not lead the Union in the direction of a strategy it could repeat, in part because McClellan and his ideas had become repellent to so many in Washington. But this meant that the Union sacrificed its best means of turning Lee's army because it gave up access to Chesapeake Bay and Virginia's navigable rivers as a base area. Bragg's experience in turning Buell in his Kentucky campaign illustrates the critical importance of access to a base area. He had turned his opponent and begun entrenching his army across his line of communications and retreat when he realized that Buell could feed from his stores on hand; so Bragg's Confederates, lacking a base area, had to withdraw and allow the Union army to march on to Louisville.

Since the perceptive Lee realized that the association with McClellan precluded Union adoption of this most menacing line of operations, he could make his dispositions without concern for the Peninsula. Moreover, Lee had learned to use the Shenandoah Valley as a base area to support a turning of his adversary. The northeast-southwest direction of the valley made this possible by leading into the rear of the Union army.

135

On the other hand, it offered nothing to the Army of the Potomac because it led progressively farther away from the rear of the Army of Northern Virginia.

Yet Halleck looked at the situation differently because he saw the Peninsula leading to Richmond and an inevitable siege. Since he did not believe that, like the city of Sevastopol in the Crimean War, Richmond must inevitably fall to the siege and not comprehending how much Lee feared the logistical difficulties of defending Richmond, he thought that a siege played into the enemy's hands. Realizing how much the thoroughly fortified defenses of the city would economize manpower, Halleck saw that a siege would free some of Lee's men to conduct politically damaging raids or reinforce Confederate armies elsewhere.

With the rejection of the Peninsula strategy for both political and military reasons, Halleck had to acknowledge the continuation of the stalemate in Virginia. Thus he and Lincoln planned to manage affairs in Virginia so as "to detach sufficient forces to place the opening of the Mississippi beyond a doubt." They soon sent an army corps from Virginia to Kentucky to operate against East Tennessee in coordination with Rosecrans, and they directed all new troops raised in the West to go to Grant to strengthen his campaign against Vicksburg. This distribution of resources gave the first priority to Grant, the second to Rosecrans, and the last to the stalemated Virginia front.

Still, the highly visible and politically important Virginia theater required a strategy. The one Lincoln and Halleck adopted had two parts. First, the Army of the Potomac would continue to "occupy the rebel army south of the Rappahannock," which gave this army the essentially political objective of keeping the rebels at least 50 miles from Washington and the Potomac River. The second part, almost surely Lincoln's idea, was to watch for an opportunity to harm Lee's army. To accomplish this, the general must "beware of rashness" and above all understand that he was not to try to besiege Richmond: The "first object was, not Richmond, but the defeat and scattering of Lee's army." For this defeat of Lee, he would have to wait "til a favorable opportunity offered [itself] to strike a decisive blow." Doubtless remembering how close the Federal armies had come to bagging Jackson during the Valley campaign, Lincoln had the conviction that, if Lee made another raid north, he opened himself to having his retreat blocked and his army forced either to fight its way through superior numbers or to scatter itself.

Thus Northern strategy implicitly took account of the major factors which conditioned operations in the Civil War. The Union high command recognized the primacy of the tactical defensive and the ascendancy of retreat over pursuit. The relevance of these varied, depending on the ratio of force to space. With a high ratio of force to space, defenders usually relied on the power of the tactical defensive; when campaigning with a low ratio of force to space, they tended to employ the greater celerity of retreat. In the constricted area of eastern Virginia, a Union army on the offensive could hardly avoid meeting its Confederate adversary blocking its path behind strong entrenchments. In the much larger spaces of the West, the attacking army had little hope of catching an opponent who could so easily retreat, often with a choice of more than one direction.

Moreover, the Union faced a significant logistical obstacle. Dependent on supply from bases in the sparsely populated South, Federal forces increasingly had to depend on the railroad, whose vulnerability the failed offensives of both Grant and Buell had amply demonstrated. Grant could still campaign by using the secure and efficient Mississippi, but the eastern armies found that Chesapeake Bay and its rivers contributed little to solving their supply problems. Even if McClellan's experience had not made a Peninsula campaign politically undesirable and its exterior lines given it some risk, any such water-based advance had little utility because it would inevitably lead to a siege at or near Richmond. Just as concentration in the West recognized the better opportunities there, so the Union strategy for Virginia made a realistic accommodation to the ascendancy of the strategic defense in that restricted theater. So the Union had evolved a strategy well adapted to the operational and political conditions under which it fought an adversary essentially identical in doctrine, equipment, and operational skill. But sophisticated and appropriate as this strategy was and effective as it proved to be in 1863, it overlooked a major part of the North's strategic problem.

CHAPTER 11

THE STRATEGIC
FRAMEWORK

———— •—◦—• ————

Classifying strategy makes it and the Civil War's strategy easier
to understand. Combat and logistic strategy offer the two basic
means of depleting the enemy forces, either directly through
combat or indirectly by depriving them of needed resources. Of
course, implementing a logistic strategy usually involves combat, but this combat is a means to the end of conquering territory or otherwise undermining the adversary's supply base.

The other classification divides strategy according to its operational approach, the hit and run strategy of raiding or the
persisting strategy's goal of seizing territory. The Napoleonic
operational strategy of concentration and turning movements
belongs primarily to persisting strategy. Political strategy,
which uses military means to accomplish political objectives
directly, does not fit into these classifications of military strategy, but its military actions do.

But these two pairs of classifications do apply equally well to
naval warfare and help illuminate the essential unity of strategy. Early in the war the navy, with totally inadequate forces,
sought to blockade southern ports. By attempting to control the
water outside the ports, the navy applied a persisting strategy
in pursuit of its logistic strategy of destroying the Confederacy's foreign trade and cutting off its critical imports.

The war brought phenomenal expansion to the U.S. fleet, which, in four years, increased from 90 to 670 ships and from 7,500 sailors to 51,500. Beginning with 1,300 officers, of whom 322 joined the Confederacy, the U.S. Navy's officers numbered 6,700 at the war's end. Much of the credit for this increase belongs to Gideon Welles, the able, energetic, and eccentric secretary of the navy. A journalist and politician who covered his bald head with a wig, he had served for three years as chief of a navy department bureau concerned with supply. This background helped the gifted secretary give perceptive direction to the navy's contribution to waging the war. The navy diverted some ships to pursue Confederate commerce raiders and some to render crucial aid to the army by controlling the inland rivers, but concentrated most of its resources on blockading Confederate ports. This fit Scott's anaconda strategy and constituted the contribution which a superior fleet could make to the war effort.

Although almost all merchant craft carried sails, only a minority used steam engines; the coal-burning steamer dominated in the fleet and complicated the task of supplying the blockade by adding coal to the food and water requirements of the blockading ships. Because fuel gave out sooner than food or water, blockaders needed to have bases closer to the blockaded ports or else spend more time returning to base and less on duty. Since many ships attempting to run past the blockading squadron would have sails alone and steamers could usually catch them, the blockading fleet wanted steamers only. Indeed, some blockade runners would have steam power and a sailing ship had small chance of catching them.

Making matters worse, a blockading ship could not employ an obvious method of conserving coal, that is, by depending on its sails most of the time, and using its engine only when it sighted a blockade runner. A steam engine required hours to heat water and make steam to operate. It needed even more time for full speed. Thus a steamer not using its engine might as well not have one if a blockade runner appeared. The quarry would have long escaped before its pursuer could steam. Accordingly, Welles and his naval leaders felt the need for bases near the ports they wished to blockade. And even so, in spite of the success in finding such bases, an average of one third of the blockading ships was absent from their stations at any one time getting essential supplies.

In capturing suitable ports or sheltered anchorages to use as bases, the naval forces would likely face gun batteries erected on shore to dominate the approaches to these desirable locations. Shore-based guns had the advantage over those on ships because they had a steady platform from which to aim and had, in masonry or earth, far better protection against the enemy's shot than a ship's side could afford. This superiority of coastal fortification made army assistance extremely important in capturing and protecting bases on the enemy coast.

But, in conducting amphibious operations against the southern coasts, the attackers had the advantage of the initiative, that is, the ability to assail an adversary's weak point without having to fear an attack from him. Though it usually required taking the enemy by surprise, the initiative could bring important victories at little cost. The fleet could land soldiers at any of many different places, arriving unexpectedly on the horizon, while the Confederate army could do nothing to threaten the U.S. Navy. An unexpected landing usually found the defenders weak, because a surprised opponent is an unready one.

In August 1861 a flotilla and a contingent of 800 soldiers descended on Hatteras Inlet, a channel between two islands which led into the spacious and sheltered Pamlico Sound on the North Carolina coast. This force easily overcame the Confederate garrisons of the small forts guarding the inlet. The navy promptly established a base there for its blockading squadron. In November another expedition, which included 27,000 soldiers, gained control of Port Royal Sound on the South Carolina coast and established a base convenient for blockading the important ports of Charleston, South Carolina, and Savannah, Georgia. In January 1862 the army took the initiative in expanding its area of control on the North Carolina coast, and the following month the navy landed 15,000 soldiers on Roanoke Island, where they overwhelmed 2,500 ineptly led and inadequately entrenched defenders. This victory received publicity and called favorable attention to General Ambrose E. Burnside, the commander of the land forces. He extended his conquest by capturing the port of New Bern, important to the Confederates because of its railroad running inland.

Capturing southern ports, which, like New Bern, had high value because of their rail connections, provided a sure means of implementing a blockade that so far had captured very few of the ships which attempted to use southern ports. By April 1862 combined operations had closed two more such ports, Fernandina in northern Florida, by capture, and Savannah, Georgia, by the capture of Fort Pulaski, which controlled the mouth of the Savannah River and access to the city and its port.

Protecting the coast from the demonstrated menace of landings became a major element in Confederate strategy as the War Department concentrated many of its newly raised troops along the eastern seaboard and Gulf Coast to meet this expected Union threat. Protecting Southern ports became a major mission for the newly organized Confederate Navy.

In his choice of Stephen R. Mallory as secretary of the navy, Davis had the same good fortune as Lincoln in his selection of Welles. A Floridian with a lifelong interest in the sea, Mallory had served ten years in the U.S. Senate and had become chairman of its Naval Affairs Committee. Combining knowledge and enthusiasm with good judgment, he made an excellent secretary. With over 300 officers from the U.S. Navy to provide leadership of a small force, he faced problems of matériel and strategy rather than manpower. After initially considering the use of iron-armored warships to break the blockade, Secretary Mallory realized the error in challenging the U.S. Navy at sea. He remained mindful, however, of the need to take the offensive with a logistic strategy against the North's commerce. To this end the government authorized privateers but only a few entrepreneurs fitted out ships to make money by preying on northern merchant ships. Government ships such as the *Alabama* played an important role. A steamer built in England, the *Alabama* cruised both Asiatic and Atlantic waters until finally sunk off the coast of France. In her 22 month career she captured 65 U.S. merchant ships. The small number of rebel raiders at sea drove up insurance rates for Union ships and caused many to change to foreign registry; but the application of raiding strategy to Yankee commerce in no way seriously impeded the export and import trade of the United States. Rebel cavalry raiders had far greater success in pursuing their logistic strategy against the supply lines of Union armies.

Nor did the Union blockade cut off southern commerce; rather it raised the costs of doing business and diminished the volume of imports and exports. The U.S. Navy was quite unequal to carrying out General Scott's prescription for a "strict blockade of the seaboard." The failure of the blockade to interdict vital Confederate commerce made the capture of southern seaports, a method used in the Mexican War, an important, and potentially conclusive, effort.

Thus, in its broader naval strategy, the Confederate Navy directed its main efforts toward building ships for coast defense and, to aid the army, for defense of the inland rivers. In pursuing this objective the Confederates built many gunboats and laid down 50 ironclad warships, all but the first five having port and river defense as their mission. Of these iron-armored ships it completed but 25, leaving its fleet inferior to the Union's even in its chosen field of port defense. The Federal navy could concentrate against a port and, though the Confederate Army could move men to counter this, the port defense ships could not make sea voyages to carry out a corresponding concentration.

The capture of ports by the Union Navy and Army ultimately had more significance than the blockade, despite the steady increase in Union ships devoted to it. But many of these vessels, converted from other duties and often old or not well maintained, frequently had a small capacity for carrying coal. Numerous ships spent much time away from their station replenishing fuel and obtaining repairs. The numbers of ships which ran the blockade of the important port of Wilmington, North Carolina, clearly shows the ineffectiveness of the blockade. During the entire war, 84 percent of the attempts to run past the blockaders succeeded, or 1½ per day. In the Gulf, the blockaders did much better, capturing more than a third of the ships trying to run the blockade in 1862 and 1863. But in 1864, when the blockade runners used more steamers, 87 percent got by and, in 1865, 94 percent. While the blockade raised the expense of imports and reduced the return on exports, essential military supplies broke through, as attested by the Confederate government's appropriating for its own use only half of the space on incoming ships.

If the U.S. Navy's logistic strategy failed to cause the Confederates great apprehension, the reverse was true of its logistic strategy on land. The defense against the Union land offensives against logistically critical areas of the South provided the keystone of rebel military strategy. The Confederacy made its decision on the primacy of territory without reference to the enemy's strategy. President Davis clearly explained the rationale when he wrote that the "general truth that power is increased by the concentration of an army is, under our peculiar circumstances, subject to modification," because "the evacuation of any portion of territory involves not only the loss of supplies, but in every instance has been attended by a greater or less loss of troops." He referred not only to the loss of potential troops but also to the greater propensity of soldiers to desert when the enemy occupied the region where their families lived, yet another motive for conserving territory and another advantage accruing to the North's logistic strategy.

The Confederacy, like the Union, could not see another strategy as a reasonable alternative. An effective defense necessarily involved defending against the kind of offensive the Union conducted. An offensive to conquer Union territory had little realism for armies which the enemy's outnumbered by two to one, and a combat strategy directed against the hostile armies had even less to commend it to the South than the North. The strategic defense does not rule out the counterattack anymore than does the tactical defense. And the strategic counterattack had the same advantage as the tactical, assailing an antagonist unready to defend and vulnerable to surprise because of his commitment to an offensive posture and goals. The strategic counterattack that recovered lost territory would augment southern strength by bringing friendly citizens and their labor and resources back into the service of the Confederate cause.

In addition to its ability to employ the counterattack as well as exploit the dominance of the tactical defense, the strategic defense could use retreat. Although retreats exposed Southern territory to occupation by Federal forces, they also presented the advancing hostile army with immense difficulties. The obstacles to supplying itself in an enemy country, on a route already scoured by a retreating army, would often delay or halt an invader. In the thinly settled South, the supply problem could impose immense delays for logistical preparations if it did not indeed preclude an advance at all. Northern armies, by having to garrison their conquests in order to prevent them from reverting to rebel control, quickly dissipated their strength and could even lose their numerical advantage. Hypothetically, a Union advance could weaken its armies just as much or more than the retreat diminished Confederate numbers. But such a strategy for the South faced a serious political objection. Retreat and loss of territory would not only discourage and possibly demoralize Southerners; it would encourage the people of the North by giving them tangible evidence of success, which would reinforce their determination to continue the war for the Union. Thus important political considerations harmonized with the military need to defend territory.

In pitting the greater strength of the strategic defense against the North's larger forces, what chance did the South have? Except in the constricted, Netherlands-size Virginia theater, the Confederate armies would usually have ample space in which to avoid their adversary. And the Confederacy's immense size as a whole precluded complete occupation. The perceptive George W. Randolph, secession advocate and Confederate secretary of war, clearly grasped the defensive power conferred by the vast expanse of the South. At the beginning of the war Randolph believed that "there is no instance in history of a people as numerous as we are inhabiting a country so extensive as ours being subjected if true to themselves."

The results of the December 1862 campaigns reinforced this assessment by showing the inability of numerical superiority to prevail over the defensive. Halleck's laboriously coordinated major simultaneous advances had failed ignominiously. Only Rosecrans's had had any success, aided by the absence from Bragg's army of a large Confederate division, futilely dispatched to aid Mississippi. This meager gain was surely a discouraging result from the application of what was clearly the best strategy. But the offensive had secured a triumph for rebels because they used it in a form in which it had a natural superiority over the defense: raiding, particularly against logistic objectives. So, in the West, favored by ample space, raids against Union communications by guerrillas and by cavalry under Forrest, Morgan, and Van Dorn actually contributed as much to the defense as the actions of the main southern armies.

Raiding is particularly well suited to implementing a logistic strategy, because supplies, bridges, and other logistic objectives, are normally weaker than a unit of enemy soldiers, the typical objective of a combat strategy. But raiders can function only in an area with a low ratio of armed force to space. The more enemy soldiers in an operational area, the greater the likelihood of encountering an adversary unexpectedly or of facing entrapment by several forces. In addition, if civilians in the area are hostile, armed, and aided by fortifications, they could so multiply the ratio of force to space as to destroy the raiders' mobility. Guerrillas, who typically employed raids, therefore had a particular desire for, and dependence on, operating among friendly civilians.

Under the proper conditions, it is clear that a strategic offensive by raiding is stronger than the strategic defensive. This is exactly the opposite of the situation of an army seeking to conquer enemy territory with a persisting strategy. Thus, the Union employed a persisting strategy of conquest to implement its logistic strategy of depriving the Confederacy of resources essential to carry on the war, and the South used a raiding strategy to carry out its own logistic strategy of cutting the communications of the invading armies.

But the Confederates did not limit their raids to those by the regular cavalry of Forrest, Van Dorn, and Morgan. Guerrillas used the raid as well, exploiting its characteristic strengths: the ambiguity of objective which facilitated strikes against a weak, surprised, or vulnerable adversary; alternative routes of withdrawal; and the greater rapidity of retreat. The Union area of occupation had become infested with rebel guerrillas in spite of an occupation policy designed to prevent this.

The state of Tennessee absorbed an enormous number of Rosecrans's and other Union troops to garrison the conquered area and support the Nashville military government of General Andrew Johnson, a former Democratic senator from Tennessee. When Union forces first occupied Middle Tennessee, they consistently applied the policy of conciliation, leaving slavery undisturbed and removing only a few blatantly secessionist officials. General Buell had announced to his troops that "we are in arms not for the purpose of invading the rights of our fellow-countrymen anywhere, but to maintain the integrity of the Union and protect the constitution." The policy, however, failed to enlist appreciable support for rebel Tennesseans or tap any hidden springs of Unionism which the policy's advocates believed existed. This response in Middle Tennessee typified that in most southern regions.

The war's bloody fighting further hardened attitudes, increased enmity, made an early reconciliation impossible and showed the failure of the optimistic conciliation strategy. But this did not have much effect on the pacification policy practiced by the army. In living off the country, the armies could hardly pay rebels for supplies; nor could it give receipts for reimbursement by the Confederate government, because to do so would be to recognize it, something completely at variance with the reason for fighting and the assumption underlying the original conciliation policy. Thus supplying troops in the conventional way involved a contradiction only avoided by providing for the armies from a base in Union territory, something which, even if possible, would impose a serious military handicap.

So the Union forces lived on the country to the degree it would support them, attempting to minimize the burden by trying to restrain individual looting and trying to take only needed supplies through the action of quartermaster and commissary officers. This method had the sound military foundation that pillaging soldiers were more likely to straggle, desert, commit rape and other atrocities, and suffer injury or death at the hands of civilians. These would both lose men and add to the number of adversaries. Since commanders did not want to increase the number of their guerrilla enemies, they did their best to avoid unnecessarily antagonizing the Southerners among whom they marched and camped.

But, though commanders could minimize these evils when on an urgent march, a stationary army could not help but destroy much even if the soldiers behaved in an ideal manner. One observer thus described the vicinity of a Union army's winter quarters: "Buildings were leveled; fences burned; . . . the wagon trains and batteries cut new thoroughfares across the estates; the feet of men, and hoofs of horses and mules, trampled fields of vegetation into barren wastes; every landmark was destroyed."

They also sought to avoid alienating their friends. If they could identify a southerner as a Unionist, they could pay him for produce taken by giving him a receipt payable by the United States. This was an uncertain and sporadically applied policy. Thus a pallid version of the policy of placating hostility remained, but it had its basis almost entirely in military considerations and owed very little to its original political inspiration.

But in many places the reception given to the occupiers compelled the Union armies to adopt a radically different policy. And few places better illustrate the cause and resulting policy than Middle Tennessee, where the occupying army faced a community controlled by guerrillas who kept the country firmly rebel in active sympathy, and who intimidated the few existing Unionists. The social pressure of ostracism, of treating them "as if they had been infected with leprosy," and, in many instances, adding "bitter recriminations," usually sufficed to suppress any expressions of support for the Federal cause. Supplementing this pressure, the guerrillas used destruction of property and physical force to frighten northern sympathizers into leaving the area.

These measures, and occasional lynchings, proved quite effective in keeping the population loyal to the Confederacy despite Union military occupation. Secessionists made examples of Unionists, kidnapping one and "literally hewing him to pieces." Hanging Federal sympathizers and leaving their bodies swinging also proved an effective deterrent. The guerrillas, operating as raiders and having the support of the population, actually dominated the country and, in one county, "shot everybody that interfered with them. If they didn't kill people they would beat them on the head with a pistol or anything they could get hold of and everybody was afraid of them." One observer dared not report them for, "if I did I would get my house burned down and everything destroyed."

Guerrilla activity extended to the countryside, where bands succeeded in deterring the flight of most slaves and capturing and returning those who attempted it. They also ambushed slaves working for the Union Army. One guerrilla recalled that "6 of us attacked a company of negroe[s] at Taylor's Camp Ground in Cannon County, killing several & wounding others & running off [the rest.]"

The rebel irregulars directed much attention to fighting the occupiers as well. In the words of a Union officer, "clothed in the peaceful garb of the citizen," guerrillas "enter our camps and pass through our lines, and the citizen's dress is generally but the disguise of a spy." But many more were said to "attend their farms in the day-time and go bushwhacking at night." They raided isolated points, lightly garrisoned posts, wagon trains, and foragers as well as ambushing messengers, cutting telegraph lines, sabotaging railway track, and burning bridges and trestles. The warfare had a ruthlessness absent elsewhere, as when partisans captured five foragers, took them away, tied their hands, and shot them. These guerrillas enjoyed an advantage denied regular cavalry; they could employ an additional mode of retreat when they resumed their guise of loyal citizens.

Guerrilla strength early demonstrated the most emphatic failure of conciliation locally, just as the course the war had taken precluded any early reconciliation. Seeing that "these people are proud, arrogant rebels," a Union general announced: "I propose, so far as I can, to let the people know that we are at war." Abandoning efforts to placate his foes and turning instead to intimidation, Governor Johnson and the army as a whole began putting Unionists in positions of political power and arming them.

The Federal government pursued this policy further. It armed local Union sympathizers and had them campaign against bushwhackers. With their knowledge of the country and its people, these "home guards" proved singularly effective. In one county a Union officer reported that "they are killing many of the worst men in this part of the State & will soon drive the guerrillas out. They are passing through the Country in small parties killing (they take none) all the robbers & Scoundrels."

Making the transition to intimidation, the Federal troops often killed captured guerrillas, frequently without trying them. But, since the raiding guerrillas usually eluded capture, the army cowed their supporters by requiring citizens in areas of guerrilla activity to pay fines for damage done. For example, when guerrillas captured and killed five Union soldiers, the authorities raised $30,000 for the dead men's families by assessing every rebel sympathizer within ten miles of the scene of the "atrocious and cold-blooded murder." In reprisal, the army also burned farms and even whole villages and occasionally took hostages. A Union cavalry unit, for instance, burned most of a village's 30 houses in revenge for having shots fired at it in the neighborhood. Most effective was the campaign to intimidate the gentry, a very influential group supportive of the guerrilla resistance. These wealthy citizens became the object of reprisals. In effect the Federal forces held them and their property hostage.

When guerrillas acted against northern sympathizers, soldiers, or property, the occupation authorities often arrested prominent citizens, usually confiscating some of their property and putting them in prison. Sometimes the government would assess all local aristocrats to pay for the damage caused by a guerrilla incident in their area. These measures had the desired effect of inducing these important people to use their influence against guerrilla warfare. Though this proved effective in nearly ending guerrilla activity, it did not come soon enough to save many large planters from ruin through loss of money, crops, animals, and equipment. The various forms of intimidation had proven effective, as a Union officer testified when he noted that a "distinguishing feature in this country is the manner in which these people are cowed by the force of the Gov't." Yet before their subjection, the guerrillas had interrupted the communications of the main armies and occupied the attention of a disproportionate share of Union troops.

Middle Tennessee was not the only area of intense guerrilla activity. Grant's department in West Tennessee, for example, met a bitter local opposition which threatened a railroad network almost as extensive and vulnerable as that upon which Rosecrans depended. In Virginia, Union forces occupied the eastern and northern fringes of the state, areas that fluctuated in size with the ebb and flow of the military operations in that stalemated theater. Union policy and rebel resistance there resembled the pattern of events in Middle Tennessee.

As elsewhere, the invaders in Virginia tried to propitiate the opposition. One Union officer, for instance, tried "to make all [citizens] I come in contact with feel as if we were not conquerors, that we did not feel exultant, . . . that we had no desire to play the tyrant." But he received no response, finding that "the tenor of society here is hostile to us. *I may say hatefully so."* Another Union officer confessed "[t]he more I see of these rebels the more I hate them." General Sherman had worried that the behavior of Union soldiers would alienate the Union's "friends" in Virginia. But the army had difficulty finding friends to lose, and the rebels had intimidated many of the few remaining ones it had.

When attempts at both official and unofficial conciliation ended, Union forces had no difficulty in applying intimidation. Many troops had early "adopted the theory that all property of the inhabitants was subject to plunder." Officers began to give their men the freedom to loot, and all suffered at the hands of the occupiers. One officer noted that "we are in effect adopting the doctrine that the Secesh have no right[s] a white man is bound to respect."

To this unsystematic attempt to overawe the rebels, the authorities added loyalty oaths, levies for damages, and reprisals such as burning houses. One witness described official destruction thus: "All day long the soldiers continue to destroy property. . . . Many hundreds of sheep, cattle and hogs & . . . poultry are destroyed. People generally are stripped of their subsistence. One half of this truly unfortunate country have been robbed to destitution & and the other half have nothing to spare for their relief." But the tenuous state of Union dominance, the division of the occupied areas among several commands, and the lack of a consistent policy to suppress dissent, meant that only the towns came firmly under Federal control.

In the countryside, however, the results of this policy varied. It cowed many, especially among the poor whites who had initially supported the war with enthusiasm. Some of these turned against the Confederacy, and others became apathetic, one caring "but little how the war ended, [just] so it ended soon." Yet the sporadic intimidation provoked a virulent hostility which took the form of guerrilla attacks on railroads, depots, and other vulnerable targets. It also provided support for the renowned and very effective guerrilla, John S. Mosby, who operated in northern Virginia. He and his small body of rangers belonged to the Confederate Army. They had a strict discipline, and carried out many daring and successful raids. But the lines of communication were too short and the ratio of Union troops to the constricted space of the northern Virginia counties too high for guerrillas to have the substantial success in interrupting communications enjoyed by those in the West.

Though supplementing and receiving support from guerrillas, raids by Confederate regulars constituted a separate problem, one extending beyond occupied territory into states as distinctly Union as Missouri, Kentucky, and Maryland. Through Maryland, for example, ran the critically important Baltimore and Ohio Railroad which linked Washington and Baltimore with Cincinnati, the Ohio River, and all points in the western theaters. Running near the Potomac in the north end of the Shenandoah Valley, the railroad offered an easy target for southern raiders, who once held a section of it for two weeks. It required strong detachments of Federal troops to protect it. Thus Maryland and the Washington area had 70,000 men largely as garrisons, amounting to over a third of Union forces available in the region.

The army purchased its ultimate success against guerrillas and a precarious security for rail communications at the expense of seriously weakening its main forces by the use of large number of soldiers in the rear to combat this powerful resistance. The main Union armies had only two thirds of their strength available, the remaining third being devoted to garrisoning occupied territory and protecting against guerrillas and raiders. The proportion the Confederacy devoted to similar duty amounted to less than a sixth, in spite of her long, vulnerable coastline. The railroad along the Atlantic coast permitted a few men to do the duty of many, the pipeline concept of troop movement making it easy to reinforce a threatened point quickly, with state-raised reserves steadily playing an increased role. Thus the Confederacy had the best of both strategies. It defended against the Union's persisting strategy with its own, exploiting the dominance of the defense; and it employed a raiding logistic strategy with cavalry and guerrillas against Union communications, availing itself of the primacy of the raid on the offensive.

A weakness in the guerrillas' situation constituted the only defect in this happy state of Confederate strategy. Just as an army needed a base area, so also did raiders. When on a cavalry

151

raid in West Tennessee, General Forrest would not just destroy Union property and live at the expense of their supplies, but secure aid and recruits from sympathetic citizens. But this was only a temporary logistic situation because Forrest had his base area in Confederate territory. There he could return to rest his men and horses and refit both. Guerrillas, who used the same basic raiding strategy, also depended on having a base area for rest and refit between raids to damage a railroad or intimidate Yankee sympathizers.

Guerrillas differed from raiding cavalry in that General Forrest's base area was secure from the Union Army unless a persisting Federal advance should capture it; but in this case he would have retreated to a new base area still in firmly Confederate territory. The guerrilla raiders, however, lived in areas conquered by the Union persisting advance. This meant that the U.S. Army would use a logistic strategy against the guerrilla base to defeat the guerrilla raiders. The usual method, employed in Virginia, involved devastating the country to make it uninhabitable for the guerrillas. Rather than do this in Middle Tennessee, which would also deprive the Federal forces of its production, the Union authorities used a political means, intimidating the countryside's leaders and coercing them to influence the guerrillas to halt their raids. This proved an effective and economical method of exploiting the control of the country which their persisting strategy had originally gained for them.

The offensive raiding strategy had a common objective with those offensive and defensive persisting strategies implemented by concentrations and turning movements. All served the strategic objectives grounded in estimates of the political situation. Like the Union, the Confederacy had started out with a political strategy, one based on influencing foreigners. The South had begun the war with a fairly high expectation of British and French intervention on behalf of its quest for independence. It assumed that its position as supplier of most of the world's cotton assured such aid. Spinning and weaving remained Britain's largest industry, and cotton was its indispensable raw material.

Southerners believed that a cessation of raw cotton exports would halt the mills and bring depression and misery to Britain, the world's leading industrial power. This would compel the British to use their overwhelming naval supremacy to open Confederate ports and so bring the world's greatest power onto the South's side. Southern leaders attached so much importance to the power of "King Cotton" that the Confederate government stopped the export of its own cotton to create a crucial shortage in European factories, thus ironically blockading itself at a time when the Union naval blockade was almost completely ineffective. Everything which was supposed to happen did, short of the British intervention. The shortage-induced rise in the price of cotton in British markets did make it a valuable enough cargo to warrant the high ocean freight rates caused by the risk of capture in running the blockade all through the war.

When King Cotton failed to secure British intervention, the Confederacy fell back on its most basic political strategy: an adamant resistance until the Union tired of the war of coercion and made peace on the basis of recognizing the independence of the Confederacy. Having begun the war with all of its war aims achieved, it had only to conduct a successful defense in order to win.

The South could still shape its military strategy to help the political goal of discouraging the Union about the prospects of victory. Lee saw this as a possible effect of his Antietam raid. When the preliminary emancipation proclamation gave added evidence of Lincoln's adamant position in favor of reunion, the Confederates looked to the public and to elections to change the Union government's attitude. When the fall elections of 1862 continued Republican domination of the Congress, Southerners began to count on the 1864 congressional and presidential elections.

Implicitly at first and explicitly by 1864, the Confederates assessed their military strategy in terms of its effect on peace sentiment in the North and the 1864 elections. In the spring of 1863 General Lee well summed up the connection between the course of the war and the Union elections. He characterized the kind of strategy and results needed to aid the peace advocates in winning the election for the Confederacy. Lee wrote his wife in April 1863: "If we can baffle them in their various designs this year & our people are true to our cause . . . I think our success will be certain." Expecting soon to establish his "supplies on a firm basis," he continued: "On every other point we are strong. If successful this year, next fall will be a great change in public opinion in the North. The Republicans will be destroyed & I think the friends of peace will become so strong as that the next administration will go in on that basis. We have only therefore to resist manfully."

To "baffle" the North's persisting strategy implied holding the territory that the Union sought to conquer. If the South could turn back every invasion and recover lost territory, as it had done in Virginia in 1862, it could show the northern voters in 1864 that the Union could not win.

The strategy of giving primacy to the defense of Confederate territory, dictated by political considerations, conformed to the military strategy of defending the armed forces' essential logistic base against the North's persisting logistic strategy. The defense of Confederate territory did rule out an alternative strategy of accepting territorial losses and the logistic impairment these entailed. Such a strategy, which employed retreat, could count on a compensating diminution of the Union armies on account of their need to garrison the occupied territory and protect their railroads from cavalry raiders and guerrillas. The application of such a strategy would reduce Confederate forces as the defending armies lost territory, but it could reasonably expect to decrease the main Union armies in the same proportion. This defensive strategy would have cost the Confederate armies fewer killed, wounded, and captured but would have lost it new recruits and increased the number of deserters who would have departed when the enemy occupied their home area. Such a strategy would have far less chance of winning the 1864 Union elections because the occupation of Southern territory would offer tangible evidence that the Union Army was winning the war. Moreover, a strategy which lost much of the South's territory to occupation would surely have caused many Southerners to see themselves as suffering defeat, to lose heart for continuing the war, and to vote for peace and reunion at the polls or by deserting the armies.

In the end, the military strategy of each belligerent served the political objective of disheartening its opponent by making victory look hopeless and encouraging its own people by giving victories. Each side sought to win by a military strategy most consistent with this political objective. Since most essential imports reached the South when needed, the Union's persisting logistic strategy of sea blockade failed to cripple the Confederacy's war effort. Yet the blockade made a valuable contribution to the political strategy by destroying the bulk of the South's wealth-producing foreign trade and consequently reducing its people's standard of living. This, together with such shortages as coffee, added to the expense and hardship of the war. It helped persuade some Southerners that independence was not worth the unexpectedly high costs of devoting resources to the war effort, of human lives lost, and of the discouragement of defeats. The Confederacy's logistic raiding strategy of using commerce cruisers failed to curtail essential northern imports and had no appreciable effect on the Union's standard of living. Consequently, it did little to increase hardship or to help persuade Northerners that saving the Union had too high a price.

The U.S. Army's logistic strategy against the South's defense had achieved only limited success in 1862, in part because the Confederacy had supplemented its persisting defense with a raiding logistic strategy against Federal communications. These communications, increasingly railroads rather than the relatively invulnerable river steamers, proved very difficult to defend against Confederate cavalry raiders and guerrillas. Controlling occupied territory and protecting communications thus absorbed as much as a third of available Federal troops. Still, the Union was raising more men, and the Confederacy would face new and more skillfully conducted offensives in the spring of 1863.

CHAPTER 12

THE MATURITY OF UNION
OPERATIONAL SKILL

———◆———

Chancellorsville, Vicksburg, Tullahoma, and Gettysburg Campaigns

Just as the soldiers became veterans, experienced in combat, inured to marching, and resourceful in caring for themselves, so also did the generals mature. Particularly did Union generals display a perceptiveness in their strategy and, in the case of Grant and Rosecrans, a virtuosity in execution which had far more to do with their victories than their slight numerical superiority. Grant commanding on the Mississippi and Rosecrans in Middle Tennessee were both veterans of the December offensives and each wiser for their experience. In Virginia, the Army of the Potomac had in Joseph Hooker, a new general, one brought up in McClellan's army but receptive to the new ideas developed by Lincoln and Halleck and emanating from Army Headquarters.

To coordinate with the advances in the West, Hooker had to do more than wait for Lee to act and then try to hurt him if he made a mistake. To do his part Hooker had a plan of campaign from Army Headquarters. Originally sent to Burnside and drafted by Halleck's brilliant collaborator, Quartermaster General Meigs, it offered the means for "a great and overwhelming defeat and destruction" of Lee's army. Pointing out that "no battle fought with your back to the North or the sea can give you such a victory" because the enemy had "shown skill in retreat," he prescribed a turning movement, by making "a march as Napoleon made at Jena, as Lee made in his campaign against Pope." To do this, he should march "up the Rappahannock, cross the river, [and] aim for a point on the railroad between the rebels and Richmond." Merging Napoleonic with Civil War lessons, Meigs's sophisticated plan would require considerable talent in execution.

At the end of April, Hooker attempted just this. With Longstreet absent, the Federals had 133,000 against 60,000. Dividing his force, with General Sedgwick and 40,000 men crossing the river just below Fredericksburg to distract Lee, Hooker, carrying more than a week's rations for the men, took most of the remainder upstream to ford the river above Lee's line of fortifications. With a movement of his cavalry confusing and distracting Lee, Hooker had the essential element of success, a turning movement which surprised the enemy. But once he reached Lee's flank, he halted rather than push on to try for the enemy's rear (see diagram of Chancellorsville campaign 1). When he announced to his troops that the "enemy must either ingloriously fly or come out from behind his intrenchments and give us battle on our own ground," he proved himself a disciple of McClellan as well as Meigs by understanding that the turning movement could induce an enemy to take the tactical offensive. But he understood the situation insufficiently because it called for him to continue his march into Lee's rear, aided by Sedgwick's simultaneous advance.

With his army between a halted Hooker on his flank and Sedgwick poised on the south side of the river, Lee resolved to exploit his interior lines rather than retreat. Concentrating first against Hooker, he avoided meeting him on his own ground with a frontal assault by turning Hooker's own turning force when he sent Jackson with 25,000 men around Hooker and onto his right flank. This attack, near Chancellorsville, forced the Union forces to change direction, which they did with the usual facility of Civil War armies. So, in the end, the Confederates faced a well-entrenched foe with his back to the river. Lee then could concentrate against Sedgwick, who had just driven back the small force which had contained him by the Rappahannock River (see diagram of Chancellorsville campaign 2).

Having pushed Sedgwick back across the river, Lee turned again against Hooker, who occupied a classic defensive position: thoroughly fortified and with his back to the river which gave him an ample water supply and protected his flanks. Nevertheless Lee resolved to attack him, his logistically founded reluctance to retreat, his pugnacity, and his unwillingness to admit defeat getting the better of his realization of the supremacy of the entrenched defense. But, before Lee could make his mistake, Hooker, apparently morally exhausted by the stress, made his own by retreating across the river. Had the inexperienced Hooker a superior to order him to stay and fight, he would doubtless have done so with proficiency and success.

Thus ended the Battle of Chancellorsville, a notable campaign compressed into a very constricted area. Again the armies showed how their superior articulation enabled them to carry out difficult offensive maneuvers while the same capability precluded the attacker's gaining an important advantage. With Union casualties over 17,000, 13 percent of their force, and Confederate at 12,764, or 21 percent, the attrition had given Hooker a very modest tactical victory. Nevertheless strategically he failed to gain territory much less do serious harm to the enemy army and, by retreating, had suffered a symbolic defeat. Though the military attrition favored the Union, the political attrition, the further discouragement of the northern public about the prospects of an early victory, favored the South.

The costly struggle took the life of the incomparable Jackson, accidentally shot by his own men. Rather than try to find a successor, Lee divided his army into three, instead of two, corps, appointing two talented men, Richard S. Ewell and A. P. Hill, to command units smaller than the brilliant Jackson's old corps.

The campaign had an important impact on Lee's thinking. He had fought at a disadvantage in order to defend the valuable supply area between the Rappahannock and Richmond. Concern for this part of his logistic base and determination to avoid fighting again in a similar position dominated his strategic thinking in the next months. Unless he could defend in a position like the Battle of Fredericksburg, he wanted to be able to retreat without sacrificing part of his base area.

Close to a railroad and navigable rivers, Hooker had few supply problems in the small Virginia theater. In the West, as long as the rivers had supplied the Union armies, they had made dramatic advances. But in the fall Rosecrans's disrupted railroads and long delay to accumulate supplies and the quick defeat of Grant's advance showed the primacy of the Confederate raiding logistic strategy. This, the difficulty of living on a country of insufficient agricultural output, and the vulnerable railroads, had thwarted every Yankee invasion. An autumn western campaign which had only gained 20 miles along the route from Nashville to Chattanooga did not promise a quick end to the war.

Instead of relying on the exposed railways, Grant used secure water transport to support his campaign to capture Vicksburg and open the Mississippi on secure river transport. But this meant that he had exchanged a serious logistic problem for an equally intractable one in strategy. His railroad-based advance to Jackson and then west toward Vicksburg would have automatically turned Vicksburg's defenses, bringing him into the city's rear and giving him the same advantage he had enjoyed at Fort Donelson. Now his river line of operations would lead him directly against the city's defenses, whose strength Sherman's experience at Chickasaw Bluffs had recently confirmed. Grant would spend the remainder of the winter trying to find a way to turn the Vicksburg defenses on the north through terrain filled with bayous, swamps, snakes, and fortified rebels.

Just as Hooker set out on his Chancellorsville campaign, Grant at last began an effective move against Vicksburg, less complicated than Hooker's but also embodying the classic elements of turning movement and interior lines. Grant's advance marked the culmination of his futile efforts to turn Vicksburg from the north while still basing himself on the river. These had included two unsuccessful attempts to float an army in bayous with overhanging trees full of snakes and Confederate batteries blocking the way, and two efforts to find or dig a water route around Vicksburg.

Finally, when the navy managed to run gunboats and supply

vessels past the Vicksburg batteries, Grant saw that he could turn the city by the roundabout southern route. He marched two of his corps past the city on the Mississippi's west bank and met ships and supplies below Vicksburg. The ships then ferried his troops across the river while distractions kept Pemberton from understanding the full significance of what was going on. To distract Pemberton he had left Sherman's corps near Vicksburg to make a "simulated attack," for which Sherman had ordered that "every man look as numerous as possible." Initially this failed, the Confederate commander commenting on Sherman's men in boats that the "display made in moving them showed a desire to attract our attention." More effective in gaining Pemberton's attention was Colonel Benjamin H. Grierson's cavalry raid, traversing 600 miles from Tennessee through Mississippi to meet Federal forces in Louisiana. Grierson's erratic movements with only 1,700 men seriously confused Pemberton.

So Grant at last had the initiative which had eluded him because of the ineffectiveness of his earlier offensive efforts, beginning with those in December. Moreover, he had attained strategic surprise when he brought two army corps across the Mississippi, 30 miles below Vicksburg, landing them below the rebel force guarding that area. With two corps against two brigades, he defeated and drove the rebels northward toward Vicksburg. Thus, by May 1, 1863, the day after Hooker had crossed the Rappahannock, Grant had established himself east of the river and awaited the arrival of his third corps, Sherman's, before marching northward into Vicksburg's rear. Grant had abandoned a plan to turn south and unite with General Banks, coming north from New Orleans, because Banks had diverted his attention from the river and marched away on a different expedition.

Meanwhile, following Johnston's reiterated instructions to concentrate all of his troops to drive back Grant, Pemberton directed the evacuation of Port Hudson and other points so as to unite all his forces for the "defense of Vicksburg and Jackson." Showing that he had grasped Johnston's instructions as well as the situation, he wrote Mississippi's governor: "I must concentrate my whole army to beat Grant's."

Although he planned to live on the country, Grant needed

additional ammunition which had to come by wagon along a circuitous and difficult route west of the Mississippi. He also had to run past Vicksburg's batteries 400,000 rations of hard bread, coffee, sugar, and salt. The delay of these and for Sherman's arrival on May 7 gave Pemberton time to concentrate his scattered forces. But happily for Grant, Pemberton changed his mind, ordered the men back to Port Hudson, and disposed his troops for defending Vicksburg instead of holding back Grant. Apparently partly prompted by a telegram from Davis, the Confederate commander fell back on the defense of fortified points, easy for one who understood these and had never commanded a field army in such a campaign. But this action meant the sure loss of Vicksburg. Pemberton's decision would have given Grant a clear path into Vicksburg's rear had Davis not sent reinforcements from Beauregard and Bragg to Jackson and ordered Johnston there to command them.

Grant, now supplied and finding in the country an abundance of corn, hogs, cattle, sheep, and poultry, moved forward with 44,000 men in three corps against Pemberton's 32,000 near Vicksburg and Johnston's 6,000 at Jackson. Marching between them, he left one corps to delay Pemberton and used his interior lines to concentrate two against Johnston. When Johnston wisely retreated northward, Grant then turned toward Vicksburg, delaying long enough to cripple any move into his rear by tearing up the railroad in all directions from Jackson. Meanwhile Pemberton had remained immobile, vacillating between his desire to remain close to Vicksburg and Johnston's orders to move onto Grant's rear.

Grant now advanced on his remaining adversary to drive him back and to reestablish his army's communications with the Mississippi north of Vicksburg. Pemberton, defending at Champion's Hill until Grant had virtually turned his flank, fell back. Deciding to disobey Johnston's emphatic order to evacuate Vicksburg, an order calculated to avoid "losing both troops and place," he instead marched his army into the city. Grant followed, reestablished his water communications, and took a position to block Pemberton's escape (see diagram of Vicksburg campaign; readers may wish to compare this with diagrams of Napoleon dividing Colli and Beaulieu, and the Ulm campaign). Grant had waged a brilliant campaign, one which

Halleck compared with Napoleon's of Ulm, but Grant always modestly shared the credit with his "best friend," John C. Pemberton. In an unfamiliar situation, Pemberton had wilted in the heat of his great responsibility and found refuge in the familiar—fortifications—and turned defeat into catastrophe by losing the army as well as the city.

Though Davis built up Johnston's army and Halleck reinforced Grant, the remainder of the campaign consisted in waiting for Vicksburg's supplies to give out, which they did on July 4, 1863. On the tactical offensive, like all such relieving armies, Johnston never led his 31,000 men in a futile battle against Sherman, with 50,000 of Grant's men barring the way to Vicksburg. Although it was a sensible decision and almost routine practice in sieges, Johnston's failure to make more than a token attempt to extricate the trapped Pemberton army caused a serious rift with President Davis, whom, in a season of other reverses, the loss of Vicksburg had "plunged into the depths of gloom." Truly a great defeat, nearly 30,000 men surrendered at Vicksburg, indicating the scale of the attrition which resulted from Grant's Napoleonic strategy. In symbolic terms, because of the great prestige of the Mississippi, the Union triumph at Vicksburg had far more weight than a victory merely signalized by a retreat.

Yet winning had little actual strategic importance because the Confederates had long had so little commerce across the river that they lost virtually nothing. The Union did, with the fall of Port Hudson, obtain the almost unhindered navigation of the Mississippi and acquire some additional areas of occupation in Mississippi, but this loss to the Confederacy was also a liability to the Union in that it required more troops for garrisoning.

This defeat represented the end of the Department of the West, an effort to supply unified command and facilitate strategic maneuver in the West. Differing views of the value of the Mississippi contributed to the fissure between Davis and Johnston, though had nothing to do with the loss of Vicksburg. The soldiers, Beauregard, Johnston, and Lee, attached comparatively little importance to keeping a foothold on the Mississippi. They knew that few supplies and virtually no troops crossed the river or, in view of the absence of a trunk-line railroad crossing the river between east and west, were likely to do so. The fall of Vicksburg could cause the South no loss of supplies or of opportunities for strategic maneuver. Further, control of the Mississippi led the Union to no other line of operations beyond a fourth railroad into Mississippi and the distinct advantage of having river lines to support any advance into Arkansas. Of course, it would have pleased the Confederate generals for the spacious state of Arkansas to swallow up more Union soldiers.

In Tennessee, however, the Confederacy stood a chance to lose the remainder of productive Middle Tennessee and the railroad through East Tennessee that connected Atlanta and the Gulf states with Virginia. Further, in spite of difficult country, that railroad would support a Union line of operations into Georgia.

Davis understood this, and he also realized the immense political significance of the control of the Mississippi. The Confederate Congress had understood well enough to have assured the Union its free navigation in peace. The river's symbolic importance guaranteed that, just as the northern public would see control of the Mississippi as a harbinger of victory, its loss could and did work so much discouragement among Southerners as to render the word attrition inadequate to describe the resulting drastic decline in their confidence in a reasonably early victory.

Thus Davis correctly saw the loss of Vicksburg as far more serious than did his generals, preoccupied as they were with their immediate strategic and logistical concerns. Moreover, Davis had much higher expectations of success than did Johnston. Convinced of the potential of Johnston's command, he doubtless based much of his belief in the practicality of using the railroad to operate in Napoleon's manner on the Shiloh and Kentucky campaigns' concentrations of the year before. In contrast Johnston, in spite of his own success in April in quickly moving men from Mississippi and Mobile toward Tennessee, still remained skeptical of his department's possibilities for maneuver. Though he had some confidence in his cavalry concentration, which Grant's use of the Mississippi nullified, Johnston feared simultaneous advances. He asked Davis which was more important, Tennessee or the Mississippi; and even considered moving Bragg's army to north Mississippi. Unlike Davis, Johnston did apprehend defeat.

Faced with an unexpected disaster of unprecedented proportions, Davis responded by blaming the commanding officer. This is hardly a surprising reaction, the most drastic response of this kind on record probably being the revolutionary French government's execution of 67 unsuccessful generals in one year, 1794. Davis did not even relieve Johnston of command, though he engaged in constant recriminations and considered a court of inquiry. And the president never regained his earlier confidence in the general, remaining prepared for him to fail in his next assignment.

He was wrong, however, in thinking that Johnston's vain effort to relieve Vicksburg involved a command failure. Traditionally a most difficult task involving both the strategic and tactical offensive, the raising of a siege in this instance involved the added complications of the invulnerability of Grant's communications and the absence of any line of supply for Johnston in an already campaigned-over country with a wrecked railroad.

Pemberton failed in command: in losing his nerve, by not acting swiftly against Grant, and then dooming his army by retreating into Vicksburg. In contrast, had Beauregard commanded, his earlier and later actions guaranteed an energetic performance in concentrating against Grant to keep him south of the Jackson–Vicksburg railroad if not to bottle him up on the river bank. In any case, Beauregard would not have lost his army. Clearly neither Longstreet nor Hardee would have responded differently from Beauregard. Perhaps the defeat itself and certainly the loss of the army resulted from Davis and Randolph's hastily and too casually giving to the untried Pemberton what proved a crucial appointment. His capable management of his fortifications and the retreat of Grant and Sherman in December 1862 provided false indications of Pemberton's capacity for field command and doubtless gave Davis confidence in the selection, making him complacent about Pemberton's competence until his catastrophic failure.

While Grant crossed the Mississippi and Hooker the Rappahannock, Rosecrans naturally received encouragement to advance again. He resisted this, pointing out that, if he could drive Bragg out of Middle Tennessee, to follow him he would have to advance through a denuded country "over obstructed roads and destroyed railroads, which we would be obliged to repair." While his army coped with these logistical obstacles, Rosecrans pointed out that Bragg could send the bulk of his army to Vicksburg. Unknown to him, Grant, Bragg, and Johnston shared this judgment. Thus, to the intense irritation of Lincoln and Halleck, he waited and further perfected the elaborate logistical preparations for his next advance.

Unlike Grant, Rosecrans had no way to revert to a river supply line, the Cumberland being behind him and the Tennessee ahead and in enemy hands. He tried to protect himself from guerrillas by garrisoning his communications and, in order better to defend against rebel raiders, requested more cavalry and even mounted infantry on mules. He worked to increase the number of his wagons and mules so that he could carry more provisions with him, and so be able to maneuver far from the railroad. This was a slow process, and his importunity wore out the welcome in Washington which his victory on Stones River had given him.

Rosecrans, who had set out to crush the enemy in battle in his Tullahoma campaign, had lost faith in combat strategy. And his generals echoed this when he asked for their opinions. Although one general noted the political significance of the Battle of Stones River, that it had saved the "Northwest from falling under the domination of the peace or coward's party," the generals agreed on its military futility. Another such battle, wrote one, would "once more prove the valor of the army" but gain no "decided advantage." Such victories were "unproductive of the grand results which make success valuable and compensate for the loss of life necessary to attain it; in short, those results which justify the fighting of battles." Another reflected the cynicism felt by the professionals towards the civilian focus on war as bloody battles when he wrote: "We certainly cannot fight the enemy for the mere purpose of whipping him. . . . To whip him would gratify our pride and delight the country, but what have we gained . . . ? The time has passed when the fate of armies must be staked because the newspapers have no excitement and do not sell well. I think our people have now comprehended that a battle is a very grave thing."

165

Instead of advocating whipping the enemy, Rosecrans's generals gave emphatic support to the turning movement as "the true line of attack." One explained it thus: The general must first act "to engage the attention of the enemy, and to march with the mass of our force upon his communications near Tullahoma. This movement, by compelling the enemy to fight us on our own battle-field, and by throwing him off his line of retreat, promises the destruction of his army, if successful." This was precisely Rosecrans's plan and, to execute it, he had twice as many ration wagons as Union armies could usually muster.

So, on June 26, 1863, just as the siege of Vicksburg was ending, Rosecrans moved with 65,000 men against Bragg's army, depleted to 44,000 by reinforcements sent to Mississippi. As a distraction, sending his cavalry and one corps westward as it to turn that flank, Rosecrans took the initiative and gained surprise when he used three infantry corps to turn Bragg's eastern flank; though he failed to reach Bragg's rear, he forced him back to Tullahoma. Not even pausing, Rosecrans continued around Bragg's new eastern flank and again compelled him to retreat, this time all the way back to Chattanooga. In spite of rain and mud and in just nine days with only 600 casualties, Rosecrans had driven the enemy back completely out of fertile and productive Middle Tennessee, a major triumph for a logistic strategy but mitigated by the necessity of coping with more guerrillas. A notable strategic victory, the Tullahoma campaign had no tactical dimension and, in the absence of a battle to signalize the retreat, only a modest effect on public opinion. Realizing his victory's lack of éclat when he had received no praise from Washington, Rosecrans reflected the chasm between soldiers and civilians when he sarcastically wrote Secretary Stanton that he hoped that the "War Department may not overlook so great an event because it is not written in letters of blood" (see diagram of the Tullahoma campaign).

As Grant settled down to besiege Vicksburg and Rosecrans perfected the preparations for his Tullahoma campaign, Lee reached a decision about his logistical and strategic problems. Though he would gladly have faced a second Burnside advance, Lee desperately wished to avoid coping with another sophisticated and probably more expertly executed effort by Hooker, and he definitely expected another soon from a general whose nickname was "Fighting Joe." So, in order to avoid fighting with his back to a valued supply area, to forestall Hooker's expected advance, and to live for a time at the enemy's expense, Lee resolved on another raid north of the Potomac. He could easily pass around Hooker's western flank by entering the Shenandoah Valley base area and finding along this route north ample forage for his animals and food for his men.

Since Lee had successfully rebuffed Seddon's request for reinforcements for Vicksburg in May, his raid did not relate to relieving the siege of Vicksburg. So, in spite of what he had earlier written about offensives as the way to relieve threats against other armies, he had his attention focused entirely on his own problems. In early June 1863 he began his march past his adversary's flank, not to reach his rear but to carry out a raid into the prosperous farming area of southeastern Pennsylvania.

Typically, raiders could evade pursuers because they could move as fast or faster and need not fear being cut off because they had many alternate routes of retreat. Illustrative is Grierson's raid in which he had entered Mississippi from Tennessee and left it by riding into Louisiana. But on his Pennsylvania raid Lee had to return the way he had come because the seaboard to the east and mountainous terrain to the west enclosed the theater of operations. Consequently, Union forces in superior numbers stood a very good chance of blocking his retreat and forcing him either to fight on the tactical offensive or disperse his army to escape through the gaps in the Union screen. Either alternative was likely to cost him heavily if he did escape. Though Lee probably trusted to his superior adroitness in maneuver to surmount this obstacle, he also doubtless counted on the political inability of the Lincoln administration to let him roam freely in Pennsylvania while the Federal army deployed to intercept his retreat instead of opposing his advance.

When Hooker followed Lee, he did as expected and kept to the east and in touch with the railroads running west from Baltimore and Philadelphia, thus confirming Lee's supposition that the enemy would not try to trap him. But a latent concern may have inspired Lee to suggest to Davis that General Beauregard come from Charleston with a few men to take a position in northern Virginia where he could appear to threaten Washington. Though correct in this political judgment, Lee does not seem to have considered all the political ramifications of his raid.

He understood that the Confederacy's task was to "baffle" Union efforts to subdue the South. But to make a raid, certain to be seen by people in both North and South as an invasion with the aim of conquering territory, necessarily involved eventual withdrawal if only because the army would exhaust the supplies in the area it controlled. But Lee must have overlooked that withdrawal equaled retreat, the symbol of defeat, and so would depress southern spirits and elevate northern morale and give support to those Northerners who desired to prosecute the war to victory. As a consequence, though the demonstration that the Union was vulnerable to such a raid would have favorable symbolism for the South, the chances seem to have favored more political attrition in the South than the North. This would certainly be the effect if Lee fought, as the raid made possible and some officers expected, a defensive battle in a strong position like Fredericksburg. Even if he were victorious, as was almost certain, his inevitable withdrawal would, like that after Antietam, make it seem a defeat and so assure a negative balance in the political scales.

So Lee's men marched, the units fairly well dispersed to make the most of the foraging opportunities, while the Union army followed, more compactly deployed. On June 28 it also received a new commander when Hooker resigned. Halleck, very glad of Hooker's departure, had confidence in his successor, George G. Meade. A West Pointer, former engineer, and Mexican War veteran, Meade, like Hooker, had grown up in the Army of the Potomac, rising from brigade to corps command. Irritable, secure in the responsibilities of command, and moderately aggressive, he had a realistic and careful military attitude. Moreover, his impregnable imperturbability, together with an engineer's eye and a discerning grasp of any tactical or strategic situation which rivaled Lee's, made him a first-rate general. He did not command the affection of the men as had Hooker, but he had their and the officers' confidence. The Army of the Potomac at last had found its general.

While moving northwest toward Lee, Meade also laid out a line of defense adjacent to a railroad to which he could fall back. Meanwhile, Lee, with most of his cavalry absent and thinking that he had found Meade's army dangerously dispersed, concentrated and attacked the Army of the Potomac. But Meade's army closed on the battleground at Gettysburg, Pennsylvania, as quickly as the Confederates (see diagram of the beginning of the Gettysburg campaign).

A much-discussed three-day battle followed, one which had the outcome expected when Lee's well-commanded, veteran army assailed Meade's army, similar in strength, quality, and leadership. The troops which rushed to the vicinity of Gettysburg on the first day of the battle fought and established the fishhook-shaped conformation of the battle line. When Lee attempted to turn Meade's left on the second day, his attack met formed Union troops who thwarted him with a capable and determined resistance. The battle ended on the third day after the Confederates made Pickett's charge, a doomed frontal attack that failed so emphatically that the Union chief of artillery believed he could have stopped it without the infantry.

Just as at Antietam, Lee delayed a day before withdrawing in order to show his army and others that the enemy's tactical effort had not compelled retreat. Lee had won the Battle of Antietam because he had accomplished his objective of repelling McClellan's attack. But Meade had won at Gettysburg for the same reason, defeating Lee's attempt to drive him back.

Meade followed Lee and briefly caught him with his back to the Potomac, but he did not attack his well-entrenched foe before Lee slipped away to Virginia. Meade's failure to take a chance on what he deemed a hopeless attack, one tactically comparable to any fight Johnston might have made to relieve Vicksburg, caused Lincoln particular anguish; at the beginning of the campaign he had devoutly wished that he could have ignored political consequences and had Meade try to trap Lee and force him to fight his way out of Pennsylvania. Lincoln's disappointment made him overlook the degree of success which his strategy of hurting Lee when he made a mistake had gained through the attrition in the battle.

The battle hastened Lee's withdrawal by intensifying the logistical factors which would have forced his departure in any event. Lee had found his foragers already bothered by Pennsylvania militia, not useful in battle but annoying and even dangerous to men searching for food and fodder. The Confederate army's need to keep concentrated in Meade's presence made it, as President Davis pointed out, impossible "under such circumstances for General Lee to supply his army for any length of time." With access to a railroad to Baltimore, Meade had no such constraint.

This logistical situation also answers the question of what would have happened had Lee won the battle. The same logistic factors still would have forced him to retreat. He might have followed Meade to his next position but could hardly have tarried. That he might have "destroyed" such a combat-seasoned and well-commanded force as the Army of the Potomac runs counter to what happened in the Civil War and in over two centuries of European campaigning with similarly armed troops. Some have speculated that, had he won, Lee could have captured Philadelphia or Baltimore. But they fail to explain how, had he not departed the city as soon as he arrived, Lee could have returned south through the entrenched lines of a besieging Union army. General Beauregard's relieving army would have had even less chance to raise that siege than Johnston's did at Vicksburg.

Lee, who offered President Davis his resignation, did, however, evaluate the campaign as a "general success." When Davis agreed, he, like Lee, considered only the strategic objectives, living at the enemy's expense and not having to defend along the Rappahannock, from which the campaign had kept him absent for nearly two months. But most people could not imagine that such a spectacular operation had to do only with the parochial concerns of Lee's army. The tactical outcome differed markedly from the strategic, Lee's casualties numbering over a third of his army and Meade's more than a quarter of his. The men Lee lost, perhaps as many as 27,000, reduced later by recovered wounded and returned missing, amounted to more than 10 percent of all the Confederate armies, Meade's about 5 percent of all the Union's forces. Realizing that the tactical results had produced a defeat of attrition, President Davis summarized the lost tactical opportunity for a victory of attrition when he later wrote that, "had General Lee been able to compel the enemy to attack him in position, I think we should have had complete victory."

After the war Longstreet stressed this point, and, immediately after the battle, Brigadier General Wade Hampton, a highly regarded cavalry commander badly wounded in the campaign, expressed the view of the officers who had understood that the battle strategy was to seek a repeat of Fredericksburg. Writing his cousin J. E. Johnston, Hampton explained: I "thought the advantage we would have in Penn was that we should not be compelled to look for strategic points," as when defending the Rappahannock line to protect the foraging area southward, "but only critical ones, so that we might choose our own points at which to fight. But we let Meade choose his position & we attacked."

Had Lee, following the original strategy, waited in a strong position, his raid would have put political, if not military, pressure on Meade to attack. This strategy would have pitted political against logistic necessities, as Meade resisted pressure to drive back the insolent rebels and Lee tried to supply his concentrated, stationary army. But Lee obviated this contest by succumbing to the temptation to exploit enemy weakness to assail what he thought was a dispersed adversary.

As after Antietam, the battle aggravated the negative symbolism of the inevitable withdrawal. But Davis saw the raid itself as the chief cause of political attrition when he noted that it "impaired the confidence of the southern people so far as to give malcontents a power to represent the government as neglecting for Virginia the safety of the more southern states." Beauregard spoke for the malcontents when, even before the Battle of Gettysburg, he asked "of what earthly use is this 'raid' of Lee's army into Maryland, in violation of all of the principles of war? Is it going to end the struggle, take Washington, or save the Mississippi Valley?"

In the spring campaigns of 1863 Union generals had done well, those on the offensive showing their facility with the turning movement and General Meade displaying his steadiness and competence in the Gettysburg campaign. The North had attained tactical victories of attrition as well as those of symbolic and political value at Vicksburg and at Gettysburg. Though with more morale than strategic substance, Federal control of

171

the Mississippi did some strategic harm to the Confederacy and provided some benefit to the Union. The Tullahoma campaign, though lacking military attrition and the symbolic éclat of a victorious battle, nevertheless had provided the major strategic gain of cutting the direct rail link between Richmond and Chattanooga and completing the conquest of Middle Tennessee.

In both Tennessee and Mississippi success had rewarded the Union strategy of concentration in the West. The western victories owed more to sound strategy and outstanding execution than to a preponderance of force. Grant, after all, with over half of his forces garrisoning West Tennessee and guarding railways, barely outnumbered Pemberton. All three spring offensive operations had the same essential elements of strategic success, a turning movement facilitated by surprise attained by distracting the enemy. When Grant faced a divided enemy, he made the most of the situation by marching between them to gain and use interior lines.

Hooker's failures in execution gave Lee an opportunity to use his own interior lines and carry out a surprise turning movement, depriving Hooker of his victory. Hooker and Pemberton seemed to share the inability to bear up under the responsibility of command. The other defeated general, Bragg, had done well in extricating his army from two threatening enemy moves.

But the southern losses in Tennessee stimulated the malcontents Davis had criticized, the Confederacy's Western Concentration bloc, which had reached full flowering. With Longstreet, an acquaintance of Senator Wigfall as well as a member, promoting to both Lee and Seddon the Beauregard plan for concentration in Tennessee, the bloc's ideas would soon have their fruition.

CHAPTER 13

THE CHICKAMAUGA AND CHATTANOOGA CAMPAIGNS

Following the Confederate losses in the West and Lee's withdrawal from Pennsylvania, the Western Concentration bloc increased its agitation and sought a nationwide concentration for an offensive against Rosecrans's army, still perceiving it as the point of Union strategic weakness. Losing Middle Tennessee to Rosecrans's Tullahoma campaign in June gave added urgency to the appeal which Beauregard had sent in May to Wigfall, Johnston, Bragg, and doubtless others. Beauregard proposed using 30,000 men to reinforce Bragg's army to attack Rosecrans suddenly, with the result that he "would be either totally destroyed or the remnant of his forces would be speedily driven beyond the Ohio." Following a march westward to block the Mississippi, Grant, turned by this maneuver, would be "compelled to fight his way through a victorious army equal to his own in strength, on its own selected battle-field."

Such extravagant language and fantastic forecasts characterized much of Beauregard's writing and certainly undermined his credibility—but only with those who did not know him. In person he had for many a compelling magnetism and demonstrated a clear grasp of any strategic situation. His confidence and optimism communicated themselves to those around him. Yet, in action, he was competent, circumspect, and orthodox, completely belying the air of unreality in his writings. But his eccentricity in the presentation of his plans militated against his selection for a more responsible command; this has made many historians and others skeptical of his ability as a general in spite of its demonstration on several occasions.

In the summer of 1863 the Western Concentration bloc displayed the extent of its influence as it exerted itself to have the Davis administration adopt its proposal. The president received a plan like Beauregard's from his friend Bishop/General Polk, saying it represented the ideas of "the most intelligent circles" at Bragg's headquarters. With Bragg also lobbying for it, as well as Tennessee legislators, Wigfall, and probably others, the bloc deluged the administration with its campaign for an offensive against Rosecrans. Halleck had unintentionally given the plan's proponents an opportunity through his failure to give Grant a new objective after the fall of Vicksburg. Instead, the general in chief had taken some of Grant's men for a project to capture much of Arkansas and so free troops for use east of the river. Although this campaign led to the fall of Little Rock in September, Halleck had left Grant quiescent and Johnston free to reinforce Bragg.

In early August of 1863 President Davis advocated a scaled-down version of Beauregard's concentration when he proposed to detach men from Johnston to Bragg and send him most of the troops in East Tennessee to enable him to take the offensive against Rosecrans. But Bragg demurred, believing the concentration inadequate unless the Union army moved closer. Disappointed, Davis nevertheless showed he knew the command lesson Halleck had taught Lincoln, when he admitted: "However desirable a movement may be, it is never safe to do more than suggest it to a commanding general, and it would be unwise to order its execution by one who foretold failure."

Meanwhile, Rosecrans, who had kept his distance from Bragg's army, had readied himself for a new advance by repairing the Nashville & Chattanooga railway and accumulating supplies. Resisting pressure from Washington to move sooner, he waited until August 16, when the corn had ripened and could provide for his men and animals. Using a bombardment of Chattanooga and confusing movements up river to distract Bragg, he crossed his main force below the city. Here he faced eastward and began marching over a series of ridges toward Bragg's rear and the rail connection with Atlanta.

On August 21 Bragg ordered General Simon B. Buckner with the infantry of his East Tennessee department to join him, abandoning Knoxville to an army under Burnside, which had just moved into East Tennessee from Kentucky. On the same day Bragg telegraphed to Richmond the signs of Rosecrans's advance and appealed to Johnston for reinforcements. With the War Department supporting Bragg's request, Johnston began dispatching over half of his infantry, 9,000 men, the next day.

Also during the last week in August, Lee came to Richmond for almost two weeks of conferences with Davis. These talks familiarized Lee with the whole Confederate situation and, though he did not entirely abandon the idea that he could help Bragg more by turning Meade back, he did not strongly resist the president's idea to send Longstreet and two divisions to reinforce Bragg. He did, however, decline the president's request that he go to Tennessee and take personal command of the multi-departmental concentration in its counterattack on Rosecrans. Since Burnside had taken Knoxville and blocked the direct rail link between Richmond and Chattanooga, Longstreet's men had to take a long detour through the Carolinas and Georgia. Nevertheless, even without interior lines, the initiative and strategic surprise made the concentration effective. Longstreet and five brigades arrived in time to play a key role in the battle which drove Rosecrans back (see the diagram of the Chickamauga concentration; readers may wish to compare this with Shiloh concentration and Defense of Mantua siege 1–3).

In crossing the mountains to cut Bragg's railroad, Rosecrans had spread his army over a 40-mile front by using three roads. This made his army vulnerable, but his belief that Bragg's evacuation of Chattanooga indicated his retreat toward Atlanta made him complacent. While Bragg had spent a week in ineffectual efforts to exploit his antagonist's dispersal and an unsuccessful effort to overlap his north flank, Rosecrans concentrated his army. So Bragg fought an essentially frontal battle at Chickamauga against his adversary's proficient and determined defense. But, when a mistake in orders withdrew a division from the right of Rosecrans's line and Longstreet burst through the resulting gap, Rosecrans lost his defensive battle and retreated to Chattanooga. Here Bragg followed him, taking up a position on the heights above the city and controlling its rail and water communications. The disorganization of the retreating Union army was so great that Bragg's depleted army might have pursued and inflicted severe casualties. Still, in his advantageous position, Bragg then proceeded to try to starve out Rosecrans.

The Battle of Chickamauga had more strategic significance than most Civil War battles because it was a major strategic victory achieved by again using the telegraph and the railroad to carry out a Napoleonic concentration over an immense space. It drove back Rosecrans, essentially nullifying the gain he had made in his crossing of the Tennessee and preventing him from taking a position where he could threaten northern Georgia. Whereas the battle yielded the South a substantial symbolic victory, it also gave the Federals a tactical victory in terms of the attrition, a loss of 16,170 compared to the Confederate's 18,454, the frontal tactical offensive having cost the victor more than the vanquished. Though the losses were fairly close as a percentage of the armies engaged, the South suffered double the percentage loss of total forces in the field.

After a season of victories, the defeat and retreat of the slow but heretofore victorious Rosecrans came as quite a shock to Lincoln, even though he had learned of the Virginia reinforcements bound for Bragg by September 14, almost a week before the battle. This intelligence had required no immediate action, because Halleck had already ordered Grant to send substantial reinforcements to Rosecrans.

But the Virginia reinforcement of Bragg presented an opportunity for a Union concentration in time, by Meade advancing upon the weakened Lee. Though willing to fight Lee, Meade, explaining that he still lacked a sufficient superiority to break out of the stalemate, wrote "In fine, I can get a battle out of Lee under very disadvantageous circumstances, which may render his inferior force my superior, and which is not likely to result in any very decided advantage, even in case I should be victorious." Much discouraged by this declaration of the weakness of the offensive and the implied bankruptcy of the strategy of simultaneous advances, Lincoln noted that for "a battle, then, General Meade has three men to General Lee's two. Yet, it having been determined that choosing ground, and standing in the defensive, gives so great advantage that the three can not safely attack the two, the three are left simply standing on the defensive also." Concluding, he pointed out that, "having practically come to the mere defensive, it seems no economy to employ twice as many men for that object as are needed."

When news of Chickamauga came in and the Union command realized the rebel success in achieving a consequential strategic victory, Lincoln, Halleck, and Stanton met with the principal cabinet members, the secretaries of state and treasury. Stanton proposed to aid Rosecrans by sending "30,000 men from the Army of the Potomac. There is no reason to expect that General Meade will attack Lee, although greatly superior in force; and his great numbers where they are, are useless. In five days 30,000 could be put with Rosecrans." Skeptical, Lincoln commented: "I will bet that if the order is given tonight, the troops could not be got to Washington in five days." But Stanton replied: "On such a subject I don't feel inclined to bet; but the matter has been carefully investigated, and it is certain that 30,000 bales of cotton could be sent in that time by taking possession of the railroads and excluding all other business, and I do not see why 30,000 men cannot be sent as well. But if 30,000 cannot be sent, let 20,000 go."

Showing their disillusionment with concentration in time, Lincoln and Halleck yielded to Stanton's insistence after only a brief argument in favor of an offensive by Meade. The Union railways almost met Stanton's ambitious schedule, delivering the first of the 20,000 men, commanded by Joe Hooker, over a 1,200-mile route in 7 days, and the last 4½ days later. This amounted to only two thirds as much time as southern railroads had needed to deliver Longstreet's smaller force over 200 fewer miles. Thus the Union had interior lines, but the Confederates had taken the initiative, attained strategic surprise, and driven Rosecrans back.

Learning of the dispatch of Hooker and anxious that no more Federal reinforcements go west, Lee advanced and succeeded in turning the west flank of the now also-weakened Meade. But the astute Union commander kept out of danger by falling back until he had gotten as near Washington as Manassas. Finding the Army of the Potomac entrenched ahead of him and the country denuded of supplies, Lee fell back to his old position, Meade following and repairing the railroad.

Meade's next move, a carefully planned turning movement, showed how a lack of surprise can give the initiative to the defender. Counting on rapidity of movement rather than a distraction in front or on the western flank, Meade moved around Lee's eastern side and, after delays, deployed at right angles to his line. But, instead of facing the hostile flank, Meade found that the alert Lee had taken the initiative and entrenched his men on a seven-mile front, facing their adversary. After Meade wisely declined to make an assault, Lee planned to emulate his Chancellorsville maneuver and turn Meade's abortive turning movement. But he too suffered surprise when, the initiative passing to Meade, Lee moved into position to attack, only to find the Union lines vacant and his foe en route back to his old position. So ended, in early December of 1863, the year's campaigning in Virginia.

Meade had given up men to help Rosecrans, but more men could not solve his problem; and Rosecrans, not knowing what would, seemed paralyzed by defeat and indecision, "confused and stunned," as Lincoln aptly expressed it, "like a duck hit on the head." Just as the Virginia reinforcements arrived, Lincoln combined Grant's Department of the Tennessee, Rosecrans's of the Cumberland, and Burnside's of the Ohio into the Military Division of the Mississippi under Grant. The gifted and imaginative Sherman succeeded Grant and the stalwart and thorough General George H. Thomas replaced Rosecrans, who took command in Missouri, leaving the capable John M. Schofield available to come to Tennessee. The ample fund of excellent western generals with military reputations adequate to fend off political aspirants for the commands enabled Lincoln to make this wise reorganization. It created an organization similar to that of 1862 under Halleck and corresponded to the now-defunct Confederate Department of the West.

When Grant came to Chattanooga to take personal command, he found a besieged army on half rations with many horses dead and the remainder emaciated. More men could not survive in Chattanooga. Supplies came by wagons over a roundabout route, and even these were not safe, since Bragg, relying on his favorite strategy, sent his cavalry to raid them. Though they burned 300 wagons and captured 1,800 mules, the raiders failed to strike the crippling blow of seizing the depot at Murfreesboro. Grant then had Thomas make a surprise attack to open a short route along the Tennessee River, which then brought in enough supplies for the army. In spite of the failure of his raid to have a decisive effect and the enemy's success improvising an adequate supply route, Bragg felt confident enough to send Longstreet 100 miles northwest to try to recover Knoxville from Burnside. But the inept Burnside stymied the accomplished Longstreet by staying within his fortifications.

When Sherman finally arrived from Mississippi on November 15, 1863, Grant was ready to bring him and Hooker into Chattanooga and to try to drive Bragg back. Positioning Sherman on the left, Hooker on the right, and Thomas in town in the center, Grant had his flanks move forward in a systematic approach. But on the third day, both Hooker and Sherman stalled. Grant ordered Thomas to capture the Confederate trenches at the bottom of Missionary Ridge, the hill in front of his position. This the Federal soldiers easily did. They then followed the retreating Confederates up the hill, captured the main entrenchments, and drove the demoralized rebel army from the field. Thomas owed part of his success to the spirit his men displayed and part of the rebel defenders at the bottom of the hill. In an entrenched skirmish line, they had orders to fire a volley and fall back on the main line at the top of the hill. But the Union troops exceeded orders and promptly followed the fleeing skirmishers up the hill. This meant that many of the defenders at the top of the hill, facing both friend and foe approaching their works, withheld their fire for fear of hitting their own men.

Thus the Battle of Chattanooga, like Chickamauga, had witnessed a successful frontal assault and, at Chattanooga, against an adversary with ample time to entrench. The battle yielded a modest attrition, 5,800 Union and 6,600 Confederates. Its strategic value lay in the recovery of what Rosecrans had gained by his August turning movement and then lost to the Confederate concentration in the Battle of Chickamauga. Chattanooga showed consistency with other battles when Grant abandoned his effort to follow Bragg upon finding the rebels strongly posted on hills, facing their would-be pursuers. Still, the Federal army's secure position below Chattanooga meant that it definitely closed the most direct rail line from Richmond to Atlanta and poised the Yankee army for a continuation of its advance, Atlanta being about the same 100 miles away as the army had traveled from Nashville to Chattanooga. The one encouraging fact for the Confederates was that 21 months had elapsed between the fall of Nashville and the secure capture of Chattanooga, a statistic that did not auger well for a quick capture of Atlanta.

So the Western Concentration bloc had finally secured their offensive concentration, but to conduct a counteroffensive. Though not living up to Beauregard's impossibly optimistic forecasts, the Confederate concentration had driven Rosecrans back and placed him in a serious predicament to hold Chattanooga, the fruit of his second advance. But, when the South's concentration ceased to be a surprise, the campaign became another stalemate along the railroad in Tennessee in which Union reinforcements from Mississippi and Virginia countered those the Confederates had already dispatched to Bragg. Then Grant had driven Bragg back from Chattanooga, regaining control of the railroads which connected Nashville, Chattanooga, and Knoxville. Thus the campaign had required the Federal armies to engage in a two-month struggle and fight two big battles to engage and consolidate the fruits of Rosecrans's and Burnside's easy victory of maneuver during August and September.

The Battle of Chattanooga had great symbolic significance in encouraging the North and discouraging the South. It also ended activity on that line of operations until the end of the winter. Longstreet wintered near Knoxville, basing himself on the East Tennessee & Virginia railroad, doing little beyond causing Grant anxiety. Grant continued to keep his headquarters in Chattanooga, where the winter afforded him and his staff and confidants an opportunity to think deeply about Union strategy for the coming year.

CHAPTER 14

THE INCEPTION OF
GRANT'S RAIDING
STRATEGY

―――◆―――

Meridian Campaign

In spite of the opening of the Mississippi and the conquest of Middle and East Tennessee, the Union's persisting logistic strategy did not work rapidly enough. The stalemate in Virginia, the slow progress along the railroad from Nashville into Georgia, and the work of Confederate cavalry raiders and guerrillas on the western army's vulnerable communications did not presage more rapid progress. These problems had long occupied the thoughts of Grant and Sherman.

Grant saw little of Sherman that winter, but he received stimulating ideas from General W. F. "Baldy" Smith, a veteran of the Army of the Potomac who had served as an engineer officer in Rosecrans's army. Smith brought to the problems of the Virginia front a distinctively McClellanesque perspective, for he, like so many generals in that army, remained loyal to their army's creator and first chief, and to his strategy. Thus he contributed pertinent knowledge and perceptive questions to the unsystematic discussion of strategy which was taking place among Grant, his staff, and visitors such as Sherman.

Because of his connections in Washington, Grant had good reason to think about strategy beyond his own huge western command. Elihu B. Washburne, the influential Illinois congressman who had secured his appointment as brigadier general, had become Grant's first important friend. He then acquired another valuable contact in the eminent journalist, Charles A. Dana, a special agent of the War Department sent by Stanton to Grant's headquarters in the winter of 1863 to observe and report on Grant's performance. Soon Dana reversed roles and became part of an informal organization of Grant supporters which included Washburne and General James Harrison Wilson, who soon became the chief of the cavalry bureau; all three of them lived at the same boarding house when Dana returned to Washington to become an assistant secretary of war. Halleck, in some ways Grant's mentor, lent at least tacit support to an increase in Grant's influence.

In the winter of 1864 Washburne introduced a bill to create the grade of lieutenant general, hitherto not used in the Union Army because, as it had only been held by George Washington, it seemed almost profane for anyone else to assume the rank. After checking to find that Grant had no immediate political ambitions, Lincoln supported the bill which Congress passed, all understanding that the appointment would go to the victorious general from the West. As the highest-ranking general, the lieutenant general would become general in chief, with, as it worked out, Halleck becoming his chief of staff. Grant was ready for this responsibility and brought to Washington a new approach to Union strategy.

Unlike Lee and Halleck, Grant had risen slowly, gaining ultimately not just a fine seasoning in command but a different outlook on the war from that more easily acquired in the capitals or in the small, stalemated Virginia theater. Though lacking also their high intelligence, Grant used well the time it had taken him to rise by making the most of this opportunity to reflect on the strategic problems he faced. In this he had assistance from William T. Sherman, West Pointer, Mexican War veteran, and artilleryman, who had left the army to become a lawyer and college president. Intuitive as well as analytical in his thinking, the vivacious Sherman had become a fast friend of the meditative Grant. They then developed into quite effective collaborators in evolving what became the new Union strategy.

Their experience in West Tennessee and along the Mississippi convinced them of the futility of trying to occupy enough of the South for the persisting logistic strategy to work. They doubted the possibility of depriving southern armies of sufficient men and resources to weaken them enough to give the Union victory. Actually it seemed to work the other way, with occupation of the country requiring more men than the rebels lost by the contraction of their base. Sherman summed this up well in writing that, "though our armies pass across and through the land, the war closed in behind and leaves the same enemy behind"; so he saw, for instance, no chance of operating a "railroad running through a country where every house is a nest of secret, bitter enemies."

Grant and Sherman found the remedy for this strategic impasse in abandoning the persisting strategy of territorial conquest and adopting raiding as the means of carrying out the same basic logistic strategy. Heretofore, only the rebels had made extensive use of raids. Early grasping the power of such raids, Sherman had envisioned one to "break up absolutely and effectually the railroad bridges, mills, and everything going to provide their armies." Yet to make these "useless for a whole year" would require not the cavalry raids used by the rebels but action by infantry and engineer troops who would have the time, temperament, and tools to do a more thorough job of destruction.

The plan Grant evolved for 1864 envisioned three gigantic raids aimed at destroying the transportation and supply system that supported the principal rebel armies. For one of these, Sherman would first lead the three armies of his Military Division of the Mississippi to capture Atlanta, and then he would make a raid either to the Gulf or the Atlantic coast and so cut the east-west railroads that linked the seaboard states to Georgia, Alabama, and Mississippi.

The second raiding force, coming from General Banks's command west of the Mississippi, would land at Mobile, long a favorite objective for Grant, raid inland at the same time Sherman moved, and cut the railroads between Mississippi, Alabama, and Georgia. The third raiding force, of 60,000 men gathered from the forces in Maryland, Virginia, and the Atlantic coast, and likely commanded by "Baldy" Smith, would start in southeastern Virginia, raid through North Carolina, break both railroads between Virginia and the Carolinas, and end by capturing the important port of Wilmington, North Carolina (see diagram of Grant's planned raids).

As a result of these three raids, every Confederate state east of the Mississippi would lose its rail connections to the others, two major rebel ports would fall, and the raiders, in addition to living at the enemy's expense and taking much livestock, would wreck many foundries and mills important to the war effort. Without these logistic resources, the Confederacy would no longer be able to maintain such formidable armies as those of Lee and Bragg.

Grant's concept made a major change in the strategic means, though not the objectives, of Federal military strategy. The following table shows the four kinds of military strategy:

	Persisting	Raiding
Combat	#1	#3
Logistic	#2	#4

Union strategy had been to use #2, a persisting logistic strategy, to conquer territory to deprive the enemy armies of the supplies and recruits they needed. Grant changed the army's strategy to #4, a raiding logistic strategy. The navy still used #2, its persisting logistic strategy of blockade. Abandonment of the persisting strategy had two principal advantages. First, Union armies would no longer have to occupy additional territory and devote much of their manpower to controlling civilians, combating guerrilla and cavalry raiders, and protecting railroads. Second, the persisting strategy had necessarily involved combat with the main Confederate armies in order to conquer territory, with the Union armies having to use the weaker tactical and strategic offensive against a highly competent and dedicated enemy. Grant's main strategy no longer had much dependence on combat, because raiders pursuing a logistic strategy avoided hostile armies in order to destroy depots, factories, and bridges.

Confederate strategy would remain unchanged, at sea still depending exclusively on #4, with its commerce raiders like the *Alabama.* On land, it would continue the mixture of #2 and

#4, but, if Grant's raiding strategy became fully effective, the armies would have no persisting invaders to resist, and the cavalry and guerrillas would find that raiding armies had no communications to raid. This would reduce the Confederate armies to fighting at a huge disadvantage against offensively dominant raiders bent on destroying their base. This occurred, but not to the extent it might have had Grant's plans worked out as he intended.

Before his appointment as lieutenant general in March 1864, Grant responded to Halleck's request for ideas for the 1864 campaign by sending him his plan for the North Carolina raid to occur late that winter. In an uncharacteristically disorganized letter, Halleck showed that he did not understand it, seeing it as just another water-based turning movement. Though he cited lack of men as the reason for not implementing it, its similarity to the ideas of McClellan, now the prospective Democratic presidential nominee, was enough to assure its disapproval. Still, the plan for western raids would have remained intact had General Banks, scheduled to land at Mobile in the spring, not made what he projected as a quick raid up the Red River in Arkansas. Here a fall in the water level trapped the Federal fleet, further delaying the army until its engineers could raise the river and extricate the ships. As this removed the Mobile raid from the schedule of spring operations, Grant planned a later capture of Mobile and for Sherman to direct his raid there after he had taken Atlanta.

Since Sherman would pursue a persisting strategy until he had captured Atlanta, Grant could not immediately implement his large scale raiding strategy. But Grant and Sherman had given the concept a successful test in February 1864, when Sherman marched 150 miles from Vicksburg with 21,000 men, mostly infantry, to raid the railway junction of Meridian, Mississippi. Concerned that the rebels might use their railroads to concentrate against Sherman, Grant supplied a variety of distractions to "confuse the enemy," including threatening movements by the fleet near Mobile. But Sherman's main security lay in the offensive dominance of the raid over a persisting defense. Once on the march to Meridian, Sherman planned to "destroy the [rail]roads east and south of there so effectually the enemy will not attempt to rebuild them during the rebel-

185

lion. He will then return unless the opportunity of going into Mobile with the force he has is perfectly plain." Though Sherman's raid caused anxiety in Washington, Grant knew that Sherman could march as fast as his adversaries and, with a choice of routes of withdrawal, would "find an outlet. If in no other way, he will fall back on Pascagoula, and ship from there under protection of Farragut's fleet."

Faced by feeble opposition, Sherman easily occupied Meridian, did his work there, and returned to Vicksburg. He had neither sought nor fought any battle. In spite of his advance deep into enemy country, he made no effort to occupy more of the South. But he accomplished the objectives of the logistic strategy by raiding rather than conquest.

Aiming primarily at crippling the railroads, he had destroyed 115 miles of railroad, 61 bridges, and 20 locomotives. In the process, he had "lived off the country and made a swath of desolation 50 miles broad across the state of Mississippi," at the same time returning with prisoners and "about 10 miles of negroes." Because of the long, hard work of the foot soldiers, the infantry raid did a great deal more damage than the cavalry could accomplish. Sherman owed his success to the size of his force, which both supplied ample labor and meant that he did not have to flee when the rebels concentrated a few men against him. Thus "for five days 10,000 men worked hard and with a will in that work of destruction. . . . Meridian, with its depots, store-houses, arsenals, hospitals, hotels and cantonments no longer exists." Sherman's Meridian raid confirmed the effectiveness of Grant's new raiding logistic strategy, the product of his intellectual collaboration with Sherman.

Though Grant had developed a new logistic strategy which promised to accelerate the destruction of southern war resources, even as general in chief he could not immediately implement it for the 1864 campaign. Since only Sherman would raid, his advance became the strategic centerpiece of the 1864 campaign. But, before beginning his raid, even Sherman planned a persisting advance at first, to capture the important industrial and transportation center of Atlanta. The 1864 spring campaign would have to begin much like those in 1863 and earlier.

CHAPTER 15

MILITARY/POLITICAL CAMPAIGNING

Spring and Summer 1864

Unable initially to rely on his new raiding strategy, Grant depended on the persisting strategy with the now-standard concentration in time. He essentially replicated Halleck's carefully concerted advances and diversions of December 1862. Although in his memoirs, Grant shows he thought that he had originated the idea of simultaneous advances, he did have exceptionally good coordination but without having to synchronize Rosecrans. Although Longstreet had returned to Virginia in the early spring, the fear of another rebel western concentration like that of Chickamauga dominated Grant's initial strategy. He counted on keeping Lee so occupied that he could not detach troops to oppose Sherman in Georgia.

For his two main armies Grant had excellent generals, better than those of 1862. The now-seasoned Meade commanded the Army of the Potomac and Sherman the western forces, the same command Grant had just left and Halleck held in 1862. Though this was his first such responsible assignment, Sherman had ample experience in independent command and thrived on the opportunity the 1864 campaign presented. Grant placed his headquarters in Virginia, with Meade's army, and Halleck still managed the staff in Washington.

Grant fashioned an elaborate Virginia campaign with troops from West Virginia and those defending the Baltimore & Ohio railroad making diversions in the western part of the state and the Shenandoah Valley. Meanwhile, Meade would advance upon Lee while an army of over 30,000 men came up the James River to break Richmond's southern rail communications by digging in south of the city. When Meade had advanced far enough to break the railroad north of Richmond, Grant anticipated that the lack of supplies would cause Richmond to fall. And, he believed, with surprise and vigorous leadership, the powerful force from the James had a good chance of taking Richmond immediately.

Unfortunately for Grant, this promising campaign depended in large part on General Benjamin F. Butler who commanded the army destined to move up the James. A prominent Massachusetts Democrat, Butler had supported Jefferson Davis for the presidential nomination at his party's 1860 national convention. Lincoln's desire to attach this man to the Union cause, together with Butler's energetic action as a brigadier general of militia at the beginning of the war, warranted him a succession of commands. After gaining a favorable impression at their meeting, Grant confirmed him in command of the surprise attack on Richmond from the southeast.

In the West, with the exception of Banks, who was stranded in Arkansas, Grant had outstanding commanders: Sherman, having followed Grant in command of the Military Division of the Mississippi, and the brilliant, young General James B. McPherson, who succeeded Sherman in the Army of the Tennessee. Thomas, proven in capacity at the Battle of Chattanooga, continued to command the large Army of the Cumberland. Burnside returned to a corps command in Virginia, opening the small Army of the Ohio to John M. Schofield, McPherson's equally able but less seasoned West Point classmate. Sherman would command them as a group, maneuvering them as the Confederates did their large corps. This near-perfect command, made up of Halleck and Grant protégés, contrasted sharply with the Confederacy's difficulties in the West.

Upon his defeat at Chattanooga, Bragg had resigned his command, accomplishing what Davis and Seddon had sought the previous winter. Recognizing Bragg's administrative capacity, grasp of strategy, and knowledge of the workings of the armies in the field, Davis placed him in charge of military operations at Confederate Headquarters in Richmond, the post Lee had held in the spring of 1862. Yet, since Davis and Bragg would not make a team as Davis did with Seddon and Lee, this promising move to strengthen headquarters did not work as well as hoped. By appointing a thoroughly discredited general to the post, the president had cost his administration some of its credibility and support.

Davis then offered the command of the Army of Tennessee to its best corps commander, William J. Hardee. Far more than merely reliable as suggested by his nickname "Old Reliable," Hardee was an excellent choice; but he declined, probably feeling more comfortable in a subordinate position. The president then selected J. E. Johnston, about whom he had misgivings. After the fall of Vicksburg an observer reported Davis denouncing Johnston "in the most violent manner" and "attributing the fall of Vicksburg to him & to him alone, regretting that he had been sent to the West." Further, Johnston had become the general around whom the administration's critics had rallied.

Even in the unlikely event that Davis had appointed Johnston to appease such critics, their antagonism to the president would have rendered it a futile gesture. Having Johnston as the focal point of a factional dispute would certainly taint Davis's judgment of his ideas and performance. Unwilling to have Beauregard, Davis should have turned to Longstreet, Hardee's equal and favorably known to the army in Georgia by his crucial part in securing the victory of Chickamauga. Lee would not have thanked Davis for taking away his best corps commander now that Jackson was dead and, if asked about the selection, as he most likely was, Lee certainly recommended Johnston.

So Davis made the appointment and replaced Johnston in Mississippi with General Polk. He elevated to corps command in the Army of Tennessee John B. Hood, aged 32 and a West Point classmate of McPherson and Schofield. Initially commanding a Texas regiment, Hood had made a reputation as a skillful and courageous fighter while a brigade and division commander in Virginia and at Chickamauga, where he lost a leg. As a corps commander he would write letters to Davis, criticizing Johnston's circumspect strategy, from the perspective of an audacious and offensive-minded brigade and division commander.

A final surge of activity by the Western Concentration bloc also contributed to Johnston's potential difficulties. It generated a blizzard of proposals for western offensives of one sort or another. Beauregard produced several, Polk sent one from Mississippi, Kentucky generals another, and Longstreet several from near Knoxville. With the leisure of the winter lull in operations enabling him to visit Richmond, Lee, having regained his strategic perspective, took an active and well-informed part in the discussion of western strategy. With Bragg in Richmond, and in agreement with Beauregard's outlook, and Longstreet corresponding with Lee, the idea of a renewed western offensive became a subject much discussed by Davis, Seddon, Bragg, and Lee.

This deliberation resulted in a striking departure from the usual relation of headquarters with department commanders: a plan of campaign devised in Richmond and pressed on Johnston. Davis lent himself to this innovation for various reasons. When he stressed the "importance—I may say necessity —of our taking the initiative," he doubtless expressed not only his desire to recover the recent and serious territorial losses in Tennessee and Georgia but his concern for southern morale and the northern political situation. With the northern presidential election just a half year away, the wish to influence the attitude of the Union public supplied part of Davis's motivation for an offensive to "inspirit" the army in Georgia and "the country and depress the enemy, involving the greatest consequences."

Thus, in the winter of 1864, President Davis made a proposal for an offensive by Johnston, an unusual procedure in itself but even more so in that he recommended that it take place in the winter. In that its substance reflected not just the desires of the Western Concentration bloc but combined two major themes of Confederate strategy, the plan had nothing out of the ordinary about it. As in the Shiloh and Chickamauga campaigns, the plan envisioned a concentration of troops moving by rail from Mississippi and South Carolina joining a union of Johnston's and Longstreet's forces near Knoxville in East Tennessee. In emulation of Bragg's Kentucky campaign and Lee's consistent practice, this combined force would march between Knoxville and Chattanooga to turn the Union armies back or compel them to assume the tactical offensive.

The proposal to schedule the offensive in March and April doomed the plan. The Army of Tennessee lacked enough wagons to carry supplies for the campaign through a thoroughly foraged East Tennessee. Johnston stressed this, pointing out that it would avail the concentrated forces nothing to turn Knoxville because the army would not have enough supplies to wait "long enough to incommode the forces there," concluding that the move would have to "wait for the grass of May."

Yet, as Johnston knew, this would doom the movement because the Union army would have concentrated and readied itself to move also. Assuming that Grant would command in north Georgia and would have an immense army for a May offensive, Johnston urged countering this by making the contemplated concentration immediately. He proposed that he would then use his stronger army to cut the railroad between Chattanooga and Knoxville while maintaining contact with his own rail communications. To restore Knoxville's vital supply line, the Union army would then have to attack, giving him the opportunity to fight on the tactical defensive and the chance to invade Tennessee after his victory. This proposal for immediate action provoked no response, in part because everyone soon learned that Grant would be in Virginia rather than Georgia.

Accepting the plan's fate, Longstreet pressed for a raid, the other strategy which had served the Confederacy so well. Longstreet's idea involved penetrating Kentucky with a sizable force of infantry, mounted on mules and horses which could better traverse barren areas rapidly. Once the force had reached the enemy's rear and found food and fodder, Longstreet planned to break the railroad line and force the Yankees out of northern Georgia, just as raids against railroads had stymied Buell and Grant in 1862. Seeing the primacy of the raider, Longstreet pointed out that his infantry "could destroy any mounted force that the enemy could bring against us, and it could avoid any infantry force that might be too strong for us." But

191

Longstreet's plan foundered due to the lack of horses and mules to mount his men. If it had not, he would have found his projected route through the mountains utterly impassable for the large force he envisaged. In recapitulating almost every Civil War strategic idea, plans for the Confederate winter offensive testified to their wide currency, even to Longstreet's anticipation of Grant's use of infantry for raiding.

Soon after the collapse of these plans, Longstreet's divisions returned to Virginia. Still, an offensive mindset remained in Richmond with Davis, Bragg, and perhaps Seddon. Hood's letters to Davis also played a role in sustaining the dream of a politically influential offensive. But now both South and North fixed their eyes on Virginia, where the celebrated Lee was about to face the North's champion, Lieutenant General Grant, clothed in the rank held only by the revered Washington.

Grant felt the pressure of popular expectations. He understood that the public saw victory not in terms of strategic objectives attained but as the more dramatic fall of a city or a battle with victory graphically illustrated by the retreat of the hostile army. If Butler carried out his mission, Grant would likely achieve at least an impressive retreat by Lee and, perhaps the finest trophy of all, the fall of Richmond, the rebel capital. Meanwhile, Meade had the mission to engage Lee closely to keep him from detaching troops to act against either Butler or Sherman.

The campaign saw two masters of their craft commanding soldiers seasoned in combat. With his superior numbers and ample logistic preparations, Grant could hold the initiative by turning his adversary. But, without the element of surprise, this could produce no result beyond forcing Lee back: Grant, at first attempting no important distractions, found it almost impossible to take his wily and alert antagonist unaware.

In early May 1864 Meade's army, numbering about twice Lee's 64,000 men and with Grant present and directing its movements, crossed the Rappahannock and Rapidan rivers upstream. Grant then marched to turn Lee's eastern flank, enabling him to draw supplies first from Fredericksburg and then from the Virginia rivers. Lee's move to thwart this turning movement resulted in a battle in a place so overgrown with wood and brush it bore the name the Wilderness. Here the

Confederates repelled Federal assaults but their counterattacks met the same fate. Grant then turned again, but, a little farther south, met Lee blocking his path. Here, at Spotsylvania Court House, he assailed his entrenched adversary in a protracted, futile effort to give the public a famous victory.

The soldiers on both sides well understood this stalemated war of a high ratio of force to space, and they most diligently and adroitly practiced the ancient art of field fortification. A Union observer reported:

When we arrive on the ground, it takes of course a considerable time to put troops in position for attack, in a wooded country; then skirmishers must be thrown forward and an examination made for the point of attack, and to see if there be any impassable obstacles, such as streams or swamps. Meantime what does the enemy? Hastily forming a line of battle, they then collect rails from fences, stones, logs and all other materials and pile them along the line; bayonets with a few picks and shovels, in the hands of men who work for their lives, soon suffice to cover this frame with earth and sods; and within one hour, there is a shelter against bullets, high enough to cover a man kneeling, and extending often for a mile or two. When our line advances, there is the line of the enemy, nothing showing but the bayonets, and the battle flags stuck on the top of the work. It is a rule that when the rebels halt, the first day gives them a good rifle-pit; the second, a regular infantry parapet with artillery in position; and the third a parapet with an abatis in front and entrenched batteries behind. Sometimes they put this three days work into the first twenty-four hours.

The observer neglected to mention that the attackers always dug in also, protected in their skirmishing and against counterattacks. Clearly these men needed no West Point instruction as to the value of field fortifications.

While Grant was campaigning from the Wilderness to Spotsylvania Court House, Butler had come up the James River with 33,000 men and landed between Richmond and Petersburg. Anxious and overestimating difficulties, he halted: He did little more than raid the railroad between those two cities, which stimulated a rush of rebel troops up the coastal pipeline as well as the arrival of General Beauregard to take personal command of the Confederate forces. In his attack on Butler, the outnumbered Beauregard failed to cut him off from the river but did drive him into a neck of land with the James on three sides. Here the Confederates built a line of entrenchments to keep Butler securely corked as in a bottle, a simile Grant used in his report.

Unable to drive Lee back in a battle, Grant turned his right again, well back toward Richmond. After seeing no opportunity for an attack, he turned Lee again until he had reached the position of McClellan's right in June 1862 and could draw his supplies from the York River. Logistically a good situation, it was politically embarrassing to have campaigned so hard only to arrive at the place Lincoln's likely opponent in the 1864 presidential election had reached so easily in 1862. Here the disastrous Battle of Cold Harbor occurred where a hopeless Federal frontal assault lost 7,000 men in less than an hour. Badly managed by Grant and Meade, this attack, like Lee's on Meade's center at Gettysburg, was a blunder which even the best generals commit from time to time.

With careful preparations for the march and river crossing and admirable work by the engineers, Grant next took Lee by surprise. Distracting him for the first time, Grant shrewdly made it appear that he was attempting to turn him only a few miles beyond Lee's south flank. Again using the initiative conferred by his numerical superiority and the offensive, Grant, undetected, moved virtually his entire army south of the James River and toward the key rail center of Petersburg, 25 miles south of Richmond. Here the Yankees faced elaborate fortifications but practically no troops under the command of General Beauregard (see diagram of Grant turning Lee from the Wilderness to Petersburg).

Leading the first corps to arrive, General Baldy Smith, wary of losing his command in another attack like Cold Harbor, delayed so long that he did not breach the defenses until dark. The next day Hancock, well named "the superb" on account of his usual energy and acumen, also acted sluggishly. These delays were costly for they enabled Beauregard, who was conducting a frantic and imaginative defense, to obtain reinforcements from Lee. Enough of these arrived in driblets for Beauregard to hold back the increasingly powerful and deter-

194

mined Federal attacks. After three days, Grant, now facing a strong, entrenched defense, realized that he had lost his opportunity to capture Petersburg and began building siege lines. The siege of Petersburg lasted until the spring of 1865 because the Union army could not interdict Richmond's ample communications. The siege disproved two assumptions: that Richmond would fall to Union siegecraft and that the rickety Confederate logistic organization could not supply Lee's army in Richmond.

Even before losing nearly 70,000 men in six weeks, approximately double the Confederate losses and about an eighth of all Union soldiers present for duty, Grant had been trying to cope with the unfamiliar experience of failure. Initial over-optimistic reports from Secretary Stanton had raised popular expectations about the course of the campaign in Virginia. Stanton represented Grant's turning movements and Lee's withdrawals as pursuits of a beaten foe and even reported to the state governors a rumor that Lee had retreated from Spotsylvania west toward Lynchburg. Having to keep in step with Stanton's management of the news and election year needs by interpreting his costly operations as victorious, Grant proclaimed that "Lee's army is really whipped" because a "battle with them outside of their entrenchments cannot be had." Under other circumstances Grant would not have made this claim, since he would interpret a resort to entrenchments as sensible behavior when it occurred with his own soldiers. After the war Grant further developed this thesis to say that the heavy fighting had made Lee's "a far different army from that which menaced Washington and invaded Maryland and Pennsylvania. It was no longer an invading army."

The attrition thesis subsequently came to justify a campaign that was an inevitable result of the high ratio of force to space which had produced a stalemate in eastern Virginia since the beginning of the war. From a strategic standpoint Grant intended only to keep Lee from reinforcing Johnston. He would not have adopted a wasteful and ineffective combat strategy when he expected soon to unleash his powerful, new logistic strategy in the form of Sherman's raid. But in these circumstances Grant argued that attrition of manpower vindicated, and presumably inspired, the heavy fighting even though bloodless turning movements could have brought the army into the same position. Of course attrition is the by-product of combat but, to make a positive contribution to winning the war, attrition must use up a higher proportion of the adversary's men than of one's own. By losing men in the same proportion as Lee, Grant's operations failed to provide attrition useful to the North.

Moreover, the morale of the Federal army suffered seriously. One of Grant's staff, an advocate of the battles fought, admitted in his diary that the "troops do not fight as well as when we started. Best officers and best men gone—losses enormous." And he later cited others: "Hancock saying with 12 brigades he has lost 25 brigade commanders and his men are not half as good as when we started. Meade is doubtful if our men can be relied on as yet." Having fought mostly on the defensive, usually entrenched, the Confederate soldiers maintained their morale far better than the Union men, many of whom had participated in unsuccessful assaults which they saw as unwise and futile.

So many casualties in such a short time contributed to their demoralizing political effect. For example, Grant had lost in six weeks about as many men as the 1862 battles in Virginia in over six months. And this represented more than mere compression in time. The change in the ratio of losses must have contributed to the public's dismay. Considered as an effort at attrition, Grant's campaign compared unfavorably with the Union's five principal offensive battles east of the valley in 1862: Whereas Grant suffered about double Lee's casualties, Union generals McClellan, Pope, and Burnside lost only about 40 percent more than the Confederates, clearly effective as attrition in view of the Union armies' overall two to one numerical superiority.

So, not surprisingly, in the operations in Virginia in 1864 the North had suffered more political attrition than the South. The huge Union casualties incurred to return to a familiar place caused a revulsion in the public and a disillusionment with battles as the essence of warfare. The campaign and the resulting siege only confirmed the existence of a stalemate in Virginia, but Lee's successful defense against the redoubtable Grant gave heart to the Southerners. In July 1864 Lincoln revealed how politically sensitive the casualty issue had become.

Noting a telegram from Grant to Sherman which said that he would make a "desperate effort" to keep Lee from reinforcing Johnston, the president promptly telegraphed Grant that he hoped "the effort shall not be desperate in the sense of great loss of life."

Someone might have seen in the fighting in Virginia in 1864 a parallel in the Battle of Malplaquet in 1709, in which the Duke of Marlborough had suffered double the French losses in forcing an orderly retreat upon the strongly entrenched Marshal Villars. And Malplaquet cost the British much political attrition. The opposition British politicians called Marlborough "the butcher," and the battle provided an impetus for his recall from command, a change in the party in power, and the British seeking peace. In the summer of 1864 the parallel extended only to some calling Grant a "butcher" and a strong display of peace sentiment among Democrats and some Republicans as well. Some Republicans, dissatisfied with Lincoln, gave support to the presidential candidacy of General Frémont, a third party which might split the vote enough to give the 1864 election to the Democrats.

If Grant had foregone his attempt to meet popular expectations by trying to signalize his advances with victorious battles, his simple campaign of turning Lee back would have certainly disappointed the public, but perhaps less than a campaign with battles characterized by heavy losses. Moreover, had the army not made frontal attacks, Smith and Hancock might have been less gun-shy before Petersburg and so taken the city, a well-merited and potentially significant reward for the strategic surprise gained by Grant's masterfully executed turning movement against Lee. The long siege of Petersburg vindicated Halleck's judgment that Lee could so economize on men at Richmond that he could even transfer some elsewhere. Agreeing with this judgment, Grant telegraphed Sherman to expect Johnston to receive 25,000 reinforcements from Lee. Grant's expectation that Lee would send a third of his army on an offensive mission west clearly indicates that he did not actually believe Lee's army was "really whipped." Clearly Grant did not deceive himself while attempting to place his campaign in the most favorable light for the public.

When, in June 1864, Lee detached a corps westward, it aimed

197

at recovering the Shenandoah Valley, the scene of operations intended to distract Lee. In May, Grant's distracting force under General Sigel had advanced into the valley from the Baltimore & Ohio railroad. It had met defeat in battle and retreated so precipitously that soldiers who had said they fought with Sigel later said they ran with him. But a Union army quickly returned under David Hunter, an adequate general, and overwhelmed the small rebel force left in the valley. Just after Cold Harbor, Lee sent the capable and resourceful General Jubal A. Early to the valley with his corps, one of the three composing Lee's army.

Acting with admirable dispatch and effectiveness, Early drove Hunter from the valley and acted to help peace partisans in the North's coming elections. Crossing the Potomac, he levied contributions on two Maryland towns, brushed aside an improvised Federal force, seemed to menace Washington, and returned to the valley. This two-week campaign was so obviously a raid that Early's withdrawal did not appear as a retreat. This campaign, as well as another foray at the end of July, one that reached into Pennsylvania, acutely embarrassed the Lincoln administration.

Early's operations had made an admirable riposte to Grant's advance, but the Confederates could not agree on whether they had helped northern peace advocates. Some Southerners believed that Early's raids would provoke Northerners to rally to the Lincoln administration and to the war effort, while others agreed with President Davis that finding "the evils of war at their own door" would cause more people in the North to "sustain the policy of stopping the war." Doubtless the raids did daunt some and intensify the resistance of others, the balance of political attrition probably being favorable to the Confederacy.

Early's raids required Grant to commit more than comparable forces to the valley line of operations, almost 50,000 men under General Philip H. Sheridan, a cocky and aggressive little man of considerable ability. Receiving regimental command from Halleck, Sheridan had risen in the west until Grant had brought him east to infuse the cavalry of the Army of the Potomac with energy. Charged with halting further raids and recovering the political losses inflicted, Sheridan began organizing an army. He took men from the forces he found in northern Virginia and in Washington, joined them with two corps from Grant, one originally brought by sea from west of the Mississippi to reinforce the Army of the Potomac. He then had triple Early's force.

Without flashy battles and spectacular raids, Sherman's simultaneous advance from Chattanooga toward Atlanta lacked much news value. But the public did not have the same expectations of him as it had had of the lieutenant general in the East. Like Grant, Sherman had substantial numerical superiority, 90,000 men to 60,000. Sherman used this advantage to turn Johnston out of one elaborately entrenched position after another. With no need to attack his adversary in battle, Sherman had only one minor engagement at Kennesaw Mountain, fought in part to show Johnston that he could not count on the Union army never assaulting his field fortifications. Otherwise, Sherman's campaign followed Grant's, with numbers and the offensive supplying initiative. Without surprise, however, the turning movements only forced the enemy to fall back. Both Sherman and Johnston waited to catch the other at a disadvantage, but each proved too wary and skillful to give his antagonist an opening.

Although both sides fortified thoroughly, they suffered casualties from the process of scouting and feeling out their adversary. In May Johnston lost 9,187 men killed and wounded to Sherman's 10,528. This amounted to over 15 percent of Johnston's force but less than 12 percent of Sherman's. This adverse ratio, based on not necessarily dependable numbers, contrasted with Grant and Lee's comparable percentages and requires an explanation in view of Johnston's caution and the care with which he dug in, including even his skirmish line. The unentrenched feeling-out process offers part of the explanation, as does the Union army's entrenchment on the offensive and refusal to attack a fortified adversary. Union numerical superiority provides still another part of the explanation because it meant that often Confederate soldiers had more men shooting at them and consequently had a greater opportunity to be hit. During this campaign Sherman's soldiers made invidious comparisons between their losses and the far heavier

199

casualties of the Army of the Potomac, a contrast which elevated their respect for their own general and fostered a real affection for him.

All of Sherman's turning movements went according to plan, but the need to rebuild the railway increasingly slowed his advance as did a season of hard rains. Well prepared and hard working, the engineers repaired and rebuilt trestles and relaid track. Good management of the single-track line permitted it to supply an army that was too large and concentrated, and moving too slowly in a thinly settled country, to obtain more than a fraction of its supplies from the countryside.

By the end of June, after almost eight weeks of campaigning and a 50-mile advance, Sherman again faced an elaborately entrenched Johnston in front of Marietta while he worked out another turning movement. Then young John M. Schofield asked Sherman whether "Johnston, in anticipation of your present movement," could "bring up to Marietta two or three weeks' supplies, close the gorge of his line in [the] rear of Marietta, and meet you there in a strongly intrenched position with a greater amount of supplies than you can carry." Thus he posed the problem faced by Bragg in September 1862 when he turned Buell only to find the Federals better supplied and able to wait until he had to march away from their rear.

Having "contemplated every move upon the military chessboard," Sherman gave a quick answer. Although he did not think Johnston would want Sherman "between him and the rest of the Confederacy," he explained that he would cope with the situation in Schofield's question by immediately starting the raid which he planned to begin after the fall of Atlanta. Sherman's armies would simply march south to the vicinity of Atlanta "and destroy all his railroads before he can prevent it." Though Sherman was correct in thinking that Johnston did not want him behind him, his answer to Schofield would apply equally well if Johnston could, as had Lee in Virginia, turn Sherman to compel his retreat. Sherman could simply ignore the Confederate army by becoming a raider and set out early on his planned march to emulate the model of the Meridian raid in destroying railroads, factories, depots, and agricultural supplies.

By mid-July of 1864, Sherman had turned Johnston back to

the outskirts of Atlanta, having advanced about as far as Grant in Virginia but taking a month longer (see diagram of Sherman turning Johnston from Dalton to Atlanta). Both Grant and Sherman had entrenched as they advanced. They had driven back their adversaries, in the same way, by turning them. Sherman owed his much-slower progress to the need to rebuild and defend his railroad, while Grant could rely on the water communication accessible to his left flank provided by Chesapeake Bay and its tributary rivers. In his 1862 advance on Corinth, Halleck, who also entrenched on the offensive and advanced by threatening his adversary's flanks, had moved even more slowly than Sherman because he had to corduroy muddy roads rather than repair railroads. In his Tullahoma campaign Rosecrans, with his double proportion of wagons, had made the best rate of advance, going half as far as Sherman, 40 miles, in nine days. Lee, in his Gettysburg campaign, had gone farther and faster but, as a raider, had no need of communications nor any possibility of having any.

Sherman had made his advance in spite of committing large forces to protecting his rear. And Johnston had received the reinforcement of General Polk's 12,000 men, virtually all of the infantry of the Department of Alabama, Mississippi, and East Louisiana. Although Polk's force equaled the number Johnston had earlier said would enable him to take the offensive, he did not attack nor did he catch Sherman at a disadvantage. As Johnston approached the outskirts of Atlanta, President Davis replaced him with General Hood. Unaware of Davis's need for reassurance that he would defend Atlanta, Johnston did not tell the president his plans; he had been equally uncommunicative before Richmond in 1862. Actually he had little to tell beyond his plan to lengthen Sherman's vulnerable supply line before he acted. Doubtless, as at Richmond in 1862, he planned to attack Sherman when vulnerable, just as he had attacked McClellan. After the war Johnston said that he intended to have the Georgia state forces hold the city's fortifications while he used his entire army to turn Sherman. This would have made an interesting campaign. If successful, it could have presented Sherman with a different version of Schofield's question, that is, the choice of falling back or beginning his raid without capturing Atlanta.

But Johnston failed to allay Davis's anxieties, which were particularly intense due to the forthcoming Union presidential election. A winning offensive, for which President Davis yearned but which Johnston insisted was impossible, would have a powerful effect in encouraging the sentiment for peace in the North. But the Confederate hopes for that election imperatively demanded a successful defense of Atlanta to match that of Richmond. Davis's pre-existing feelings about Johnston and the use of the general by captious critics of the administration must have influenced the president. So did General Bragg's mistaken belief that Johnston's army had far more men than its general admitted. Moreover, Hardee, whom Johnston had excluded from his counsels in favor of Hood, had written of his doubts about the general's willingness to fight. And, Hood, on whom Johnston depended to carry out an attack but who never found the moment right, reported to the opposite, that he had urged the offensive but Johnston would never order it. Thus, with the approbation of the cabinet, Davis relieved Johnston. As a replacement, the president chose Hood, who had insisted that he could conduct the politically crucial offensive to drive back Sherman. Lee had distinct reservations about this selection.

Another possibly significant decision affecting this critical campaign was Davis's refusal to order the incomparable Forrest and his cavalry from Mississippi to ride against Sherman's vulnerable rail communications. In the autumn of 1863, Johnston had done this from his Mississippi army in an ineffective effort to aid Bragg's siege of Chattanooga. Nevertheless, Johnston continued to believe in the cavalry raid as a winning strategy and repeatedly requested the War Department to order the raids. But Davis declined because he felt Mississippi was too vulnerable. Polk, the department commander, had exceeded his instructions when he took virtually all of his infantry to reinforce Johnston and become a third corps of the Army of Tennessee. And Sherman successfully distracted the Confederate president by deliberately sending raids into Mississippi which, though Forrest defeated them, must have seemed from afar to be important invasions. Thus, reinforced by his chief of staff Bragg, who, though an original convert to the cavalry raid, had apparently lost his faith in it, Davis refused to order it.

In fact, Sherman's preparations indicate that even Forrest could have failed. Sherman had 72,000 men at the front and, all the way back to Louisville, 68,000 protecting his rear against guerrillas and raiders. At Nashville, Chattanooga, and Allatoona, about 25 miles north of Atlanta, he had provisioned and fortified bases. In between, every railroad bridge had the protection of a blockhouse with a garrison of at least 20 men, and all the railroad stations had entrenched detachments. South of Chattanooga these defenders amounted to an average of about 230 men per mile of track. In view of these large forces, the facility and rapidity of railroad repair, and the reserve of 20 days' rations that Sherman kept with his army, it seems doubtful that the raiders could have halted him the way they had Buell two years earlier.

Thus Grant's orchestration of the strategy of synchronized advances had made substantial progress, bringing Meade's army to Petersburg and Sherman's to the outskirts of Atlanta. The campaign in Virginia had pressed Lee so closely that neither Davis nor Seddon had thought of sending men to reinforce the army opposing Sherman.

Though a strategic success, his campaign had failed politically. The northern public did not view the costly campaign from the Wilderness to Petersburg as the succession of glorious victories painted by Stanton. Nor did many see the siege of Petersburg as more than a deadlock with no end in sight. That this siege merely epitomized the stalemate long existing in Virginia meant that the public correctly perceived how dim were the prospects of an early decision in Virginia. In the east the campaign seemed clearly a political defeat.

In the West, where the lower ratio of military force to space had hitherto enabled the Union to make gains, Sherman seemed stalled before Atlanta. Still, since he had a far greater likelihood of success than the Army of the Potomac, his capture of Atlanta before the presidential election had assumed major importance to the Lincoln administration. The fall of the city would show the public that Union armies were not locked in a hopeless deadlock in Georgia, too. Moreover, the capture of Atlanta would strike a double blow to southern hopes for gaining independence at a reasonable cost. The symbolism of the fall of Atlanta and the strategic value of the city would dispirit them; but they would feel even greater discouragement from the weakening of the northern peace advocates on whom they pinned such high hopes. So, if Sherman took Atlanta, he would achieve immensely significant political results, more important than the military value, even though it would set the stage for his raid.

CHAPTER 16

THE COLLAPSE OF THE CONFEDERACY

Atlanta to Appomattox

Political and military developments had interacted throughout the war; the news from the armies had a dominant part in determining the popular estimate of the likely cost and length of the war. By 1864 the relationship between military events and public attitudes had fostered explicit efforts on both sides to direct military operations so as to influence public opinion, particularly in connection with the northern elections.

In the last months of 1864 military events did influence politics, just as many leaders had assumed all along. In the North the response took place largely at the polls. In the Confederacy much of it occurred in the armies where desertion became more of a political act, reflecting the judgment that independence was costing too much. Both of these political acts had major military consequences.

The influential military events had much to do with John B. Hood, who had assumed command of the Confederate army defending Atlanta. Apparently generalizing his offensive tactical success in overrunning defenders' positions as applicable to strategy, Hood attacked Sherman's army as soon as it crossed Peachtree Creek and reached the outskirts of Atlanta. Though in motion and not well disposed to resist his first effort, the Union soldiers quickly improvised entrenchments and turned back an essentially frontal assault. Then, showing what he had learned fighting under Lee, Hood sent Hardee's corps around the Union army's left flank, only to have the Yankees establish a line of defense at right angles to their front and so thwart the turning movement. Hood, in a third offensive in eight days, again struck and failed when again the Federal soldiers threw back the rebels with the aid of hastily prepared entrenchments.

After a month's lull during which Hood's cavalry raided, but did not decisively interrupt, Union communications, Sherman moved his whole army past Atlanta's west side and reached the city's last rail link, a dozen miles to the south. Unable to drive the Yankees away and apparently not interested in learning who could last the longest without rail communications, Hood evacuated the city on the last day of August 1864.

During Hood's time in command he had suffered 27,000 casualties compared to 21,000 for Sherman's army, a very substantial Union tactical victory in terms of attrition. But, important as Atlanta was as a railroad junction, its fall did not sever the Confederacy's east-west communications. Though this limited the victory's strategic importance, it did nothing to diminish the symbolic significance of the fall of the city. As an immediate political consequence, in early September, General Frémont abandoned his presidential candidacy with its potential for diversion of votes from Lincoln. At the end of August the Democratic national convention finally met to adopt a platform and nominate a candidate for president. For many months the Confederate newspapers had watched northern political developments with care, reporting every evidence of peace sentiment and its strength among the Democrats. In fact, southern morale was high because many expected the Union's fall election to produce conditions for a favorable peace. Actually this expectation indicated that many Southerners had already paid for independence as much in casualties and hardship as they believed it worth. Linton Stephens of Georgia, brother and collaborator of the Confederate vice president, summed up this thesis about southern morale: "It has been sustained, and the collapse prevented even up to this time, only by the hopes which our people had from the peace party in the North." If Stephens had made a correct judgment, a failure of peace in the fall would mean southern civilians and soldiers in large numbers would abandon the war effort, whether or not their leaders reflected their view.

The Democratic convention adopted a platform favorable to peace but it had too much ambiguity to hearten Confederates very much. As one newspaper expressed it, the fall of Atlanta so affected the North that "All Yankeedoodledom is clapping hands, and huzzaing and flinging up caps, as though there was no longer a 'live rebel' in all America." Another soberly assessed Atlanta's effect on the election: "It will render incalculable assistance to the party of Lincoln, and obscures the prospect of peace, late so bright."

Southern hopes suffered further disappointment early in September, when the Democratic nominee, General George B. McClellan, clarified his stand on the issue of peace with the South, insisting that there could be no peace without reunion. One Confederate summed up the situation created by McClellan's nomination: "It effectually destroys the hopes that we had begun to entertain of an early termination of the war and renders the success or failure of his canditure a matter of comparative indifference."

As Southerners were digesting all this bad news, Lincoln had some good news from Virginia. Sheridan's large army, advancing south in the Shenandoah Valley, drove Early's corps back and in the best way possible, with two victorious battles within four days, adding to the new aura of military success surrounding Lincoln's candidacy. Sheridan then utilized his victory to move infantry and cavalry over much of the Shenandoah Valley, destroying 2,000 barns full of wheat, hay, and farm machinery as well as 70 mills, full at this harvest season. Thus he effectively executed his orders to disable the valley as a base area "so crows flying over it for the balance of the season will have to carry their own provender." With this traditional application of a defensive logistic strategy, he prevented the valley from functioning as a base area for rebel armies. Then in October Sheridan narrowly turned back a surprise attack by Early, yet another victory in battle for the northern public and still another discouraging reverse for Southerners.

Beneficial as were these last victories to Union morale and

Lincoln's candidacy, the president may not have needed them. He won with 55 percent of the popular vote and an overwhelming 212 to 21 majority in the electoral college. And, considering Democratic nominee McClellan's strong stand to continue the war, the Union may not have even needed Lincoln to win the war. Yet these very events, the fall of Atlanta, McClellan's insistence on reunion, and the reelection of Lincoln, so disheartening to the rebels, created a political environment for which the Union president was ready. In December 1863 Lincoln had promulgated his peace terms and, instead of asking for unconditional surrender, invited the states in rebellion back into the Union if 10 percent of the voters in 1860 would take an oath of allegiance, create a state government, and abolish slavery. By thus offering these nonpunitive terms of reconciliation, he reduced the cost of defeat to the South.

Even though a perceived threat to slavery had sparked the secession of the deep South states in 1860 and 1861, the prospect of giving up slavery to return to the Union no longer seemed too onerous a condition. The Confederacy was ready to take steps to dismantle it by preparing to enlist slaves in the army. That between June and December 1864 the number of absentees from the ranks of the rebel armies rose from less than 40 to 53 percent shows the effect of Lincoln's offer for reconstruction as well as the Southerners' discouragement with the way defeat and deprivation had raised the present and prospective cost of independence.

With the fall of Atlanta, Grant and Sherman turned to the long-planned raid. Since Grant had brought men from west of the Mississippi to Virginia and rebel activity west of the river occupied the remainder of the Union troops there, Grant again had to postpone taking Mobile. With no force at that port for Sherman to link with, the lieutenant general thought a raid to Savannah a better choice, because it would "sever the connections between Lee's army" and "the rich districts of Georgia, Alabama, and Mississippi." But he and Sherman did not definitely decide whether the raid would aim for the Atlantic or the Gulf if only because, as Sherman expressed one of the raider's traditional strengths, "having alternates, I can take so eccentric a course that no general can guess my objective."

In early October while Grant and Sherman matured their

revised plan, Davis conferred with Hood and made a speaking tour to try to elevate public morale. The president and Hood then launched an impressive riposte in Georgia while Forrest was already, albeit belatedly, raiding Sherman's communications in Tennessee and Sherman was strengthening his rear-area garrisons and preparing for his raid. Then, in a move characteristic of Lee, Hood marched past Atlanta on the west. This turning movement, which had a base area in north Alabama, drew Sherman after him as Hood, avoiding battle, kept ahead while wrecking sections of the railway. The sight of Sherman moving north through Georgia, rather than south, doubtless diminished somewhat the éclat of his capture of Atlanta but failed to have the symbolic effect of a major defeat, in part because Sherman still held Atlanta.

Hood's turning movement delayed Sherman's raid, but Hood's destruction did not cripple the railways, as Sherman's organization quickly repaired each of the breaks in the road. Nonetheless, Sherman came to the realization that he could not both keep Atlanta and carry out his raid. Consequently he began strengthening Tennessee, which Thomas was to defend should Hood cross over from Alabama. If pressed, Thomas could fall back behind the Cumberland River, its high water in the winter patrolled by the always perfectly cooperative navy, protecting his flanks and offering an almost invulnerable route for supply.

Characteristically, as Sherman prepared to carry out a logistic strategy by raiding, he saw that the movement was "not purely military or strategic." Knowing that the march of any army, much less a hostile army, would result in great losses, Sherman realized that much political intimidation was implicit in what he was about to do. When he added the destruction of railroads, shops, mills, and agricultural resources that supported the rebel war effort, he saw that the military march would have a major political by-product.

His friend Halleck, now clearly understanding Grant's logistic strategy, had already noted the decisive military impact of Grant's plans on the rebels, so that "deprived of the grain, iron, and coal of Northern Georgia, Alabama, and Mississippi, and the harbor of Wilmington closed as effectively as Mobile, Savannah, and Charleston now are, they can hardly hold out in strong force another year." Having assured Sherman of the consonance of his plans with international law, Grant's chief of staff stressed that Sherman "would destroy every mill and factory within reach." Although Halleck did not "approve of burning private houses or uselessly destroying private property," Sherman should take or destroy "whatever may serve as supplies to us or to the enemy armies." He also agreed with the political component, noting that for two years he had urged intimidation because "we have tried three years of conciliation and kindness without any reciprocation" beyond guerrilla warfare.

But Sherman saw in his raid something more sophisticated than intimidation. He believed that to march 250 miles through Georgia, going to the sea or the Gulf rather than returning the way he had come, would have considerable symbolic effect, because it would "illustrate the vulnerability of the South." Although it would "make its inhabitants feel that war and individual ruin are synonymous terms," Sherman saw the psychological impact of the symbol as more important. For, "if we can march a well-appointed army right through his territory, it is a demonstration to the world, foreign and domestic, that we have a power which Davis cannot resist."

Knowing that a march in which the commander condoned pillaging could lose many men through desertion and could exasperate rather than dismay the civilian population, Sherman ordered that officers have charge of all foraging. Anxious not to alienate those not already hostile, he prescribed that "soldiers must not enter the dwelling of the inhabitants or commit any trespass." Moreover, they were to "refrain from abusive or threatening language" and, to the apparently loyal, they could give receipts for what they took. Further, in appropriating what the army could use or destroying what the rebels needed, the Federal soldiers were to place the burden on the rich, whom Sherman saw as almost uniformly hostile. But, he instructed, "should guerrillas or bushwhackers molest our march, or should the inhabitants burn bridges, obstruct roads, or otherwise manifest local hostility, then army commanders should order and enforce a devastation more or less relentless," including mills, houses, and cotton gins otherwise exempt.

Thus politics, as much as logistic military strategy, suffused Sherman's order as he aimed at avoiding making new enemies while intimidating those already hostile. And he was ready to carry out the logistic strategy, having a specially equipped engineer regiment for wrecking railroads. The engineer troops would build fires to heat the rails which, with special tools, they would then twist around telegraph poles. The result earned the nickname "Sherman neckties." Repair required either new rails or rerolling those so artfully tied.

On November 12 Sherman at last embarked "on the projected grand raid." In spite of having 60,000 men, the great size of the state—almost 60,000 square miles—made it simple for Sherman to use the ambiguity of his objective and confusing movements to avoid the small rebel force opposing his raid. Rather than going to the Gulf, Sherman marched to the Atlantic at Savannah, reaching it on December 10 and making contact with the fleet and his new base on December 13. During the march, he adopted a system of foraging by which each day officers led out bands of picked men who roamed the countryside to bring back supplies for the army. Ideally the foragers walked out and rode back on captured horses and mules, but some parties rode in order to reach more distant sources. The small bands of Yankee soldiers faced considerable danger from state forces. Units from General Hardee's Department of South Carolina, Georgia, and Florida hovered around the army, as did armed civilians. Moreover, a Confederate cavalry division led by the able and aggressive "Fighting Joe" Wheeler tracked the army, sometimes behind it and sometimes lurking ahead. This environment, and the practice of the Confederates of killing captured foragers, doubtless helps explain the Union army's very low level of straggling and desertion.

Officers did an effective job of protecting civilians from harm and their property from wanton destruction. But, if any hid or destroyed food or fodder, the soldiers ruthlessly burned houses and barns, just as they did if they found bridges burned or encountered an ambush. The harassment of the regular and irregular troops rather than the opposition of a field army distinguished this march from others, as did the very thorough foraging and the systematic destruction of a broad range of war resources. The army took over 13,000 head of cattle and the equivalent of almost 6,000,000 rations of beef and bread. In addition to appropriating, as a military resource, nearly 7,000 horses and mules and killing many others, the army destroyed 90,000 bales of cotton and numerous sawmills and cotton gins as well as foundries, textile mills, and warehouses of a vast assortment of goods. All of this made this march bear much harder on the people than usual for the passage of even so large an army.

When he reached Savannah, Sherman reported that he "had not lost a wagon on the trip, but have gathered a large supply of negroes, mules, horses, &c. . . . We have utterly destroyed over 200 miles of rails, and consumed stores and provisions that were essential to Lee's and Hood's armies." Sherman estimated the losses his army had inflicted at $100,000,000, the army using a fifth of this amount, with the remainder "simple waste and destruction." Though it met little opposition requiring retaliation, the raid inflicted damage which proved quite intimidating. Inevitable pillaging intensified the ordinary harm done by the army's passing, as did the ruin of resources of use to the rebel armies, such as killing horses that the Federal army did not want to take with it.

These losses, computed in dollars rather than casualties, reflect the very substantial logistic losses inflicted by this campaign, while the prolonged interruption of the railroads showed the extent of the strategic victory for this new raiding, logistic strategy. The political impact of the raid contradicted the lesson of the Union's experience in Virginia, that sporadic or unsustained harshness tended not to intimidate but, rather, to arouse a more active animosity. But Sherman's raid had an opposite effect.

Still, from a political point of view, Sherman's raid through Georgia was not an isolated event; it came last in a series, each of which reduced the popular hope for a victory at a reasonable cost. After Hood's failure to drive back Sherman in August 1864 came the fall of Atlanta, McClellan's insistence on reunion as a condition of peace, Early's defeat in the valley, Lincoln's reelection, and, finally, Sherman's raid. Each forecast a longer struggle and caused more Southerners to decide that independence was not worth its ever-escalating cost. Before his march to the sea, Sherman, who in 1862 had expressed concern about soldiers' behavior alienating Virginians, shrewdly saw that the essentially unimpeded passage of his army would have far more symbolic importance and psychological effect than even that of a resounding victory in a major battle. Davis stated it succinctly when he wrote that "Sherman's campaign has produced [a] bad effect on our people. Success against his future operations is needed to reanimate the public's confidence."

Upon Sherman's recommendation, Grant gave up his idea for the army to position itself at Augusta and authorized a raid into the Carolinas. Later Grant supported this operation by sending a strong contingent to Wilmington, already captured in January by a smoothly conducted combined operation. This gave Sherman a terminus for his raid and a base should he wish to resume a persisting strategy.

Though the raid nullified the success of his turning movement against Sherman, Hood, instead of following his antagonist, extended his spectacular northern Georgia campaign. At last receiving a command consonant with his strategic inclinations, Beauregard, coming from Virginia to command Hood and the Alabama-Mississippi department, reluctantly approved a move about which Davis had great reservations. So Hood's and Sherman's armies marched away from one another, each commander convinced that he could harm the other more by going into the other's territory.

Starting after the presidential election in November 1864 and the beginning of Sherman's march, Hood moved from northern Alabama toward Nashville, repairing the rail line so as to make a permanent occupation. With his army depleted to 40,000, he faced the wary Thomas, on the defensive with more men but many of them newly enlisted. Finding Schofield with much of Thomas's force 70 miles south of Nashville, Hood turned Schofield back twice. Then the Confederates found Schofield with 32,000 men, dug in at Franklin with his back to a river and his flanks thus protected. In assailing Schofield in the Battle of Franklin, Hood lost 6,200 to 2,300, a ratio much surpassing Fredericksburg and a fine Union victory of military attrition. Rather than give Hood a chance to turn him, Schofield then withdrew to join the remainder of Thomas's army in Nashville.

In early December Hood arrived at the outskirts of the fortified city of Nashville, its flanks protected by gunboats patrolling the Cumberland River. Camped in the open with a tenuous supply situation and Thomas's 49,000 men snug in town and supplied by water and rail, Hood's 31,000 men seemed to have no reason to be there. Though traditional generalship prescribed that Thomas should let Hood's army waste away in the open in the winter, the political embarrassment of a rebel force in a position abandoned almost three years before compelled Thomas to take the offensive. This he did in the middle of December 1864, adeptly combining distraction and concentration in the two-day Battle of Nashville, which drove the rebels in headlong retreat. The winter march of demoralized troops caused substantial losses as did the pursuer's capture of the wounded from the two battles. The loss of morale in the defeated army amounted to even more than its casualties. As Hood led his army in the retreat from Tennessee, his men, hearing the rumor that Uncle Joe Johnston would again command them, sang a song. To the tune of the "Yellow Rose of Texas," the army sang the "Gallant Hood of Texas."

> So now I'm marching southward;
> My heart is full of woe.
> I'm going back to Georgia
> To see my Uncle Joe.
> You may talk about your Beauregard
> and sing of General Lee
> But the Gallant Hood of Texas
> played hell in Tennessee.

Thus ended the Confederacy's last riposte. Hood soon resigned, ending a tenure marked by an unfortunate mixture of insight and obtuseness that may sometimes have reflected the stress of command.

With Sherman beginning 1865 by moving into South Carolina, Grant projected additional raids. Since, with the fall of Wilmington and Sherman's raiding north toward North Carolina, Grant had at last accomplished his North Carolina raid, he ordered the reminder of his 1864 program, a raid from Mobile, whose port the navy had already closed. With 38,000 men gathered from Tennessee and Banks's department, the capable and thorough General E. R. S. Canby landed at Mobile in March

1865 and took the city at the beginning of April. He was then ready to carry out Grant's usual instructions for a logistic strategy: "to prevent, as far as possible, the planting of a crop this year and to destroy their railroads, machine-shops, &c. It is also important to get all the negro men we can before the enemy put them in the ranks." When he had completed this task, Grant directed Canby to "take such positions as can be supplied by water." With these secure water communications he would thus "occupy positions from which the enemy's [rail] roads in the interior can be kept broken." The war ended before Canby could do much more than capture Mobile.

In addition to the two big infantry raids, Sherman's and Canby's, Grant directed four formidable cavalry raids. The most important of these began in Tennessee, led by his protégé, General James Harrison Wilson, the former chief of the cavalry bureau and a young general with flair and a penchant for the initiative. Wilson had over 13,000 cavalry, mostly armed with magazine rifles, which he led from Tennessee into Alabama, following Grant's instructions to "destroy the enemy's line of communication and military resources" by defeating Forrest in order to take the armaments center of Selma, Alabama. Here the raiders wrecked foundries, rolling mills, machine shops, factories, railroad cars, and locomotives as well as destroyed quantities of supplies. Grant's other cavalry raids included two from the Mississippi, designed to create confusion to help Canby and Wilson, and another raid, planned but never carried out, would have entered South Carolina from Tennessee to "destroy the railroad and the military resources of the country." Grant made clear that "this expedition goes to destroy and not to fight battles."

At the last minute Grant added an "additional raid" by Sheridan from Winchester to Richmond to "destroy the railroad and canal in every direction, so as to be of no further use to the rebellion." All of these raids, he explained to Sheridan, "were all that will be wanted to leave nothing for the rebellion to stand upon." Sheridan's men destroyed every bridge and miles of track and, in addition, damaged the James River canal, which he believed had been the "great feeder" of Richmond. They destroyed every lock and much of the bank of the canal as well.

As Grant at last set in motion his long-contemplated logistic raids, the Confederates acknowledged the failure of Hood by changes in Richmond: the resignation of Secretary of War Seddon, and his replacement by Major General John C. Breckinridge, one of the Democratic presidential nominees in 1860 and a division commander of proven competence. Congress also created the post of general in chief for Lee, a post that added little to the informal power which he had enjoyed whenever he had been close enough to Richmond to exercise it. This appointment did not displace his chief of staff Bragg, because the president had already sent him to command in North Carolina. These changes did nothing for the management of the war but may have given a small lift to public morale.

General Hardee, as commander of the Department of South Carolina, Georgia, and Florida, had principal responsibility for facing Sherman, but he acted under the supervision of Beauregard. They had pitifully inadequate forces, many of them reserves intended to man coast defenses and consisting of men either too young or too old to be eligible for conscription. The Army of Tennessee was on the way to join in the defense of the Carolinas, but many from this great but now discouraged, even hopeless, army failed to arrive, having deserted along the way. A telegram Hardee received from Augusta illustrated the magnitude of the problem: "Nine hundred men from the West have arrived; one-half deserted."

Sherman's men noted a weakening of the spirit of the rebels who remained with the colors, one commenting: "We think here the rebs are about whipped for they won't give Sherman battle any more." Another noted that "the thing is fast dwindling away." That 3 Union soldiers captured 73 Confederate cavalrymen confirmed the soldiers' impression of the feebleness of the opposition. General Lee later noted the same phenomenon, commenting that the actions of the troops defending Richmond "were not marked by the boldness and decision which formerly characterized them. Except in particular instances, they were feeble; and a want of confidence seemed to possess officers and men. This condition, I think, was produced by the state of feeling in the country, and the communications received by the men from their homes urging their return and abandonment of the field."

216

In giving unity of command to the forces opposing Sherman by appointing J. E. Johnston over generals Bragg, Beauregard, and Hardee, Lee charged him with the conduct of the defense of the Carolinas. This Johnston did with commendable energy, insight, and, even, virtuosity, but to no avail. Sherman's army, in touch with Wilmington as a base, proved too strong for the Confederates to do more than briefly delay. Sherman's men continued in North Carolina the thorough work of logistic destruction perfected on the Meridian raid and practiced so well from Atlanta to South Carolina.

Grant's strategy had confronted the Confederates everywhere with everything from substantial cavalry forces to large armies, all in confusing and destructive motion but without dependence on communications; the Confederacy proved powerless to stem this deluge of Union raids.

Grant expected Sherman's application of logistic raids to result in "the discomfiture of Lee's army," but the Confederate logistic organization, seemingly always on the point of total collapse, continued to feed his army even without touching a one-week reserve long held for emergencies. But, in late March, when Grant sent Sheridan's cavalry and two infantry corps on a raid around to the south of Petersburg's defenses to break the railroad to the southwest, their success meant Richmond no longer received adequate supplies.

Immediately evacuating Richmond, Lee had a day's start on Grant; but when faulty staff work did not send the supply reserve along, Lee halted for a day in a largely futile search for supplies. This enabled Grant to move parallel with him and block the route to Lee's objective, union with Johnston in North Carolina. Essentially conducting a continuous turning movement until near Appomattox Court House, where his cavalry blocked Lee's further progress westward, Grant at last reached his adversary's rear. Rather than fight, retreat, or disperse, Lee, responding very accurately to the mood of the South, capitulated. Johnston soon followed, as did the armies farther west, and the Civil War concluded with no residual resistance at all.

Sherman had brilliantly executed the raiding strategy he and Grant had devised. Adventitiously, his strategy provided an antidote to Hood's skillful use of the defensive turning movement after the fall of Atlanta. Sherman also contributed to vic-

217

tory by the political attrition of his capture of Atlanta and the power of his raid through Georgia to serve as a symbol of Confederate defeat. A formidable Confederate war machine still existed at that point, but it was quickly melting away. During the fall and early winter of 1864–1865, 40 percent of the armies east of the Mississippi deserted. The rebel soldiers, finding the cost of victory more than they wished to bear, were voting for peace with their feet. Their sentiments did not differ from those at home. Political attrition had won the war before the military attrition of Grant's logistic strategy could bring military victory.

CHAPTER 17

THE CONDUCT AND CHARACTER OF THE WAR

The commanders in chief conducted their wars with a high degree of competence. Some have seen in Davis's confidence in his knowledge and understanding an unwarranted arrogance which resulted in a domineering attitude and an unwise interference with his subordinates. Yet he gave few directions, and most, such as telling J. E. Johnston to reinforce Beauregard at Manassas, had good effects. And, when ordering reinforcements from Charleston and the Gulf to Tennessee after the fall of Fort Donelson, it is hard to see much arrogance in the acknowledgment of "the error of my attempt to defend all the frontier, seaboard and inland." So, though no more inclined than most to see or admit mistakes, Davis had no illusions of infallibility.

Yet, having learned the army from the bottom up as a junior officer, regimental commander in combat, and secretary of war, Davis joined almost unequaled experience with intense interest and great native ability. He displayed a clear mastery of Napoleonic strategy and combined the expertise needed for command with a temperament which enabled him, unlike some of the generals, to bear great responsibility without flinching. He used his talent and knowledge to create and operate a traditionally decentralized military command. Sometimes he erred on the side of insufficient central direction, as when he allowed the West to go without guidance for much of 1862, but this certainly constituted a lesser evil than too much central control. When events marched ahead of the organization, his departments, called theaters and armies in the twentieth century, sometimes became poorly arranged. This occurred initially when he created too many departments oriented toward the coast and, later in the West, when Bragg, leading an army in Kentucky, could not command his big department.

Most of the South's organizational difficulty concerned efforts to decentralize the command of Tennessee, Georgia, Alabama, and Mississippi, a region which enemy action had deprived of its excellent water and rail communications. The area gained this needed direction with J. E. Johnston's Department of the West but lost it when Johnston went to command the Vicksburg relief forces. Then, after more than a year of controlling two departments from Richmond, Davis decentralized again when he sent Beauregard to command Georgia, Alabama, and Mississippi. So Davis strove for an organization which would enable him to decentralize all but the most important strategic decisions. And these often kaleidoscopic changes did not typify workings of the Confederate command system. For example, for almost two years Lee and Beauregard commanded the Atlantic seaboard, and Davis made the logistically independent trans-Mississippi a separate department and entrusted it for more than two years to the competent direction of Edmund Kirby Smith.

Thus much of Confederate strategy revolved around the efforts to supply unity of command to the different theaters of war. Determinations about organization, and in particular the creation of the Department of the West, constituted important strategic choices. In his other type of strategic decisions, Davis treated the theaters as one, under his own command. Then he effected concentrations, as he encouraged his commanders to do, using the telegraph and the railroad. He did this when he brought troops from the southern coast to Richmond in June 1862, and on a national scale, he acted twice, with the concentrations of the Shiloh and Chickamauga campaigns. In addition, Davis sometimes gave advice to commanders, in those cases demonstrating his grasp of lines of operation and turning movements, the basic concepts governing army maneuvers. His mastery of strategy and his consistent application of it makes his management of it deserving of high praise.

Likewise, the president showed real insight when, realizing the vulnerability of the Confederacy to a logistic strategy, he made his strategic objective the preservation of territory rather than a futile effort to overthrow enemy armies. Nor did he, as many critics have thought, respond to the idea of states' rights by dissipating military resources on the defense of unimportant places. Rather, increasingly he guided his military strategy so as to influence the 1864 Union elections. He did this by demonstrating the ability of the Confederacy to resist invasion, but not by dispersing his effort. Instead, he kept most forces in a few main armies and defended important and vulnerable ports with a few men, using the railroad as a pipeline full of troops, a concept which he hoped would also enable Johnston to operate in Napoleon's manner in the West.

In attempting to have a pipeline between Tennessee and Mississippi, Davis had adopted for national use a concept first employed by departmental commanders. But he could not give a similar stimulus to guerrillas, one of the Confederacy's most powerful raiding weapons, because their operations depended entirely on local initiative. The impetus for the other, the cavalry raids, usually came exclusively from the theater commanders. Moreover, when, in 1864, he had the opportunity to order a raid by Forrest on Sherman's communications, he seemed not to understand what a decisive weapon the cavalry raid had proven to be in the West.

In evaluating Davis's performance, the quality of his command appointments play a critical role. At the beginning most were good, those in Virginia, the West, and South Carolina, Georgia, and Florida going to A. S. and J. E. Johnston and to Lee, the stars of the U.S. Army who had joined the Confederacy. Following Lee on the coast came Pemberton, quickly succeeded by the versatile Beauregard, followed by the seasoned Samuel Jones, and finally the accomplished Hardee. Most of his departmental selections would exhibit the same pattern of placing in command experienced regulars who performed well. Controversy over his appointments focuses on a few, principally on his clinging to Bragg, justifying Pemberton, and removing J. E. Johnston. His defensive response to criticism of Bragg was a natural reaction when he knew that many of the critics were politically hostile to the administration. But he had sought to replace Bragg and only failed when Johnston refused to take his place. Critics who see Davis as typically keeping inept favorites in command seem to generalize from too few cases, having to include Bragg and Pemberton among the president's pets. It would have a better foundation to criticize Davis for too much reluctance to relieve commanders. Perhaps too much sensitivity to the feelings of the individuals restrained him. Lincoln removed generals more readily than Davis, but he had more places, like Minnesota and California, to relegate discarded commanders than did the Confederate president. As to his judgment in making appointments, it is easy to sympathize with his distrust of Beauregard but not with his delay in looking to the lieutenant generals for replacing Bragg, something he had done when he appointed the unsuitable Holmes to the trans-Mississippi and then replaced him with the capable Kirby Smith, whom he promoted to full general. More may sympathize with the appointment of Hood if they see it not merely as replacing Johnston with someone who promised to defend Atlanta but as a desperate gamble to gain victories which would help peace forces in the North and head off Lincoln's reelection.

If the president's strategy was well-conceived and executed and his appointments mostly sound, his conduct of the Richmond headquarters did not meet the standards shown in his command and strategy. He had recognized the need for a general in chief when he appointed Lee in March of 1862, but he then failed to fill the position for a year and a half after it became vacant. His respect and affection for his friend Lee and the availability of his advice in long letters and sometimes in person must have helped make Davis overlook this need, as doubtless did the lack of an appealing prospect for appointment to the position and his ability to discharge the duties himself. Though his talent and Seddon's outstanding gifts and temperament made the headquarters work fairly well, Davis wore himself out, becoming sick, giving important problems inadequate consideration, and losing the patience, which he had displayed early in the war, to deal tactfully with people.

Yet he seems to have had fewer defects as military commander and strategist than many historians have found in him and displayed more insight and ability than they have noted. His performance as commander in chief surpassed his accomplishments as a political leader.

Whereas Davis had a six-year presidential term and could not succeed himself, Lincoln had constantly to orient himself toward the 1864 election upon which the fate of the Union might well hang. Thus he made political patronage a more important factor in appointments to all but the command of the main armies; even so, McClernand and Banks had major commands in opening the Mississippi. But Lincoln could draw on a larger pool of soldiers from that corps of officers which the government had opened to talent instead of privilege and molded with a thorough and challenging training at West Point. Many of these had matured in the promising environment of a regular army influenced by West Point, the Mexican War experience, Winfield Scott and other talented leaders, and the institution's dedication to the service of the country.

There is a symmetry between the Union command problems in the East, where the main army had five commanders in a year, and Confederate difficulties in the West. Many of the Federal generals in Virginia gave their allegiance to McClellan, still their army's informal leader, and so made it hard for Pope, Burnside, Hooker, and Meade to secure the kind of loyalty which would have helped them do their best. In the West, where Halleck had led the armies to victory until he became general in chief, his appointees consequently had a legitimacy and commanded a loyalty lacking in Virginia. In the Confederacy, Lee's quick successes enabled him to make Johnston's army his own, but, in the western army, some remained loyal to Beauregard.

When Lincoln appointed Meade, also Halleck's choice, he had found a commander with the tactical insight and facility as strategist to enable the Army of the Potomac to play its assigned modest role in the stalemated Virginia theater. Thus the Union solved its command problem with a general loyal to McClellan's memory but able to comprehend and implement the Lincoln-Halleck strategy. And, when the slow but adroit Rosecrans failed after Chickamauga, Lincoln and Halleck could draw on an ample supply of proven western commanders. The Confederacy was not so fortunate.

Like Davis, the Federal president seemed never to lose his nerve or the confidence to remain effectively in command. Lincoln early grasped concentration in space and time and the maneuver of armies and, more slowly, learned the dominance of the defense and the inherent indecisiveness of military operations between similarly armed adversaries. In thus understanding the war as the soldiers saw it, he differed from many civilians, including the intelligent John Hay, Lincoln's secretary. This well-informed young man illustrated the gap between the views of the civilian and the soldier when he obviously relished what he saw as the discomfiture of the regulars and their respect for the power of the defensive as he noted the incident of "a Western brigade plunging over an open field under the direct fire of an earthwork, crossing a slough, cutting through an abattis, and storming the work successfully, thus performing four impossibilities." The generals reciprocated, disparaging the civilians frontal combat view of war, as when Meade criticized what he understood as Secretary Stanton's "cry 'Fight, fight—be whipped if you must, but fight on,' as very much of the bull-in-a-china-shop order, and not creditable to his judgment."

Some scholars have believed that the civilians properly understood war as attacking and destroying the enemy army and viewed Union generals as obtusely failing to comprehend this obvious truth. By generalizing from Lincoln's instructions to Burnside, Hooker, and Meade to aim at Lee's army rather than Richmond, they had placed him on the side of the civilians rather than the soldiers. But this thesis about Lincoln fails on the ground that he never gave such instruction to commanders in other theaters, and because those to the Virginia generals clearly related to his and Halleck's desire to avoid a siege, to their aim to keep Lee away from Washington and the Potomac, and to their hope to hurt him if he made a mistake. Thus Lincoln sided with his soldiers against the sometimes vociferous criticism of belligerent, almost blood-thirsty civilians and supported them in acting according to what history, their war experience, and their respect for their adversary taught them was a realistic logistic strategy.

This sharing of the soldiers' view enabled him to understand and work with his generals. In spite of differences in background and temperament which made it impossible for them to make a team as did Davis and Lee, Halleck and Lincoln collaborated well enough to execute simultaneous advances, formulate a strategy of concentration in the West, and to recognize the stalemate in Virginia and to develop an approach to make the best of it. With its implicit persisting, logistic strategy, the Union command dealt realistically and wisely with the primacy of the defensive and the special logistic obstacles of operating large armies in North America, strategic problems different from the Confederacy's.

In coordinating a decentralized system of departments, Lincoln faced the same tasks of command as Davis. After fumbling with the appointment of McClellan and experimenting with the War Board, Lincoln wisely chose Halleck as general in chief, a move that also strengthened the headquarters staff. Using the relations begun by the War Board, Halleck created, as an informal organization, a functioning general staff. Since such informal relationships are a normal part of any organization, the Confederacy's staff undoubtedly worked together in a different and more effective way than indicated by the organizational chart showing distinct bureaus. But the Union's, more purposefully created, guided by Halleck and his capable assistants, and aided by such brilliant men as Quartermaster General Meigs and railroad executive and Assistant Secretary of War Thomas A. Scott, worked far better, particularly in insuring excellence in the management of the Federal Army's difficult logistics.

In the war's final year, after at first misunderstanding Grant's strategy, Lincoln and Halleck fully embraced his raids. Throughout the war, Lincoln had a deep and constructive involvement in initiating and executing Union strategy. Yet, although the president followed military events with avidity and participated in decisions to move troops from one theater to another, he did not have to perform Davis's difficult and draining military duties. This gave him much more time for the politics of mobilizing support for the war and to secure his reelection. So Lincoln, in turning out to agree, rather than disagree, with his generals, loses a certain distinctiveness but

225

gains ample stature through his understanding of military realities, his constructive role in military command and strategy,
and his astute handling of the political aspects of his duties as
commander in chief.

Except for Randolph's sponsorship of the Confederate Department of the West and Stanton and Seddon's advocacy of
particular interdepartmental troop movements, it is difficult to
attribute to the opposing secretaries of war any definable influence on strategy. Stanton gave an outstanding performance
as a manager, as did Seddon also, proving a most effective
collaborator with Davis in implementing strategy through departmental reorganization and by troop transfers between departments.

Lee's influence derived not so much from his two brief terms
as general in chief but from his role as Davis's informal adviser.
But even here, their harmonious personal relations and their
common use of the Napoleonic and Mexican wars for understanding strategy makes it difficult to define with precision
Lee's role in high command and strategy. On the other hand,
some have seen Lee as bidding for a concentration of Confederate force in Virginia and an effort to win the war through a
decisive battle. Most of the evidence for this rests on Lee's
resistance to reinforcing Tennessee or Mississippi in the spring
of 1863. Some, such as Beauregard at the time, have linked the
Gettysburg campaign with raising the siege of Vicksburg. But,
in the absence of contemporary evidence for this, the logistical
and strategic reasons special to Virginia seem quite sufficient to
explain Lee's strategy.

In fact, when Lee was experiencing serious dissonance between his role as army commander and his understanding and
approval of the strategy which urged him to send men west, he
resolved it by opposing any movements to concentrate. After
this episode passed, Lee did bring up the idea that he make
another raid north as an alternative to sending Longstreet to
aid Bragg, but accompanied the suggestion with no bizarre
justifications. Later, when he believed that the main Union
effort in 1864 would come in the West, he thought Longstreet
might have to remain there. So it is hard to find Lee advocating
a concentration in Virginia comparable, for example, to that
adopted by the Union for the West.

This interpretation of Lee as seeking a concentration in Virginia has a close relation to one which sees Lee as a visionary seeking to annihilate the enemy army in battle rather than, as Lee wrote, aiming to "baffle" rather than destroy the enemy. In this way he, like many others, believed the Confederates could "resist manfully" and so discourage enough Northerners that the peace candidates would win the 1864 elections. Lee's actions conform more to this militarily realistic and politically attuned strategy than to the thesis that he believed he could destroy an enemy army in a major battle, something not done in Europe since 1704 at Blenheim. Thus these critics of Lee censure him for doing what others blame northern generals for not doing, trying to destroy their enemy in battle.

It seems much more likely that Lee had the same view of military reality as the northern generals. After learning his lesson in the Seven Days' Battles about the cost and difficulty of a successful turning movement and a pursuit that hurt the pursuer less than the pursued, Lee followed the conservative strategy which he and Davis had agreed upon. When he set out to drive back Pope, he aimed to do so without a battle; and, when Jackson reached the the Union rear, the position from which Napoleon had won his Marengo and Ulm campaigns, Jackson deliberately abandoned it when he moved away from Pope's communications. Of the campaign to drive Pope back, Lee wrote that it had met all of his objectives except avoiding battle.

At Antietam, as at Second Manassas, Lee's strategy enabled him to fight on the defensive in a battle in which he could hardly have harbored expectations of destroying his enemy. But at Chancellorsville, Hooker, well coached by Meigs, turned Lee and made him choose between taking the offensive or retreating. Yet he avoided a frontal fight by turning Hooker's turning movement. Like the others, this battle, initiated by the enemy while part of Lee's army was away with Longstreet, hardly seems the scene of action calculated to annihilate the opposing army. And Lee's conservative strategy paid off: In 1862 and 1863 he fought on the defensive more than the average Confederate general, won a higher percentage of his battles, and suffered fewer casualties.

In view of Lee's three defensive battles in a row, Second Manassas, Antietam, and Fredericksburg, his avoidance of a major frontal attack at Chancellorsville, and his brilliant but careful defense in 1864, Gettysburg stands out as an aberration, and particularly the frontal attack by Pickett on the third day. What seems best to exemplify his strategy is not his quest for a battle of annihilation but his innovative defensive use of the turning movement and the raid. So Lee's success as a realistic and innovative strategist, his wonderful audacity based upon a just appreciation of his opponents and of military possibilities, and his superb operational skill give him a valid claim to greatness.

Beauregard's influence over Confederate strategy, exerted through the Western Concentration bloc, had a good effect in encouraging Davis and Seddon to exercise more control. After the war, he expressed his goal as seeing "the whole theater of war as one subject of which all points were but integral parts." In his grasp of Napoleonic warfare he seems to have differed little from Lee, Davis, Bragg, or J. E. Johnston.

Halleck, as unmartial and unprepossessing in appearance as he was unphotogenic, did not seize the public's imagination, difficult for a headquarters general in any case. And the curt, sometimes abrasive way in which he commanded further diminished his appeal. He did not prove himself as a battle commander, made a poor start as general in chief in the Antietam campaign, and, by keeping Grant quiescent, allowed Johnston to reinforce Bragg for the Battle of Chickamauga. Nevertheless, Halleck's achievements entitle him to great respect as a discerning, almost prescient, strategist, superb manager, and excellent judge of people. He showed these qualities in the Fort Donelson and Shiloh campaigns, in his conduct of the Washington headquarters, by his lucid and penetrating strategic directions to new commanders, by his inauguration of systematic simultaneous advances, and in his development of a strategy for Virginia and advocacy of concentration in the West. He fostered Grant and Sherman; Meade may have owed his appointment to him; and McPherson, Sheridan, and Schofield got early commands from him.

Halleck survived in a difficult environment. He served Lincoln and his country by working with the aggressive Stanton while disagreeing with his view of warfare and trying to conciliate the many Union politicians with their favorite generals or campaigns. Many decisions, reflecting the resolution of political, military, and bureaucratic vectors, he found uncongenial or quite wrong, but he carried them out loyally while sometimes letting a commander know that he understood the defects of those decisions.

Grant, too, lacked a martial appearance or much personal magnetism, but his success as a field commander appealed to a public which tended to see war as little more than battles. He lacked the high intelligence of Lee and Halleck, their engineering aptitude, and their knowledge of military history and operations. He differed also in that Lee and Halleck came to the war as commanding generals. They learned less than Grant in the course of the war, not only because they had less to learn but because they missed some of his opportunities. Like them, Grant also possessed much of that ability for seeing interrelationships, making valid inductions, and identifying critical variables, so essential to managers and to those who administer, maneuver, and fight armies amidst the fog and friction of war. He learned from his varied experiences and those of others, reflected on the nature of the war, and possessed an imperturbability which awed his friend Sherman. Grant learned from Halleck but benefited most from his collaboration with the brilliant and imaginative Sherman in developing a different strategic approach to the war. After ample opportunity to observe and much time for reflection, one of Meade's most discerning staff officers decided that what made such an ordinary man exceptional was that Grant did "everything with a reason; he is eminently a wise man."

Just as a person can find one Lee by concentrating on the Seven Days' and Gettysburg campaigns and another by looking at his others, so it is easy to see different Grants, depending on which campaigns one takes as representative. To focus on his 1864 campaign, and even more so with the siege of Petersburg added, makes Grant appear merely determined, combative, and, to some, a convinced practitioner of a combat strategy in battles or through attrition. Yet in his masterpieces, Vicksburg and the movement to Petersburg, Grant turned his adversary in a consummate manner. In the stalemated Virginia theater he failed, as he was almost bound to do in an area with such a high ratio of force to space, particularly when facing such a finished operational master as Lee.

Most evaluations of Grant as strategist stress his war of attrition in 1864, even though attrition was more a rationalization for his failure to do more, and accept his assertion that he introduced the first successful simultaneous advances in 1864. But Grant's claim to greatness lies not in better concerted advances or in his casualty lists in Virginia in 1864 nor even his considerable operational skill; it lies in his thinking through the Union's strategic problem and finding an innovative solution. The political objectives of the raid had existed since primitive war, but in its military objectives, the railroads, Grant aimed at what made the Civil War distinctive, the dominance of base-dependent logistics for field as well as siege operations, the joint contribution of a sparse population to supply the need and the railroad to provide the means. Thus Grant used armies to execute a military raiding strategy when the industrial revolution had given it immense new effect.

Although Grant's logistic raiding strategy has never received much recognition because it failed to win the war, it would have, had the war lasted long enough. And its political by-product, the intimidation engendered by his raids and their psychological effect as symbols of defeat, made a powerful contribution to inducing the South to give up its quest for independence before Grant's strategy could have its decisive military effect.

Because the Union raids, particularly Sherman's, contributed to victory primarily by their political rather than their military impact and because Sherman was the exponent of their potential political power, some have seen them primarily as old-fashioned political raids and have credited Sherman with conceiving as well as executing them. Certainly Sherman, in his collaboration with Grant, had much to do with devising the basic logistic military strategy, but Grant had the power and took the responsibility for deciding to depend on raids rather than continuing the persisting strategy. In doing so, he directed Sherman to destroy "war resources," the objective of a logistic military strategy. Still, Grant was certainly not oblivious of the likely political effects of such raids. On the other hand,

Sherman had the idea of the raid in the Carolinas, superseding Grant's of positioning Sherman's army so as to continue blocking the Confederacy's southeastern rail network.

As the foregoing strictures indicate, not all have agreed that both belligerents conducted the Civil War with a high level of competence. Adherents of McClellan's Peninsula strategy long criticized Lincoln as substituting his amateur judgment for Mc-Clellan's sophisticated strategy. More recently, others have praised Lincoln for opposing—and assailed Union generals for following—an obsolete strategy of conquering enemy territory rather than seeking to destroy enemy armies in battle. Now we can see that McClellan had the best approach to reaching Richmond for a siege, but we can doubt the merit of besieging the Confederate capital and disapprove if it implied emphasizing deadlocked Virginia rather than exploiting the strategic opportunities offered by concentrating in the West. We also can see that attempts to destroy armies in battle were as unlikely to succeed in the Civil War as in wars in the preceding centuries, something Lincoln came to know almost as well as his generals.

Except for Bragg, Pemberton, and Hood, most Confederate generals long received relatively little censure. This is partly due to the tendency to see the war's military operations in terms of Virginia campaigns, which made its principal generals, Lee and Jackson, seem better than the Union commanders, especially Pope and Burnside. Later critics of Lee, starting with B. H. Liddell Hart, deprecated him as too belligerent and held him responsible for incurring too many casualties in a vain effort to win significant victories against the dominance of the tactical defensive. That Lee fought more on the defensive than the average Confederate general tends, along with other comparative data, to keep this reproach from being a decisive indictment against him. Although he did fight unnecessary battles, he also sought to avoid them.

Indeed, critics of rebel tactics have indicted the whole Confederate Army for tactical incompetence for believing in the efficacy of frontal attacks. But the failure of the southern armies to attack more often than the Union or to display an inferior combat effectiveness makes that an unlikely hypothesis. On both sides, some commanders, from lieutenant to general,

231

could not think beyond a frontal attack, but many more frontal assaults occurred because the front is where the defender preferred to receive an attack. A good system of drill, and thorough practice with it, made it easy to change the front to face an attack or to retreat to avoid fighting in one direction when the foe attacked in another. The real disparity in casualties comes from Confederate strategic blunders in trapping themselves and surrendering 55,000 men in Fort Donelson, Arkansas Post, Vicksburg, and Port Hudson.

Those who see the advent of the muzzle-loading rifle as greatly changing combat, even to shifting primacy from the offense to defense, overlook the traditional dominance of the tactical defense. Nor was the systematic use of entrenchments an innovation, being older than the Romans who learned daily entrenchment from the Greeks who had adopted it from Asiatic armies. Yet the thoroughness of the use of entrenchments by both armies owes something to the engineering curriculum of West Point. Having the same doctrine, both armies combined this tactical insight with their mastery of the essentials of Scott's methods and Napoleonic strategy to apply a doctrine distinct from and, in view of the increased range and accuracy of the rifle, in advance of the European for use with Civil War armies.

Excellence in their tactical and operational doctrine is only one aspect in which both sides fought the Civil War with well-above-average skill. The South was an underdeveloped country and the Union was still largely agricultural and only somewhat ahead, yet the belligerents displayed a wide-ranging competence in developing war machines the match for those in Europe. With sophisticated tactics, logistics, and strategy adapted to the industrial revolution and low population density, and political aims and strategic means usually well harmonized, the combatants conducted their war well.

After starting with hopes for a political compromise, the North began with a persisting logistic strategy, seeking to cripple the rebel armies by seizing much of the territory that supplied them. Realizing the menace this presented, the Confederates defended with the same strategy. They implemented it with Napoleonic operational concepts and the use of counteroffensives to recover lost territory and drive back invaders. Soon they added a raiding, logistic strategy, employing guerrillas as well as cavalry and directed largely against rail-roads. When, as was often the case, the rails supplied armies which were unable to support themselves by what they could glean from the countryside, raiding became a powerful defensive strategy that could halt the advance of major invading armies. Not only did the dominance of defense over offense in a persisting strategy aid the Confederates, but they also exploited the offensive primacy of the raider over the defender. They had the best of two strategic worlds.

But in 1864 the Union began to substitute raids for persisting advances by armies in prosecuting their logistic strategy. By the beginning of 1865, Sherman was commencing his second raid and Grant projected five more and planned no further operations to conquer territory. The Union had made almost a complete transition from a persisting to a raiding logistic strategy. The offensive ascendancy of the raid helps explain the ease with which Union armies marched into the heart of Georgia, South Carolina, North Carolina, and Alabama.

Throughout the war, the navies pursued consistent strategies. The North followed a persisting logistic strategy with a blockade, and the South used a raiding logistic strategy with commerce raiders.

At the operational level the Confederates displayed great skill in using the railroad and the telegraph to adapt Napoleon's strategy of concentration in space to vast distances. The First Manassas, Shiloh, Seven Days', and Chickamauga campaigns were the most notable instances of the use of this strategy; and in all but Chickamauga the Confederates had the assistance of interior lines. The Union made this strategic maneuver twice. Before Shiloh, Halleck directed Buell to reinforce Grant, and after Chickamauga, Hooker went from Virginia to Tennessee to reinforce Rosecrans. Instead of carrying out more concentrations in space, the Union depended on the concentration in time of simultaneous advances. In December 1862 the Union's simultaneous advances caught a large rebel division leaving Tennessee too soon to fight at Stones River and arriving in Mississippi too late to have much part in turning back Grant and Sherman.

Both sides converted the turning movement into a fine art. Lee and Bragg introduced it as a defensive means of driving

233

back the enemy without the necessity of fighting a defensive battle, and Rosecrans and Sherman perfected it as an antidote to the high ratio of force to space along the railroad between Nashville and Atlanta. In the use of raids the antagonists displayed more difference. The Confederates employed theirs on the defensive and the Union on the offensive, as one would expect, both having railroads as their principal objective. Southern raids commenced early in the war and had the greatest military effect. Their raids by cavalry and guerrillas contributed importantly to absorbing one third of northern manpower.

In spite of their significance, command and strategy do not usually receive a large place in explanations for the outcome of the war, only the thesis of Confederate tactical incompetence proposing a purely military explanation for Confederate defeat. Yet, though some have seen the navy's blockade as a major factor, it is now clear that it did nothing decisive to handicap Confederate armies. On the other hand, its disruption of the South's profitable foreign trade reduced its people's standard of living which, along with shortages, raised the costs of the war. Nor did domestic supply fail, the Confederate government and southern entrepreneurs filling most military needs not met by imports and the railroads successfully meeting minimum requirements till the end.

Long an influential explanation of the war's outcome was the interpretation that states' rights defeated the Confederacy by attracting large Confederate forces to the defense of unimportant points and by the states holding back substantial resources from the common war effort. It is now clear that, after an initial overcommitment to coast defense, the Confederacy conducted an effective local defense with minimum force. The North committed proportionately much more to protect its communications. Further, though the states held back some manpower, they had organized more into a military force which they could call up for brief service.

Of even more assistance to the common cause, the states' support for their men in the army and, of particular value, for the soldiers' families made powerful contributions to combat effectiveness and the sustainment of civilian and military morale. Thus, not surprisingly, Confederate generals, rather than

234

complaining about states' rights, looked upon the states as another military resource and viewed their activism as a powerful aid to the war effort. Further, national action, in the form of early enactment of conscription, gave the Confederate government more control of manpower than the Union, even after the North's belated institution of its draft.

The many interpretations which have assumed that the South could have won if the states, the blockade, the railroads, or insufficient industry had not kept it from having enough supplies, seem inadequate to explain the outcome. Military explanations abound, but most come from advocates of the decisiveness of a particular campaign or battle. Clearly, when one compares the consequences of victory rather than defeat for any campaign or battle, or the reverse, and keeps in mind the powerful constraints of logistics and the realities of the strategic situation, all of the Civil War battles and campaigns have little military potential for changing history. In this they do not differ from most others in military history.

So, though most Civil War battles had importance for their military or political attrition, few had much strategic significance. The Union victory at Stones River, for instance, yielded an advance of 20 miles toward Chattanooga, only a minor strategic victory; the rebel victory at the First Battle of Manassas gained an equally minor strategic victory by preventing the Federal army from making an advance similar to that after Stones River. To change the outcome even of Antietam and Gettysburg, often regarded as strategically significant, would have little strategic effect; but a defeat at Antietam would doubtless have increased Confederate casualties considerably. On the other hand, the Battle of Chickamauga had the valuable strategic result of nullifying most of the success of Rosecrans's crossing of the Tennessee and turning Bragg out of Chattanooga, and the Battle of Chattanooga achieved the undoing of Chickamauga. Big advances, such as those resulting from the Fort Donelson, Peninsula, and Tullahoma campaigns, depended on maneuver rather than victory in battle. Sherman's campaign to take Atlanta illustrates this well because it involved only one minor offensive battle, and that a defeat.

The lack of major strategic significance for most of its battles does not distinguish the Civil War from most other wars. But the combination of its four-year duration and relatively high frequency of battles did set it apart from many others. These two attributes caused it to inflict comparatively heavy combat casualties on the belligerents. In this respect it had much in common with the two great European wars of the twentieth century.

What importance then has the aggregate of military activity, as reflected in the casualties? Did, for example, the South conduct too active a defense and lose more men than it could afford? A Confederate military strategy designed to minimize the military attrition of killed, wounded, and missing would have involved more retreats and fewer counteroffensives. If this strategy had advocates, they could have reasonably argued that the Union's cost in men of occupying conquered areas, of coping with guerrillas, and guarding against the raids of regular cavalry would have absorbed enough Union troops to offset the diminution of the Confederate forces through the loss of part of their country. They could also have pointed out that the fewer casualties occasioned by this strategy would also have helped to offset the effects of the loss of territory. Opponents could have argued that the loss of manufacturing and natural resources, of the working population that also supplied recruits, and the desertion of soldiers from occupied areas would have caused the retreats to weaken the Confederate armies more than the other factors diminished the main Union forces.

But, independent of the merits of retreat to economize on casualties, such a military strategy would have conflicted with the most promising political strategy. Yielding more of the Confederacy to invaders would have cost much political attrition in the South in the form of discouragement at home and increased desertion of disheartened troops. More importantly, it would have subverted the Confederacy's principal political strategy for victory: fighting so as to enable the northern advocates of peace to win the 1864 election. Of course, the effects of Union occupation on slavery would have entered into any serious discussion of this strategy.

Increasingly and more explicitly, the Confederacy came to base its strategy on northern peace partisans winning the 1864 elections. To do this the South had to look invincible by holding, and even regaining lost, territory. Giving up significant parts of the South would sustain the Union public's confidence in victory by providing constant increments of measurable progress toward the conquest of the Confederacy. Gains by Union armies would enable northern voters to see victory looming ahead and encourage them to vote to continue the war in 1864. Of course, the South's political strategy of protecting territory failed because, by October 1864, the Union had conquered enough of the Confederacy to persuade Union voters to carry on with the prosecution of the war. In fact, Northerners did not even have the choice of a peace candidate in the 1864 election. This profoundly discouraged Southerners, because so many had looked forward to victory coming as a result of a peace party winning the Union election.

As the trend in the strength of Confederate forces shows, the events of the fall of 1864 clearly brought the war to its political end. The last full count, as of December 31, 1864, showed 326,000 men available, 72 percent of the peak strength of April 1863. But the percent absent in 1863 amounted to 27 percent compared with 53 percent in 1864. Desertion had caused the greater attrition. And this process continued. Lee's army, for example, lost nearly 8 percent to desertion between February 15 and March 18, 1865. So, whether or not the Confederacy had enough men to continue a resistance, clearly soon it would not. After the fall of Atlanta, the reelection of Lincoln, Sherman's raid through Georgia, and Hood's debacle in Tennessee, more and more Confederates saw the price of independence as higher than they wanted to pay. It had already cost far more than they had expected in 1861, and no one could any longer see a point, as in 1864, when continued resistance might make the United States decide that saving the Union was costing it too much.

Other factors also had an influence on the many individual decisions to abandon the Confederacy. A significant number of Southerners, often those most confident at the outset of the war, had come to accept the impossibility of victory. The loss of battles and territory had destroyed their belief in victory, which they had originally derived from the conviction that the South enjoyed God's favor. Since defeats had persuaded them that God did not side with them, they felt the uselessness of continued resistance.

Others began to value the Confederacy less because, when its government planned to arm slaves, it took a step which implied emancipation. Since the preservation of slavery had precipitated secession and the creation of the Confederacy, it was for many the cornerstone of their nation. This tacit abandonment of slavery as a war aim so diminished the value they attached to the Confederacy that it made them less willing to pay any more for it.

Slavery had played a major role in southern nationalism because it had so much importance in distinguishing the Confederacy from the Union. Language, religion, and history, the usual roots and supports of nationalism, differed little between the sections. Slavery had provided the principal distinction between them, and many Southerners had proclaimed it as the foundation of their civilization. But, deprived of this support, southern nationalism still had to carry most of the burden of justifying a separate country.

Military victories and defeats had essentially similar effects on the northern and southern populations' perceptions of the likelihood of victory. But the war imposed greater burdens on Southerners, particularly the whites. Though ineffective in denying the South essential imports, the blockade, by disrupting the South's highly productive foreign trade, reduced its standard of living, already diminished by the costs of the war effort. Further, the free, decision-making population probably bore more than a proportional share of this decline in real income because a higher percentage of slaves were already very close to or at the subsistence level. This group of whites also had to endure the onerousness of all of the military service and casualties. That about 2.2 percent of the Confederacy's white population died as a result of the war while only .7 percent of the Union's inhabitants lost their lives gives one measure of the comparative cost of the war.

The unblockaded North had a smaller decrease in its standard of living, and virtually the whole male population shared the hardship of military service and casualties. Further, a greater rate of enlistment of recent immigrants and the recruitment of southern blacks to fill some state quotas slightly diminished the demand for military service by the northern decision-making group. Consequently the Southerners who could make the choice between war and peace had incurred a proportionately greater burden and expense for their war than had the similar group of Northerners. So, although the North might not have desired the restoration of the Union as much as the South wanted its independence, with a much lower cost in terms of casualties and reduced living standards, the North could be more willing than the South to pay the price of victory. However strong or weak Confederate nationalism may have been, it did not prove strong enough to motivate a continuation of resistance beyond the disappointment of the last four months of 1864.

To continue the economic analogy, Southerners could also look to the alternative to independence, Lincoln's plan of reconstruction. Lacking vindictiveness, Lincoln welcomed the seceding states back into the Union on the same basis, except for slavery, as before. With slavery apparently doomed in the Confederacy, emancipation became less of an obstacle to reconstruction. And, with the elimination of the operation of the three-fifths rule, the reunited southern states would have enhanced strength in the House of Representatives. So the cost of defeat to Southerners could seem quite modest if they could reconcile, as many did, the dissonance associated with losing the war.

Thus political factors, as in most wars, determined the outcome, but the symbolic effect of victories and defeats and the human and economic losses caused by the conflict had a more than usual part in shaping critical political attitudes. Thus, with some lacking enthusiasm for the altered war aim of independence without slavery and others feeling God was against their cause, Southerners had to make a choice between more war or a resumption of their old places as states in the Union. Under these circumstances, their Confederate nationalism proved an inadequate motivation for a continuation of the quest for independence. And so the war ended, its outcome the result of the interaction between the motives for victory and its actual and prospective human, economic, and psychological costs.

If the role of political factors in the war's outcome makes the Civil War similar to other wars, its tactics have a distinctive quality in modern time. Most of its combat took place on foot,

239

with riflemen fighting riflemen, and even the cavalry dismounting to fight unless engaging other cavalry still mounted. Though the troops had bayonets, an insignificant amount of hand-to-hand combat actually took place. So a single weapon system, the light infantryman, dominated the tactics of the war. This had always characterized the tactics of forested eastern North America, the Native Americans and then the colonists fighting almost exclusively as light infantry. But this differed from Europe, where cavalry had a major combat role. Yet, adventitiously, the Civil War forecast the era of the demise of the tactical role of cavalry, for, from the use of the breechloading rifle in the Franco-Prussian War of 1870–71 to the machine gun in World War I, enhanced infantry firepower largely confined the horsemen to their strategic mission of reconnaissance.

Thus began an era of European tactics largely devoid of cavalry, which reached its apex in the early years of the First World War on the western front and then began to recede, when rapidly improving aircraft began to fill the role of light cavalry and the newly developed tank came to assume the heavy cavalry's old tactical role. So Civil War tactics belong to a brief, distinctive period in the history of modern tactics in the Western World, while being a continuation of the tactical dominance of one weapon system which had long typified fighting in eastern North America.

The war's logistics marked the real debut of motorized logistics over land and of base-dependent armies, both of which have distinguished so much of twentieth-century warfare. The railroad provided the means to begin this change, while the low intensity of agricultural production created the need. Motorized logistics played a larger role in the Civil War than in the later Franco-Prussian War, because armies in North America had greater need to bring food and fodder from the rear to feed their armies. Due to the war's length and strategic complexity, troop movements by rail had an almost revolutionary importance, with a significance probably not exceeded in later wars.

In its operational strategy the war was modern in that it was thoroughly Napoleonic, a trait of most large-scale wars ever since. The ground operations of the Persian Gulf conflict of 1991 illustrate this. After distracting the Iraqi command by concentrating in the south and threatening an amphibious landing, the Coalition forces turned the Iraqi army by marching past its west flank. This movement has a tangible link to the past in that the U.S. Army's 1980s manual on operations refers to Grant's Vicksburg campaign as an example of the turning movement, one that General Halleck had compared with Napoleon's of Ulm, (see diagrams of Gulf Conflict turning movement, Vicksburg campaign, and Ulm campaign).

Yet the Civil War was old-fashioned in its use of raids, virtually the oldest strategy and the traditional means of political intimidation and, militarily, of coping with a very low ratio of force to space. Similarly, guerrilla warfare is a strategy which has endured since the earliest times. Thus one might best describe Civil War strategy as multifaceted.

Raids against communications had a long and significant history. In 1758, for example, the Austrians raided and destroyed a convoy of 4,000 wagons, thus raising the siege of Olmutz and defeating Frederick the Great's invasion of Moravia. Yet, in a sense, these traditional logistic raids were also modern in that both the Union and the Confederacy directed their raids at the new and very vulnerable railroad, the precursor of the new logistics.

Some commentators have characterized the Civil War as total and modern because of the use of conscription to sustain the armies, but this did not result in having much more than 3 percent of the population under arms, about the same proportion as in eighteenth-century Europe, which also used various forms of compulsory service. Since the productivity of the economy and the consequent number of people which it can support in war have much to do with the effectiveness of such mobilization efforts, the Civil War belligerents could not easily reach the 10 percent under arms typical of the twentieth century.

Some have also seen the war as modern because of a parallel between Union raids and strategic bombing, though the raiding strategy antedates by thousands of years its use against Frederick in the mid-eighteenth century. Others have viewed the war as total because of the involvement of civilians, comparing the Civil War in this respect with the Second World War, with its systematic bombing of civilians. Though, by early inaugurating guerrilla warfare, the South first involved civil-

241

ians, the exponents of this interpretation find a more contemporary parallel with the political intimidation objective of strategic bombing and the comparable effect of losses of civilian property, an objective which Sherman included for his raids. Yet this manner of making civilians an objective of military action is far older than the Civil War.

Sherman, a respecter of history and knowledgeable about the English wars to control Ireland, would have known that his raid was a humanitarian venture compared to Irish warfare, which traditionally depended on raids to cow opponents, burning barns and villages and taking cattle being routine military operations. The English, more thorough than the Irish, made starvation a method, defeating a rebellion in the south by starving thousands to death and then seeking to resettle the land with immigrants from England.

When Confederates complained that Sherman expelled the citizens from Atlanta so he could make it exclusively a Union supply depot, the general could well have contrasted his humanitarianism with Oliver Cromwell's treatment of the rebelling Irish town of Drogheda, which had put him to the trouble of besieging it. When it capitulated in 1649, he killed the entire population, women and children included, except 30 whom he sent to the West Indies as slaves. Compared to Sherman, Cromwell seems modern indeed, even to Drogheda's overtones of the neutron bomb which was to destroy people rather than property. That 41 years later in another Irish war Drogheda surrendered without resistance to King William III exhibits the enduring effectiveness of Cromwell's thoroughgoing policy of dismaying potential rebels.

To find a parallel for viewing Sherman as implementing a change from a policy of conciliation to intimidation, one might look back in English history to the resistance offered against William the Conqueror in spite of his initial policy of confirming in their rights and power most of the lords of the land. Facing continued hostility even after replacing those that had defied him with his own men, William marched north to the center of the English opposition and devastated the country so thoroughly that many died and for years afterwards it remained uninhabited wasteland. In this way William cowed the rebels and ended overt defiance of his rule. In spite of the malevolence and viciousness of some of its guerrilla warfare, the Civil War was hardly more a total war than many others in the past in which invaders encountered or provoked popular resistance.

Yet more often Sherman saw the political significance of his raids not so much in their power to daunt as in their having a psychological impact which would help cause the South to give up. He summed this up well when he wrote that "there are thousands of people abroad and in the South who will reason thus: If the North can march an army right through the South, it is proof positive that the North can prevail in this contest." So his raids certainly had two political effects, that of intimidating those still wishing to continue the war and that of a symbol of defeat. A South Carolinian exemplified success in obtaining the latter objective when she thus reacted to events in Georgia: "I feel very blue, sometimes utterly hopeless about C. S. A. The army has walked right through Georgia, destroying cities and laying waste the country." The symbolism probably has more to do with the dislike Southerners felt for Sherman for destroying property in raids rather than killing soldiers in battles.

Yet the North's military strategy had already gained enough ground to keep it firm for the war for the Union, a northern support for the war which totally discouraged those Southerners who believed that independence had already cost as much or more than it was worth. Lincoln's offer of reconstruction made giving up a less difficult decision for many. Military events had created the circumstances demanding for the Southerners' political decisions. The military road to these political destinations was not long and hard because armed mobs chasing each other made the war indecisive. On the contrary, the armies were not mere mobs, and the length of the war testified to the dedication of citizens who became competent soldiers and who were led by excellent political and military leaders.

If contemporaries had sought an historical parallel for aid in understanding the Civil War, they might well have turned to the sixteenth-century revolt of the Netherlands against Spain. They would have found readily available a scholarly and readable source in John Lothrop Motley's well-respected and widely known four-volume history, *The Rise of the Dutch Republic*, published just five years before the outbreak of the war. Readers would have immediately noted a contrast in dealing with a

243

rebellion. They would have learned that, when the Protestants in the North became dissatisfied with the rule of their lord, the Catholic king of Spain, he sent as governor the severe Duke of Alva to suppress dissent. His rigor inspired a full-scale revolt. When the duke resorted to even stronger measures of intimidation, such as killing all of the inhabitants of a captured town, it only intensified the resistance, which also spread to the largely Catholic South.

So, rather than cowing the rebels, Alva's policy seemed to stimulate their resistance, the siege of one city lasting seven months. Without large enough forces to suppress such committed opposition, the war dragged on through the rule of two more governors until, after six years of warfare, the Prince of Parma assumed the governorship. Though one of the ablest soldiers of the age, the prince soon had enough of facing the fortified defense in costly sieges which looked as if they would go on forever. The resourceful Parma not only changed his military strategy, but, convinced of the necessity of abating the enemy's tenacious hostility, the politically astute governor concluded "that clemency is the only remedy with these people, and that the harsh punishments of earlier times merely served to embitter and exasperate them." The readers would then have noted some interesting parallels between the Union strategy and Parma's political and military measures.

Concentrating in the Catholic South, he abandoned the combat strategy of sieges and adopted a logistic strategy of controlling the river Schelde, a vital commercial artery into which emptied several other rivers. By gradually gaining control of the river, its tributaries, and of the villages where roads met, he could interdict the trade and supplies of the major commercial and industrial cities, like Brussels and Ghent. These constituted the heart of the resistance. Just as Caesar preferred to win with hunger rather than steel, so Parma reduced the cities without ever directly blockading some of them, much less assailing their formidable defenses. So gradually he secured the submission of all of them. To cut off the last, the great port of Antwerp, he had to block the broad estuary of the Schelde by building and defending a fortified bridge over 2,000 feet long, half of it floating on 32 sizeable, cannon-armed boats. This was a far more difficult task than tying Sherman neckties.

Hand in hand with the military effect and political intimidation of his logistic strategy went a conciliatory inducement to yield. Parma offered the provinces and cities the restoration of their traditional privileges and autonomy and went as far as the king would allow when he guaranteed to the Protestant minority two years to convert or emigrate. This military and political combination gained a complete and comparatively bloodless victory in the South. Parma's success laid the foundation of the modern state of Belgium.

Clearly there is a close kinship between Grant and Parma's use of a logistic military strategy. Grant's raids and Parma's interdiction of the cities' food supplies had comparable political as well as military effects. And Lincoln's reconstruction plan, like Parma's, invited the states to return with the same status they had before the rebellion. Thus two rebellions ended in response to remarkably similar military and political strategies. The principal difference between the two is that Grant's raiding strategy did not begin soon enough to have the decisive effect of Parma's logistic military strategy of interdiction.

Surely Parma justly deserved his reputation as the ablest European general of his time. But it is not presumptuous to compare the work of Lincoln and Grant to his nor place the conduct of the Civil War in a class with some of the finest examples of the art of war in the past. Clearly the war produced many competent commanders who, showing a realistic grasp of tactics and managing their difficult logistical problems well, often displayed the versatility to wage their multifaceted war with much acumen. And, usually perceptively attuning their strategy to political objectives, they showed a sophisticated grasp of modern strategy. Displaying an ability to apply elements of older strategy, they gave an innovative primacy to the logistical raid so as to take advantage of the vulnerability of the new base-dependent, railroad supply system.

APPENDIX I

THE EUROPEAN ART OF WAR

---•◆•---

Fighting with armies based on European models, Civil War commanders drew their strategy from Europe's wars. In part they followed that model because they had European tactical systems and, initially, thought in terms of European logistical methods. Since strategy depends in part on tactical capabilities and logistical possibilities, an understanding of tactics and logistics is essential for understanding strategy. The tactics and logistics of 1861 resulted from a century and a half of European development.

1. TACTICS

Early in the eighteenth century, European armies ceased equipping some of their infantry with a musket and others with a long spear called a pike and substituted an improved musket with a bayonet. This change increased firepower, and generals made the most of it by deploying their soldiers shoulder-to-shoulder in line, even clothing them in tight-fitting uniforms and hats without brims in order to facilitate close formations which had the greatest number of muskets per yard of front. They also used three ranks to fire simultaneously, one behind the other. Two worked well, with the front kneeling and the second standing, but three never gave full satisfaction. If the men of the second rank stooped to fire so that those in the third could fire over their heads, the men in the second suffered broken collarbones from the angle at which the kick of their powerful weapons struck their shoulders; and, if, instead, the third rank stepped sidewise and fired between the men of an erect second, those in the second often endured wounds in the hand they extended to hold their muskets. By the nineteenth century commanders had given up trying to have three rows fire simultaneously, adopting at last a two-rank formation, the red-coated British remembering this as the thin, red line.

But such a linear formation, usually in two separate lines three deep, proved very complicated to maneuver. Inequalities in the ground, fences, trees, copses, farm buildings, and other obstacles made them difficult to form as well as to move. Keeping each battalion of 500 or 600 men aligned and facing in the direction of the prospective advance had particular importance. Any overlap or an oblique advance could result in one battalion's firing into one of its neighbors. Such mistakes were particularly likely when the black powder smoke from a few volleys had obscured much of the battlefield. An arrayed army could march forward to attack its enemy only very slowly, often at about 75 paces per minute, well below the average 120 paces for a moderately brisk walk. But, even so, it had to make frequent halts to maintain alignment and close up gaps in the line.

This system of formation and movement made battle virtually impossible unless both sides wanted it. While an attacker arrayed his forces and then advanced to come within musket range, a reluctant adversary could form march columns and leave the field. So battles by mutual consent usually involved frontal attacks and could become very bloody when two battle lines faced each other. At the Battle of Blenheim in 1704, 2,400 attacking British troops, though suffering 800 casualties from the first French volley, continued their assault. The attacker sought to alternate firing and advancing until, as often happened, his men would advance no further and, instead of firing volleys on command, began individual fire. To reload their muzzle-loaders, the men used a ramrod to push powder, ball, and a wad to hold them into the barrel. They needed to stand in order to accomplish reloading and also to use their bayonets to resist cavalry which might attack suddenly out of the smoke of the battlefield. With men firing at each other as rapidly as possible, often at a distance of as little as 40 yards, casualties of a day's battle might reach a third of an army or even more.

Although both sides had bayonets fixed to their muskets, soldiers rarely engaged in hand-to-hand combat on the battle-field. But when a force had the discipline or morale to follow up firing by lowering its muskets and marching, or even running, toward its adversaries, they could often compel their antago-nists to break formation and flee, having experienced little or no physical contact.

Armies often augmented the advantage of the tactical defen-sive by building or improvising fortifications in the field. A less astute antagonist once complained that the Swedish King Gustavus Adolphus fought "like a mole fights underground," because he protected "himself with trenches and bastions." Defenders always sought a natural advantage, even if it were only the top of a gentle slope. When they lacked time to pre-pare bastions or trenches, they valued ditches or other cover and sought to extend or improve them. At the Battle of Lutzen in 1632, the famous general Wallenstein availed himself of a ditch crossing the front of his position. He had a rank of men with guns stand in it, protecting their legs and most of their torsos. He then improved on this position by digging a small trench behind the ditch and piling the dirt from it in its front. The shallow trench and the low parapet made of the earth from the trench made a covered position for another row of men able to fire over the heads of those in front standing in the ditch. This tactical ingenuity demonstrates what men could do in an hour or two as late as the morning of a battle.

When building field fortifications, soldiers usually dug a ditch and piled the earth behind until they had erected a breast-work to protect themselves. The ditch in front and the earth-work behind made a sloping wall which would present a serious obstacle to infantry that reached it. If they had time, the defenders would put sharpened stakes in the ditch or, as a quick expedient, construct an abatis made of fallen trees with the sharpened ends of their branches pointing toward the en-emy. An abatis not only forced the attackers to break ranks to go through it but also delayed them while keeping them under the defender's fire. More elaborate field fortifications had bastions, small forts projecting from the line of earthworks from which defenders could fire at the flank of the attackers. Bastions also made excellent locations for cannon. All these earthworks furnished fine protection against artillery fire because they absorbed the cannon balls and suffered little damage.

But the big guns could do tremendous damage to unfortified infantry in line at a distance of a half mile or even more. The successful technique required firing so the ball would pass through the line obliquely, thus knocking down men from more than one file. Experienced gunners knew that they had the best chance of hitting the lines of men by aiming so as to have the ball bounce along the ground as a flat rock skips on water, thus virtually assuring that the ball would not pass over the heads of the men. The smoothbore, muzzle-loading cannon used on the battlefield fired balls weighing from four to twelve pounds. All guns also fired loads of small shot, called grape and cannister, loaded and fired in a rack or container to keep them from scattering until they were near the enemy. Used at a range of a few hundred yards, cannon firing this small shot provided a devastating supplement to the infantry's firepower. Only with great reluctance did generals attack soldiers in field fortifications strengthened by artillery. In fact, commanders had such confidence in the fortified defense that they routinely entrenched themselves in positions with a river at their back. Instead of fearing capture if defeated they chose these secure positions because the river provided ample water and protected the flanks of the position.

Cavalry remained armed with pistol and saber, and some with short muskets, and had its greatest effectiveness when it could ride into a group of infantry and use its sabers from the riders' advantageous position on horseback. But the cavalry could rarely break through a line of men who were ready for it. The musket volleys frightened the horses and knocked down men and beasts; mounted men could not ride through three ranks of infantry because the horses always swerved, refusing to impale themselves on the bayonets. When menaced by horsemen, the infantry preferred to form into a hollow square to provide all-around defense against fast-moving horses that could surround them. But, since they could not use this in line of battle, cavalry had an opportunity to strike the flank or rear of the infantry. Flank attacks, together with assailing unready or disordered foot soldiers, gave cavalry its best opportunity for making an important tactical contribution in a battle.

Although the drama of big battles ensured that they received the attention of contemporaries and historians, sieges of cities were the most costly and usually the predominant form of large-scale combat. Yet smaller operations constituted the typical form of warfare. These involved ambushes, raids, either mounted or on foot, and attack and defense of supply convoys, small forts, villages, and manor houses. Naturally these actions rarely adhered to the tactical model of maximum firepower by linearly deployed troops used by armies in open fields. Some of the fighting which took place off the large battlefield involved skirmishing, a kind of combat in which men often fought as individuals rather than in a group. This suited raids and combat in villages and stressed an advantageous individual position rather than a formation for a maximum rate of fire.

Skirmishing also proved effective on the battlefield against the formed infantry. The skirmishers typically positioned themselves in front of the lines, taking advantage of ditches, trees, shrubs, buildings, fences, and every sort of cover and concealment offered by the terrain. From these positions they fired on their opponents and, if they could get within range of troops in line, inflicted enough casualties to affect their morale. Their covered positions made them almost invulnerable to the volleys of the line infantry. If charged by the line, skirmishers could escape by running. Vulnerable to cavalry because they lacked a defensive formation, they could usually save themselves by taking refuge in buildings, thickets, and other places a horse could not go.

During the eighteenth century the tactics of the new armies received attention from many thinkers. The French, whose army had suffered the indignity of no longer exhibiting a clear superiority over its opponents, gave much thought to tactics, especially the use of columns for attack. They developed one which was wider than it was long, a battalion having 50 men across and 12 ranks deep. This compact group of men could march rapidly over a battlefield while maintaining its simple, dense formation. With a width of less than 100 feet, it could

251

readily march around most obstacles. In facing a battalion in line of three ranks, it had markedly inferior firepower. Nor could it readily use its superior depth to overwhelm a line of musketeers, because the men in the rear added nothing to the courage of the men in front who had to advance against the daunting volleys of far more muskets.

The French remedied this deficiency in firepower by devising a drill which enabled a battalion to deploy quickly from this broad column into a line of three ranks, ready for firing. When the wars of the French Revolution and Napoleon began in 1792, the French Army had a new manual which taught this system. The drill had the additional advantage of being easier to learn than mastering marching forward in two three-rank lines, as much as a mile wide. The French had the advantage of being able to go quickly into a column from march formation and promptly advance to the attack, fighting in column or line as circumstances indicated. This gave their armies a tremendous edge over their enemies who stayed with the purely linear system. Further, the French generals could deploy some columns into line while holding reserves in column, ready to move quickly to reinforce an attack or concentrate against a weak point. And such tactical mobility and the ability to march rapidly near the enemy and go immediately into an assault permitted the French to attack their opponents' vulnerable flanks and rear. Further this new tactical facility not only gave infantry the opportunity to make flank attacks, but also made it more difficult for a reluctant enemy to avoid battle.

France's adversaries soon copied this tactical system, and it became the standard for European armies. With all armies using the new tactics, none had any advantage over the other. Defensive reserves held in column countered those committed in an assault, and defensive mobility in columns thwarted columns which threatened a defender's flank or rear. Thus the tactical defensive fully recovered its traditional and decided ascendency.

After the close of the Napoleonic Wars in 1815, European armies institutionalized the tactical changes of these wars. The doctrine for the offensive gave more emphasis to the role of skirmishers, sending many forward while holding the main body in column formations. These the attacker would commit after the skirmishers had clarified the enemy's position and unsettled its line troops by their fire. Many armies gave less attention to field fortifications than in the past; this reflected the devaluation of the entrenched defense by the French infantry's capability of outflanking a position and the greater efficacy given the counterattack by improved tactical mobility. The frequent changes of position in the course of the rapid strategic movements characteristic of Napoleonic warfare also discouraged great reliance on field fortifications.

But the wars which had transformed infantry's tactical potential had affected the tactics of cavalry hardly at all. Still armed with the saber and pistol, the horsemen had little chance of success in a frontal attack against a line of infantry or against foot soldiers formed in a hollow square for defense against cavalry. But, if they could assail a line of infantry on its flank or in its rear, mounted men could inflict severe casualties and total demoralization by attacking the disorganized infantrymen with their sabers. But the new column formations, which could face men in all four directions and make an organized use of their muskets and bayonets, were not nearly so exposed. Relying less on vulnerable lines, the foot soldiers' enhanced mobility and articulation made them better able to resist their mounted foe. Thus cavalry lost some more of its tactical value, and armies retained fewer horsemen than before the French Revolution.

Thanks to French improvements in the gun carriage and their success in making the guns themselves lighter, artillery emerged from the wars of the French Revolution and Napoleon with enhanced capabilities. The field artillery's smoothbore, muzzle-loading guns had changed little, but their lighter weight permitted more powerful and more mobile guns. Infantry remained in danger, but, if they stayed well to the rear and safe from cavalry attack, soldiers could protect themselves by lying prone. The firing of balls at erect infantry benefitted both attack and defense but aided the defense more if only because the attackers would be nearer to the inaccurate cannon; and at close range the guns could use the far more effective grape and cannister shot. Yet, the offense had possibly gained from the lightening of the guns, because the more mobile artillery could follow an attack and support it by placing its guns 300 to 400 yards from the defending infantry. At that range the infantryman's musket had little chance of hitting the cannoneers, while the defenders had to remain erect ready to load and fire rapidly and resist attack by either infantry or cavalry. But, though this use of artillery to enhance the power of the offense became established French artillery doctrine, it had not had many successes during the Napoleonic Wars and its effectiveness remained unproven.

2. LOGISTICS

When campaigning in wealthy and thickly populated Belgium, western and southern Germany, and northern Italy, eighteenth-century armies could often move on adequate and improving roads and find enough food for their men and forage for their horses. Usually they filled their needs by purchase, the armies' quartermasters then issuing food to the men and providing for the cavalry's horses and draft animals. In enemy territory and sometimes in a neutral country, the armies levied contributions on the local authorities, and these requisitions provided the money to buy local supplies. Sometimes the contribution payment came in the form of hay and oats for the horses and flour for the men's bread.

In previous centuries soldiers had often taken what they wanted directly from the local population without the formality of levying a contribution. This practice wasted supplies, not just from lack of system in issuing and storage but because soldiers often wantonly destroyed much. Moreover, it almost always aroused the hostility of the rural people who frequently resisted by hiding animals, food, and fodder stocks and so diminishing the resources available. Violence was another common result as rural people ambushed and killed, sometimes by torture, individuals and small groups of soldiers. This method not only created additional adversaries for the invaders, but also earned the political hostility of the gentry whose tenants and estates sustained damage.

During the wars of the French Revolution and Napoleon, the poorly disciplined and often unpaid French troops frequently restored to these older methods of procuring supplies. They hurt their cause severely by exciting serious political antipathy and arousing or exacerbating popular resistance, particularly in Spain and Russia. Early in the wars of the French Revolution a

French general assessed the liabilities of the French system of supply when the commented: "I fear the dreadful consequences of a retreat in a country where we have raised the inhabitants against us by pillage and indiscipline." On the other hand, the well-financed British armies always paid for their supplies, promptly and in coin, and then enjoyed the benefits of popular good will, unmolested lines of communication in their rear, and not only ample food and fodder but also the use of wagons, animals, and laborers.

By the time the French supplied themselves in this old-fashioned manner, nations had begun to follow a set of rules which became a part of settled European custom. These merely codified what the military and political leaders had found to be best for them, providing that soldiers would respect private property and, if they took any, would pay for it. European law and usage regarded the lives of civilians as sacrosanct as their possessions. Of course these rules assumed that the civilians in the invaded country would reciprocate by acting as disinterested bystanders, carrying on business as usual with the enemy as well as with friendly troops. If civilians offered resistance, their property and lives ceased to enjoy protection, the invader responding to provocation just as had civilians to the old method of supply.

Some critics have seen this exemption of civilians from all of the rigors of war, at their option, as an effete sort of war and urged that they should be treated as active enemies and their substance liable to destruction or appropriation as spoils of war. The critics' willingness to add the civilians to the numbers of the invaders' active adversaries seems to have its foundation in the expectation that an army could readily cow them into submission. But experience in earlier wars had shown that civilians were not easily cowed, while conciliation could turn civilians into willing participants in an efficient means of supplying the invader's army.

3. NAPOLEONIC STRATEGY

The armies of the French Revolution and Napoleon had a new organization which gave them a facility for maneuver denied traditional armies. Instead of infantry battalions and cavalry squadrons usually aggregated in essentially ad hoc, temporary organizations, the French permanently grouped their infantry battalions in demi brigades and these in brigades which became part of divisions. In addition to infantry, the divisions had their own artillery and cavalry and constituted the parts of an army or its subdivision, the corps. Having an army composed of divisions with their balance of all arms and their ability to maneuver, reconnoiter, and fight independently, a general could safely disperse his army but still control it. This permitted a wide dissemination to cover a broad front and to march rapidly by using many roads. But this distribution could be only a prelude to a concentration at a predetermined point or one indicated by the enemy's movements or the events of the campaign.

With enhanced ability to maneuver, generals needed to understand how to use this new mobility. The word maneuver conveys nothing about what an army should do in order to take advantage of movement to gain an ascendancy over the enemy. Events in the past provided illustrations of concepts which gave substance to the word. The model for one basic maneuver came from the campaigns of the eighteenth-century Prussian king Frederick the Great, and from the French soldier and emperor Napoleon. In 1861 the Napoleonic wars were no more remote in time than World War II is for people living in the late twentieth century, and they had exerted just as much fascination. The rapid and decisive action of Napoleon's campaigns justly served as exemplars for Civil War strategy. Early in the nineteenth century they had found an explicator of their strategic lessons in a veteran of those wars, General Baron Antoine-Henri de Jomini.

Writing many volumes of military history, Jomini became the most prominent interpreter of Napoleon and did much to give definition to the military art. His last work, *Summary of the Art of War*, contained no history beyond references to campaigns, only the conclusions from his study of warfare. His main interest lay in strategy; in this book he had striven to find the essence of Napoleon's strategic method. He summarized much of it in one of the maxims he listed under the heading "fundamental principle of war," enjoining generals "to throw by strategic movements the mass of an army successively upon the decisive points of a theater of war, and also upon the communications of the enemy as much as possible without compromising one's own."

Jomini immediately admitted "that it is easy to recommend throwing the mass of the forces upon the decisive points, but that the difficulty lies in recognizing those points." Mostly defining decisive points by implication, he prescribed "maneuver to engage fractions of the hostile army with the bulk of one's forces." He explained that making use of interior lines of operation offered the readiest means of bringing superior numbers against inferior. A line of operation, which need not coincide with a line of communication, consisted of nothing more than an army's line, or axis, of advance and retreat. Exploiting interior lines of operation for concentrating against an adversary simply meant being between separated hostile forces so as to be able to concentrate, "successively," upon first one and then the other. First noticed in the campaigns of Frederick the Great, exploitation of interior lines characterized Napoleon's early operations and exemplified their value for engaging fractions of the hostile army with the bulk of one's forces.

Although Jomini's works long remained available only in French and his *Summary* required much knowledge of military history to understand, Napoleon's campaigns could teach an interested reader the lesson of lines of operation without having a teacher. To his first command the 26-year-old Napoleon brought little experience, but he did have a mastery of the advanced French military thought of his day as well as a genius for warfare. He entered Italy on his first campaign and immediately made an offensive use of interior lines when he deliberately marched his army between those of his allied adversaries, the seasoned generals Beaulieu and Colli. His offensive giving him the initiative, he used part of his force to distract Beaulieu. Thus obtaining surprise, he could concentrate first against the Austrian Beaulieu and drive him back. Then turning against Colli, he pushed him so far and fast that his master, the King of Sardinia, made peace with France (see diagram of Napoleon dividing Colli and Beaulieu).

Three months later Napoleon found himself on the defensive as he protected his siege of the town of Mantua. He did this by spreading his army to cover all routes of Austrian advance to relieve the city. But, in so posting his forces, he did not employ the long-used system of parceling out his army in a cordon, or series of strong positions dedicated to defending particular points of ingress. Instead, he stood ready to concentrate against any threat coming from any direction, enabling him to give a demonstration of the defensive use of interior lines. When the Austrians did come in two main forces, Napoleon took advantage of his interior lines to concentrate first against Quasdonovich and, after driving him back, against Wurmser, defeating and pushing him northward also. Through treating his dispersed force as a unit and concentrating it quickly and aggressively, Napoleon gained surprise and seized the initiative. His rapid marching on interior lines had made his force, though no larger than the enemy's, superior on two successive battlefields (see diagram of Defense of Mantua siege 1, 2, and 3).

Jomini identified the strategic turning movement as the other salient feature of Napoleonic strategy. An analogy with the familiar tactical maneuver, the turning movement, helped Civil War soldiers overcome Jomini's obscure explanation and understand its strategic version. A few of Napoleon's most decisive campaigns brilliantly exemplified the strategic turning movement. In his first campaign, just after his defeat of Colli by the offensive use of interior lines, Napoleon sought to turn his remaining opponent, the Austrian Beaulieu. Finding him in a defensive position along the Ticino River, the French ostentatiously concentrated many of their troops north of the Po and along the Ticino to confuse and distract the attention of their careful opponent. Meanwhile, Napoleon attempted his turning movement when he sent a detachment on a rapid march south of the Po and across it at Piacenza in his enemy's rear. Having surprised Beaulieu sufficiently to reach his rear but not enough to trap him, the French could use the initiative conferred by the threat to the Austrian rear to force Beaulieu's rapid retreat eastward (see diagram of Napoleon turning Beaulieu).

In order to make a complete turning movement, a general had to bring the major part of his army upon his enemy's communications. He had to march around the hostile army to take up a defensive position blocking its communications with its base area. Success required surprise to keep the adversary from acting to thwart the movement. Moreover, the turning force had to have access to a base area of its own in order to supply itself in the blocking position. Napoleon carried out his first such maneuver in 1800 when he sent a small force from France through Mont Cenis pass into Italy in his adversary's front, thus distracting the Austrian commander by directing his attention to Mont Cenis. In the meantime he seized the initiative and brought his main forces over Alpine passes that led into his surprised adversary's rear. He then captured Milan and acquired in the surrounding territory a base area capable of supplying his army in its remarkably favorable position (see diagram of Marengo campaign 1).

Napoleon had succeeded in operating, in Jomini's words, "upon the communications of the enemy" and, by securing the Milan base area, not "compromising" his own. He had marched into the rear of the unsuspecting Austrian adversary, leaving him isolated between a French army on the east and France on the west. To regain contact with Austria and protect the Austrian holdings in northeastern Italy, General Melas, the experienced and competent Austrian commander, had to march east, avoiding Napoleon's army if he could. If he failed, he would have to attack it to drive it from his path. Thus, in any battle, the French would have the advantage of the tactical defensive, a major benefit conferred by having carried out a strategic turning movement. Napoleon dispersed so as to block each possible route of Austrian advance, but, having no intention of allowing Melas to bring the bulk of his army against one of these detachments, he planned a rapid concentration of his scattered troops in time to have his full force at hand to fight the Austrians when they had revealed the direction of their advance. But Napoleon had so widely dispersed his army as almost to have adopted a cordon. When Melas took the initiative and moved suddenly and rapidly, the surprised Napoleon could not concentrate all his men and came very near to losing the defensive Battle of Marengo. But he won, and the victory enabled him to block Melas's route east and led to an agreement in which the Austrians evacuated, leaving northern Italy to the French (see diagram of Marengo campaign 2).

Even if Melas had eluded Napoleon, the campaign would still have given the French the Austrian territory of the Duchy of Milan and much else of value in northern Italy. Thus even when a turning movement failed, as in the case of Napoleon's

259

against Beaulieu, it still attained an often important success of compelling the enemy to retreat.

Five years later, in a more decisive campaign, Napoleon advanced from the Rhine into south Germany with a huge army on a front of 150 miles. Leaving his cavalry to distract the Austrians by riding directly toward their army at Ulm, Napoleon made another strategic turning movement which brought his whole force into the rear of the surprised and outnumbered Austrian commander; he capitulated before the French could encounter difficulty in supplying their army in territory already scoured by the Austrians (see diagram of Ulm campaign).

4. A COMPARISON OF SOME ASPECTS OF THE WARS OF THE FRENCH REVOLUTION AND NAPOLEON WITH THE CIVIL WAR

The degree to which the Civil War shared the factors that made the wars of the French Revolution and Napoleon so decisive provides a basis for assessing the quality of the military performance of America's combatants. A comparison also sheds light on what chance the South had of winning by pitting the greater strength of the strategic defensive against the North's larger forces. The rapidity and decisiveness of most of the wars of the French Revolution and Napoleon impressed contemporaries and have remained an ideal in warfare ever since. Instead of the usual protracted maneuvers and frequent sieges, a lightning speed seemed to have taken over campaigning and wars. Many factors explain the short wars.

These short wars often involved campaigning in and the annexation of small areas, such as the Netherlands, which fell in one campaign. Small size gave the French two advantages: It gave their adversaries little room for deep retreats, and it made complete occupation fairly easy for the huge French armies. But during the Civil War, except in the constricted, Netherlands-size Virginia theater, the Confederate armies usually had ample space in which to avoid their adversary, and the Confederacy's immense size precluded complete occupation.

At first the French had a virtual monopoly on the new column-based infantry tactics and the divisional organization and a greater proficiency in their use. This meant that the

French armies in part owed their victories to a military superiority based on the possession of tactical and strategic methods which their adversaries could not immediately adopt. The Union had no such advantage because its army and the Confederates' were as identical as any two antagonists could be.

The French also had help in overcoming the traditional European military deadlock from the active political support from some of the inhabitants in the enemy countries, support given because of their sympathy with the invaders' revolutionary ideals. This proved crucial in the conquest of the traditionally impregnable country of the Netherlands. Yankees would find sympathy and assistance in only a few places in the South and an active hostility and a guerrilla resistance in most. In this respect the Union effort to conquer the Confederacy invites comparison with the conspicuous French failure to subdue Spain. A guerrilla resistance supported by national and religious antipathy to the foreigners gave the French only nominal control of much of the country and resulted in a continuous struggle against increasingly adept Spanish irregulars.

An entirely different political factor also contributed to French victories. By seeking only very limited political objectives, such as the cession of a province from Austria, its principal continental opponent, France could turn a successful campaign into a quick peace. But the North's unlimited objective, the extinction of the Confederate States of America, eliminated that route to a short war. Consequently, the Union could not rely on any of those factors which had so significantly contributed to French success a half century before. If, for example, the Civil War had been about whether Kentucky and Missouri would be Union or Confederate, it would probably have ended after the Battle of Shiloh. Thus the Confederacy, a huge country, largely united against its adversary, and using an identical military system, should expect to make a long and determined resistance against the Union, which pursued the ambitious political objective of destroying it.

THE DEVELOPMENT OF THE UNITED STATES ARMY

1. THE ARMY'S ORIGINS

The U.S. Army had developed and practiced the methods used in the Civil War. This regular army grew out of the colonial and national military experience and the development of tactics in Europe, which Americans followed and emulated. The Mexican War of 1846–48 contributed much to the new professional United States military machine by giving it its first test in large-scale military operations against an opponent also using modern European methods. From this background came U. S. Grant, R. E. Lee, and many of the other leaders who dominated command and formulated strategy.

In their wars to conquer land from the Native Americans, the English had depended almost exclusively on a militia. In the early stages of the establishment of the settlements in Virginia and New England, most colonists had guns, and virtually all served in the militia, which drilled and conducted target practice as often as one day a month. Because the wooded terrain severely limited the effectiveness of cavalry, infantry dominated among these units, in spite of the colonists' initial monopoly of horses. As the military frontiers advanced, militia service ceased to be universal, instead becoming volunteer groups which often acquired some of the character of clubs or fraternal organizations and provided a vehicle for political activity. Most units never experienced combat and had only the most elementary military instruction.

Although the United States continued to place primary reliance on the militia, it also established a regular army. Really a miniature force when compared with the extent, population, and wealth of the country, it nevertheless served as a nucleus for some of the expeditions against Native Americans. In the War of 1812 with Great Britain the army grew to almost 40,000 men, but promptly shrank until, by the 1820s, Congress had reduced it to a little over 6,000 men. Thus a country of over 10 million people had an army smaller than the police forces of large urban areas today. In reality Congress relied for defense not primarily on this little army or the essentially untrained militia but on the security provided by the absence of powerful hostile neighbors and the vast extent of the country.

The three decades of peace between the War of 1812 and the Mexican War provided the opportunity for this tiny army to convert itself into a competent professional force on the European model. Under the intelligent leadership and support of Secretary of War John C. Calhoun, the army acquired the institutions which would carry it through the nineteenth century. The army gained a staff, including engineer, ordnance, quartermaster, and commissary staffs. These provided their essential services to the line troops, the infantry, cavalry, and artillery. Remaining firmly subordinate to civilian control in fact as well as law, the army did acquire a general in chief. The position carried only vague powers but contributed to the unity of a far-flung force.

The army naturally modeled itself on that of France, our Revolutionary War ally whose tradition of primacy in military science the era of Napoleon had again confirmed. Virtually everything followed the French model, including the style of uniforms, the manuals for drill, and the combat doctrine. The army even followed the French in having an additional engineer corps, the topographical engineers, founded by Napoleon for mapmaking and reconnaissance. In the decades before the Civil War, the U.S. Army's infantry drilled with a version of the French manual, learning to maneuver in column and to form a line from a column.

The role of cavalry in the U.S. Army was the principal exception to this faithfulness in following France. Even after the settlers had built roads and cleared land, too much forested land remained for cavalry to have much tactical value. This meant that cavalry had its principal utility for reconnaissance and rapid strategic movement by road. The added expense of mounted forces further retarded the development of cavalry in the regular army. The units created consisted of dragoons, cavalry also able to fight on foot, and mounted infantry. When the frontier reached the plains, excellent horse country inhabited by Native Americans who were superb light cavalry, the army accelerated the development of cavalry. But this still left the mounted forces without any tradition comparable to that of the European heavy cavalry, which specialized in fighting mounted in battle and used sabers to attack foot formations in flank or to charge and overwhelm weakened or disordered infantry in front.

With artillery also properly equipped and drilled in the French way, all branches of the line had developed a high level of competence by the 1840s. The country's minute army had attained a quality comparable to its French model. The army could not readily import competent leaders, but the nation had taken a significant step in supplying these. President Thomas Jefferson provided the impetus for the creation of the United States Military Academy at West Point in 1802. This measure would work slowly but decisively in raising the quality of the army. In making this initiative, the president had in mind furnishing the country with engineers, and the academy based its curriculum on civil engineering, which also embodied military engineering.

Jefferson wished to use the academy to broaden access to officer ranks and end what he regarded as their domination by Federalists, the opposition party which he hated so cordially. To accomplish these purposes he allocated appointments to the academy to members of Congress, thus fostering geographical and political diversity and assuring more equality of opportunity than generally found in Europe, where aristocratic lineage usually gave immense advantages in obtaining commissions and promotions. A long time passed before most congressmen took seriously their opportunity to nominate cadets; some made appointments quite frivolously, as illustrated by the story from the 1850s of a youth who courted a young lady whose father had strong Republican convictions. The father, knowing the lad belonged to the Democratic party, successfully used his political influence to secure him an appointment to the academy at West Point, thus sending him far away from his daughter. Though casualness on the part of many congressmen hardly thwarted Jefferson's purposes, it did contribute to many academic failures.

The academy itself had gotten off to a poor start, with lax standards for behavior, curriculum, and academic attainment, and much favoritism shown by the least suitable of the superintendents. At one time cadets in attendance ranged in age from 41 down to 11, and West Point had physical standards defective enough to admit a cadet with one arm.

But in 1817 Major Sylvanus Thayer took command and introduced academic and behavioral rigor. After the cadets' initial dismay at this new regime, they came to respect Thayer and gain the fine esprit which has characterized the institution ever since. The curriculum, modeled on the French military engineering school, the École Polytechnique, consisted of four years, stressing mathematics and physics as preparation for the senior year's work in civil and military engineering. All studied French, needed to read many of the textbooks. The academy steadily improved by adding to the library, sending faculty abroad to study, and translating the French texts into English. The best graduates chose service in the corps of engineers and many of those who left the army worked in that profession. At a time when preparation for law normally depended on "reading" for a year or two under the supervision of a practitioner and medical education consisted of a one- or two-year course of lectures, open to secondary school graduates, the engineer-soldier had a far superior professional education.

West Point also provided a source of doctrine, informal but persuasive, which addressed fundamental tactical questions. Dennis Hart Mahan, professor of engineering and military art, was the source of the ideas that influenced students who graduated after he began teaching in 1830. A graduate of the academy who had learned much in four years of study in France, Mahan used his senior engineering course to teach students the superiority of the tactical defense over the offense and the importance of enhancing the power of the defense with field and permanent fortifications.

This view not only harmonized with the engineering education the cadets received, but their professor related it to their own circumstances. He stressed that, though regular troops might succeed in an assault on field fortifications, volunteers would inevitably fail. Since, in time of war, the graduates could expect to lead volunteers, this had great relevance, as did Mahan's point that they could expect volunteers to perform well on the defensive behind field fortifications. Many Civil War soldiers as old as their late 40s had exposure to Professor Mahan's congenial doctrine of the value of field fortifications, one so persuasive that he taught them to dig in even when they expected to take the offensive immediately. Some graduates received another dose of Mahan when they served on the faculty and engaged in an informal postgraduate course. Those who participated in the academy's Napoleon Club, presided over by Professor Mahan, prepared substantial papers, which they presented at meetings and which provided the basis for discussion.

2. THE MEXICAN WAR

The new army had an opportunity to show what it could do in the war waged from 1846 to 1848 to wrest from Mexico her northern provinces. The soldiers for the war came from adding enough privates to the 8,600 men of the regular army to double it in size, the units being enough under strength to absorb these new men and teach them soldiering quickly and well. Yet to fight well-armed Mexico and try to conquer so much territory required far more men than the augmented regulars. The government called for volunteers and received units from the states, and thus fought the war with a mixture of amateurs and professionals. The generals ranged from a regular who had served with distinction in the War of 1812 to one, Major General Gideon J. Pillow, who had as his principal qualification his earlier law partnership with the president. The regulars performed well, as did the volunteers when seasoned, and the mixture of professional and amateur generals did surprisingly well.

The West Point graduates were too young to have high commands, but many gained combat experience and others had the opportunity to give notable performances as informal members of the staff of General Winfield Scott. He was the general in chief of the army who had personal command of the expedition which advanced from the coast into the interior to capture Mexico's capital. Having begun his military service as a captain of artillery in 1808, he suffered two wounds in the War of 1812 and reached the rank of brigadier general before the age of 30. Having read widely in military works, tactics as well as history, Scott exercised a strong influence on subordinates, one reinforced by his imposing dimensions, six feet five inches tall and robust as well as portly. He could hardly have offered a greater contrast to Major General Zachary Taylor, the commander of the forces on the border along the Rio Grande River, who had led his men in four victorious battles. Unlike Scott, who had a taste for showy uniforms and had earned the nickname "Old Fuss and Feathers," Taylor usually wore civilian clothes and disdained formality. "Old Rough and Ready" Taylor also differed from Scott in his simple and unintellectual approach to war. He viewed it as little more than marching and fighting, unanimated by any reference to principles or the examples of the great captains of the past. But Taylor was an unequaled leader who commanded the respect and loyalty of his troops.

Thus the army, and the many volunteers who served during the war in ranks from private to major general, had two commanders worthy of emulation, each in his own way. The operations of the Mexican War also offered future Civil War commanders the experience of a variety of terrain, long marches, defensive and offensive battles, attacks on fortifications, and good practice in logistics, strategy, and tactics with smoothbore muskets.

The battles of the Mexican War provided some tactical lessons for Professor Mahan's graduates who participated. In the first of the battles near the Texas-Mexican border, under Taylor's command, the unentrenched Americans repulsed two Mexican cavalry charges and one by infantry, the United States' artillery showing its worth on the defense. In the next engagement the Mexicans fell back when assailed in the front and flank. Following this, Taylor again took the offensive, attacking the fortified city of Monterey on the north while part of his army marched around to cut the city's supply line and attack from the south. Although the assaults north of the city attained only limited success and the troops suffered heavy losses, they distracted the enemy and so helped the force Taylor had sent around to the southwest of Monterey have enough success to cause the Mexicans to give up the city (see diagram of Battle of Monterey). In Taylor's last battle, at Buena Vista, the much-outnumbered Americans repelled Mexican attacks, again saw the effectiveness of their artillery on the defense, and observed another failure of a charge by the excellent Mexican cavalry. Fortifications had played no part in these combats, except at Monterey.

These operations had witnessed some hard fighting but no operational virtuosity on either side. But, when the navy landed General Scott's force at Vera Cruz, the best American general began a drive for the Mexican capital against the experienced General Santa Anna. The first battle between these two came when the Americans found their advance blocked by a partially fortified Mexican position in rugged terrain at Cerro Gordo. Reconnaissance by young West Point engineers led to the discovery of a route by which Scott could go around, or turn, the Mexican position. Instructed to march until it was behind the enemy, the turning force, in diverting some of its strength to attack the Mexican's flank, alerted the foe, sacrificed surprise, and allowed the bulk of Santa Anna's army to escape. Meanwhile, General Pillow, with the remainder of the army, failed to execute the distracting frontal attack in time to gain the attention of the Mexicans. This tactical turning movement, brilliantly successful in spite of its flawed execution, made a profound impression on many of the participants. It also served as a model for the remainder of the campaign (see diagram of Battle of Cerro Gordo).

Having shown how to avoid relying on a frontal assault on a partially fortified position, Scott's maneuver could also have intercepted and trapped the Mexicans and compelled them to attack if they were to escape. Since Mahan's West Point pupils believed that volunteers, that is, amateurs, could not succeed in a frontal assault, the tactical turning movement had much significance for the army's thought. Even though many felt that regular troops had a reasonable chance of winning unless the defenders had good fortifications, Scott's maneuver would save the regulars the risk and casualties of a frontal assault and even shift the burden of the attack to the defending antagonist.

Like most soldiers, few academy graduates believed that the charge in front had equal or greater merit than one against the adversary's flank or rear. They knew that frontal attacks were the most common form of assault because defenders did their best to receive attacks in front where they had prepared for them. It had long proven so difficult to assail an enemy in flank that many soldiers had experienced nothing but frontal attacks. To illustrate, an eighteenth-century Prussian general, when he found his army deployed on his antagonist's flank, laboriously moved his men until he had arrayed them in his enemy's front and could attack in the usual frontal manner. This is doubtless one of the few instances of the display of a positive predilection for an attack in front. Because of the traditional preference for assailing the hostile flank or rear, Scott's maneuver, skillfully exploiting the tactical mobility introduced by the French drill during the wars of their revolution, made a great impression, especially as he made it a pattern for his Mexico City campaign.

On approaching Mexico City, when some of the American forces had attacked unsuccessfully without orders, Scott again found a way to turn the Mexicans. One brigade held the enemy's attention with a frontal assault and three brigades assailed the rear. Their surprised foe fled, leaving behind 700 dead, 4 generals and 839 other prisoners, 22 artillery pieces, and 700 pack mules. In the victory, won by the improvised but well-executed combination of a successful frontal distraction and a timely turning movement, the Americans lost only 60 killed and wounded. In the next battle, an impromptu contest between pursuer and pursued, the Americans suffered a costly repulse in their frontal attacks. But, as American troops then worked their way around the enemy flanks, most of the Mexicans retreated. In the next confrontation, the last except for the assault on the city, Scott's men drove back their adversaries in a two-hour battle of essentially frontal charges.

If the events of the battles and of the campaign had not supported the pessimists about the frontal assault, they had shown that Scott's sophisticated approach virtually obviated such attacks except as distractions to help gain surprise. By the time the army had prepared to attack Mexico City, a young West Point graduate, Lieutenant Beauregard, showed that he had discerned the pattern when he expressed concern that the city could not "be taken in the flank or rear, which was, after all, our most successful tactic with the Mexicans."

In his remark Beauregard expressed what today armies call doctrine, their established methods of carrying on war, embracing logistics as well as tactics and strategy. Now armies state their doctrine quite formally in publications dealing with each aspect, change these from time to time, and engage in much formal and informal discussion of this vital subject. Before the Civil War, however, the U.S. Army's principal formal doctrinal publications consisted of its manuals for infantry, cavalry, and artillery. These dealt with tactics only, the infantry's, based on the corresponding French publication, being the most important. But the Mexican War created an informal, unwritten tactical doctrine—to turn the enemy. The participants had derived this from their experience of the war and found it in full harmony with the French tactical manuals and the teachings of the history of the Napoleonic wars.

General Scott and his campaign probably also taught a lesson by demonstrating the intimate relationship between military operations and politics. The campaign had the political objective of taking the Mexican capital to force the cession of territory which the United States had already occupied. Success depend on Scott's ability to march through and supply himself in a hostile country. He protected his army against the possibility of dangerous Mexican popular hostility by combining rigorous action against guerrillas with paying cash for supplies, adopting a conciliatory manner in dealing with the Mexican governmental and ecclesiastical authorities, and taking care for the good behavior of his soldiers. Thus he minimized guerrilla attacks while in the midst of a gigantic and hostile country.

Before the fall of Mexico City, General Scott gave another lesson in the relationship between military action and politics. He did this by his way of dealing with a government disrupted by the stress of defeat in war, when he displayed a perceptiveness and concern for his adversary's political attitude by delaying the capture of Mexico's capital. He explained to the secretary of war that he had heeded advice not to act with "precipitation" lest he "excite a spirit of national desperation, and thus indefinitely postpone the hope of accommodation." He had the political sophistication to try to leave the Mexicans some pride.

Indirectly he probably also helped teach a lesson in military strategy. Although he made only tactical turning movements during his campaign, many officers must have seen the clear analogy between the tactical movement and Napoleon's strategic maneuver. This could well have made a knowledge of Mexican War campaigns a valuable aid in understanding Napoleonic strategy. That Civil War soldiers used the word turn for the strategic as well as the tactical maneuver suggests this. This interpretation also receives support from the failure of Civil War officers to show any evidence of understanding the strategic turning movement in terms of Jomini's approach, which depended on the theory of the base. In fact, it is hard to find Civil War soldiers making any use of the notion of the base as a line, an approach important to both Jomini and Clausewitz. Thus Scott and the Mexican War taught tactics directly, operational strategy indirectly, and exemplified the interdependence of military action and political factors and objectives.

3. THE ARMY'S TACTICAL THOUGHT

After the war, a simple change in the ammunition made a military rifle possible. The Minié bullet, with a cylindrical shape and a deep conical hollow in the rear, loaded easily but, when fired, had the essential tight fit with the rifling. Not only did the Minié rifle surpass the smoothbore in range and accuracy, but the shape and rotation of its bullet gave a higher velocity, greater penetrating power, and diminished likelihood of deflection. Slowly armies began to rearm their men using the new weapon, combining it with the more dependable percussion cap which had already superseded the flint.

Since both sides fought the Mexican War with smoothbores, the U.S. Army naturally gave thought to the effect of the increased range and accuracy of the new rifled weapon which all armies introduced in the 1850s. In adopting the newest French tactics, the army acquired one response to the increase in firepower in its new manual, *Rifle and Light Infantry Tactics,* called "Hardee's Tactics" after the officer who had adapted it from the

French. It improved battlefield mobility and deployment and provided a means of command for skirmishers so as to combine the advantage of dispersal and the use of cover and concealment with the control necessary for battlefield maneuver.

To give scattered men the direction necessary to carry out frontal or flank attacks, it established a system of more than 20 different bugle calls signaling maneuvers by the widely distributed men and their leaders. But the calls could not give distinctive orders to separate units nor could the recipients acknowledge receipt or report success or failure. So, even without the interference of the noise of a battle, such a system exceeded the capabilities of long-service regulars and was quite beyond the scope of volunteers. It was not until the handi-talkie and walkie-talkie radios of the Second World War that commanders could readily combine dispersion and control.

Consequently, after the introduction of the rifle, one manual from this era thus widely revised Mahan's hypothesis that, though a frontal assault by volunteers would fail, one by regulars might succeed. Instead, it stated that a *"cool, well-directed fire from a body of men armed with the new rifle or rifle musket is sufficient to stop the advance of any kind of troops."* In spite of the recognition of the problem presented by accurate, long-range fire, troops still had to maneuver by marching erect, usually in regiments of 400 to 700 men, controlled by their captains and colonels who sought to respond to the orders of the brigade commander. Most Civil War soldiers endlessly practiced their drill. Their proficiency not only enabled them to respond promptly and maneuver quickly and easily, but also created a habit of obedience and concerted action and a feeling of cohesion which continued even when group evolutions were inadvisable or impossible.

To the thinking soldier of the 1850s the augmentation of the already-dominant power of the tactical defense placed an even greater premium on Scott's turning movements as a route to offensive tactical success. To others—many, no doubt, who gave little or no thought to such questions—attack still meant going right ahead. Certainly for many volunteer officers this would be true.

Thus the introduction of the rifle reinforced the army's ex-

273

isting implicit doctrine of the dominance of the tactical defense, modified by the lessons of the Mexican War on the importance of the turning movement. But much of the value of the rifle's increased range and accuracy depended on accurate shooting, something unknown to most volunteers and not a skill cultivated by regulars, who, except for skirmishers, had traditionally stressed rapidity rather than accuracy of fire. Further, the rolling and often wooded terrain found in much of the United States limited fields of fire and consequently the opportunity to have a battle at much longer range than that possible with the smoothbore.

So by 1850, the United States had created a sophisticated professional army that had successfully employed its French tactics in combat, using both regulars and volunteers. This army would provide excellent leaders for the Civil War, and American education, experience, and topography would create a distinctively American approach. While the forests of the East continued to limit the tactical effectiveness of cavalry, the rifle's increment to the infantry's defensive power further diminished cavalry's offensive potential and contributed to continuing North America's centuries-old tradition of relying primarily on infantry. The advent of the rifle also harmonized with West Point's emphasis on a European as well as an American military tradition and the dominance of the tactical defensive, especially when assisted by field fortifications.

4. EXAMPLES OF THE ARMY'S MILITARY THOUGHT

It is difficult to trace the effect of education, reading, and experience on the American army officers. Occasionally there is a flash of light, as when Union Quartermaster General Montgomery C. Meigs compared Lee's Second Manassas campaign with Napoleon's of Jena and Auerstadt and used these as a basis for the plan Joseph Hooker used in his Chancellorsville campaign. Its failure to mention Jomini or use his approach to the turning movement is as significant as what he includes. But such insights into the roots of military ideas are rare indeed. Three other officers left more ample records of what influenced them. Two of these, G. T. Beauregard and H. W. Halleck, left the most ample record; they also campaigned against each other in May

1862, and both had great influence on their armies' strategies.

As a young officer Halleck wrote a book on the art of war, which had a favorable reception and a second edition just before the Civil War. Although he based his 1846 *Elements of Military Art and Science* on Jomini's *Summary of the Art of War*, he consulted many other authorities and, unlike Jomini but in consonance with his own background, he included much on fortification and its merits. In his revised edition, he included a brief treatment of the Mexican War. Moreover, he acquired a firm grounding in history and Jomini's interpretations when he translated into English Jomini's four-volume biography of Napoleon.

That Halleck's wartime correspondence practically never contains an historical allusion indicates how hard it is to induce in this way the Civil War soldier's reading. Yet, if the practices of Napoleon and the explanations of Jomini were to function as the basis for strategic doctrine, Halleck should exemplify them at work. His attention to lines of operation and his eye for the turning movement are consistent with his reading and writing but do not, of course, demonstrate history or Jomini as sources of these insights.

Beauregard, a contemporary of Halleck's at West Point, followed a different approach when, just before the Civil War, he became enamored of P. L. MacDougall's *The Theory of War*. Essentially a popularizer of the ideas of Jomini and others, MacDougall organized his book in terms of maxims and, unlike Jomini, made these meaningful to his audience of young officers by illustrating them with numerous examples from military history. By thus uniting the principle and an example, he made a work that all could read and profit from, and one which so rightly charmed Captain Beauregard.

During the Civil War, Beauregard published his own *Principles and Maxims of the Art of War* for the guidance of his officers. He began it thus:

> The whole science of war may be briefly defined as the art of placing in the right position, at the right time, a mass of troops greater than your enemy can there oppose you.
> PRINCIPLE NO. 1—To place masses of your army in contact with fractions of your enemy.

PRINCIPLE NO. 2—To operate as much as possible on the communications of your enemy without exposing your own.
PRINCIPLE NO. 3—To operate always on interior lines (or shorter ones in point of time).

With the exception of omitting a line which calls numbers two and three "secondary principles" and adding the parenthetical statement in the last line, Beauregard took this clear restatement of Jomini from MacDougall's book. Indeed, the bulk of Beauregard's booklet came from MacDougall's, also without any attribution at all. MacDougall's three principles improve on Jomini's fundamental principle of war, as does Beauregard's clarification that interior lines need not be geometrical, a wise amplification when the railroad carried so many troop movements. Though he omitted a few of MacDougall's maxims, he included the one on the value of field fortifications: *"A position cannot be too strong; lose no opportunity of strengthening it by means of field fortifications."*

Thus we know that Beauregard, who played a significant role in the formulation of Confederate strategy, had a familiarity with the ideas of Jomini. So intense is his interest in strategy during the war and so well-informed his earlier comments on the Mexican War that it is hard to believe that MacDougall, whom he recommended to his brother-in-law, was the only work of history or military art he read.

Nothing about the conduct of Beauregard and Halleck's May 1862 campaign for Corinth reveals anything about their ideas. But elsewhere, as with so many other commanders on both sides, they show the effect of the Napoleonic strategic tradition, the tactical ideas found in Professor Mahan's teaching, and the experience of the Mexican War.

Another West Pointer and Mexican War veteran, George B. McClellan left a much briefer record of his ideas and their connection with action, one quite as revealing as Meigs's. In basing the strategy of his Peninsula campaign on the strategic turning movement, General McClellan applied a concept congenial to a former member of the Military Academy's Napoleon Club. When a member, he had prepared papers on the Battle of Wagram of 1809 and Napoleon's Russian Campaign of 1812, one of them 111 pages in length. He had an intimate exposure to another major influence on the army's military thought as a member of Scott's informal staff in Mexico. When commanding in western Virginia, McClellan had written Scott of his wish to show that he was "no unworthy disciple of your school" and sent him a message that he planned to "repeat the maneuver of Cerro Gordo." In his initial plan for the 1861 Battle of Rich Mountain, he showed that he understood the fundamentals of the maneuver when he allocated one of his brigades to advance in front to distract the enemy and enable the three brigades assigned to the turning movement to gain surprise.

Thus the soldiers left us a quite inadequate record of the bases of their operational ideas. Perhaps the best indication is not the scanty evidence but the obvious harmony between their practice and those of the Napoleonic and Mexican wars. But Civil War strategy included important elements not found in these wars. Doubtless the participants improvised these as a response to opportunity and need rather than adapted them from their use in wars more remote in time. So some Civil War strategy had no ancestry, representing, instead, a recreation of past practice in response to comparable circumstances.

DIAGRAMS

BATTLE OF MANASSAS 1

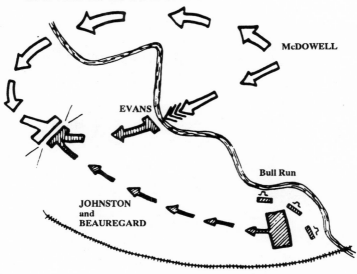

McDOWELL

EVANS

Bull Run

JOHNSTON
and
BEAUREGARD

BATTLE OF MANASSAS 2

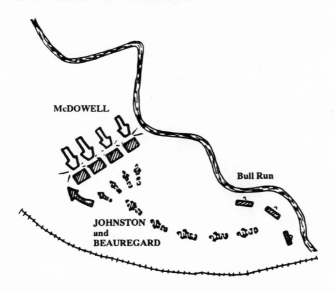

McDOWELL

Bull Run

JOHNSTON
and
BEAUREGARD

MANASSAS CAMPAIGN

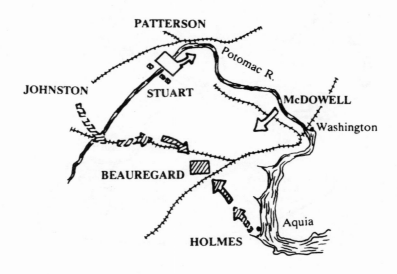

SHILOH CONCENTRATION

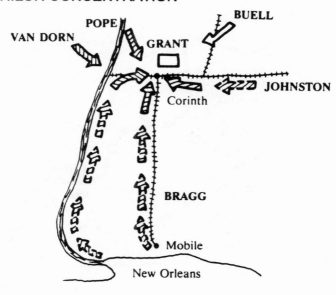

MOVE TO THE PENINSULA

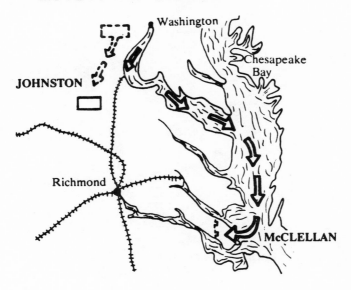

JACKSON CONCENTRATES AGAINST FREMONT

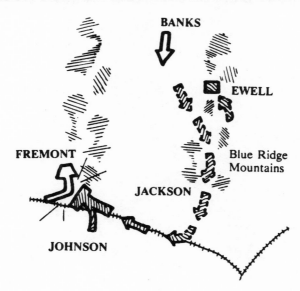

Diagrams

JACKSON CONCENTRATES AGAINST BANKS

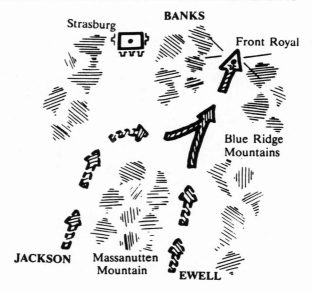

JACKSON'S EFFORT TO TURN BANKS

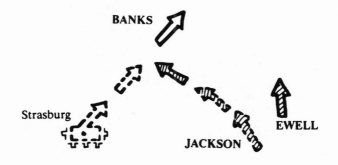

284

JACKSON PURSUES BANKS AND ESCAPES

CROSS KEYS AND PORT REPUBLIC

BATTLE OF MECHANICSVILLE

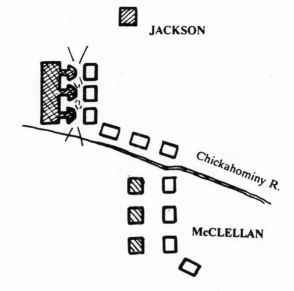

BATTLE OF GAINES'S MILL

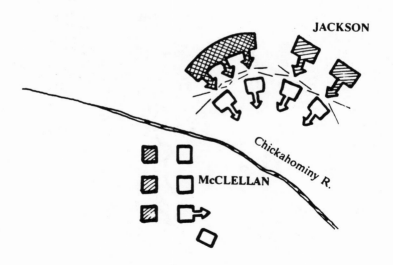

SECOND MANASSAS CAMPAIGN 1

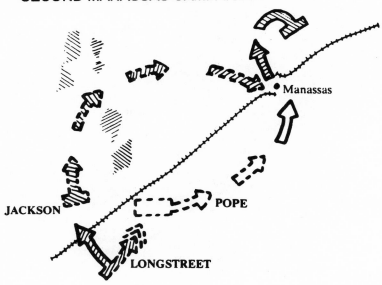

SECOND MANASSAS CAMPAIGN 2

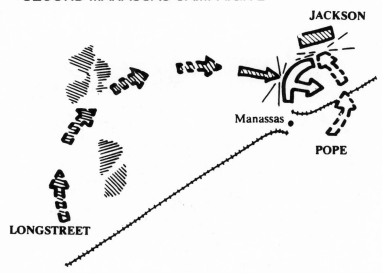

RAIDERS AND GUERRILLAS

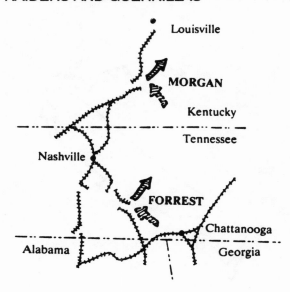

BRAGG TURNS BUELL

ANTIETAM CAMPAIGN BEGINS

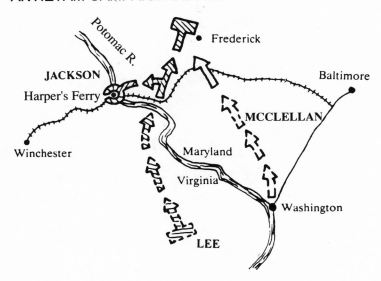

FIRST ADVANCE ON VICKSBURG

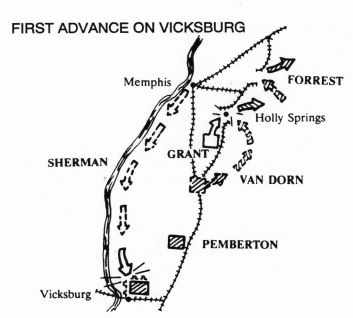

CHANCELLORSVILLE CAMPAIGN 1

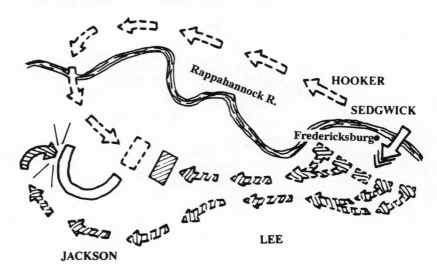

CHANCELLORSVILLE CAMPAIGN 2

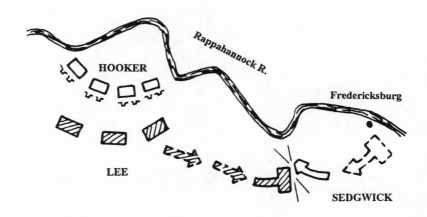

VICKSBURG CAMPAIGN

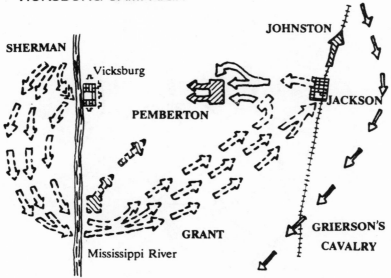

SHERMAN

Vicksburg

JOHNSTON

PEMBERTON

JACKSON

GRANT

GRIERSON'S
CAVALRY

Mississippi River

THE TULLAHOMA CAMPAIGN

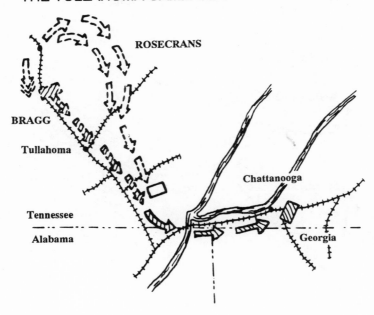

ROSECRANS

BRAGG

Tullahoma

Chattanooga

Tennessee

Alabama

Georgia

291

GETTYSBURG CAMPAIGN BEGINS

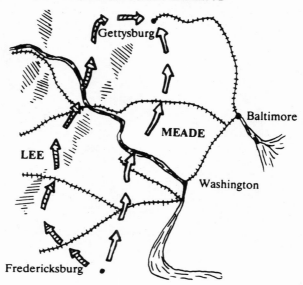

CHICKAMAUGA CONCENTRATION

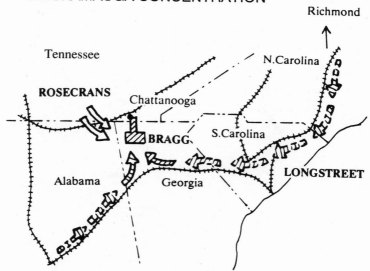

GRANT'S PLANNED RAIDS

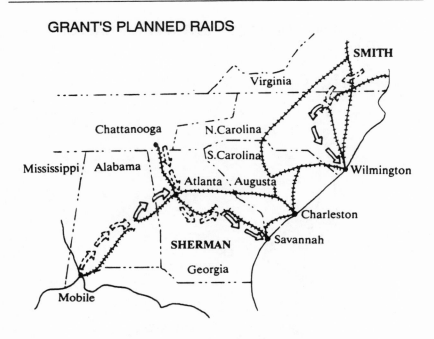

GRANT TURNS LEE FROM THE WILDERNESS
TO PETERSBURG

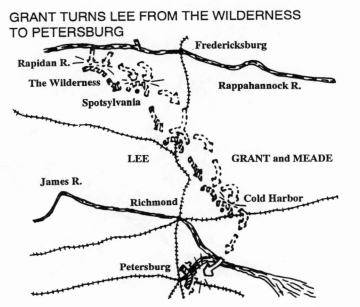

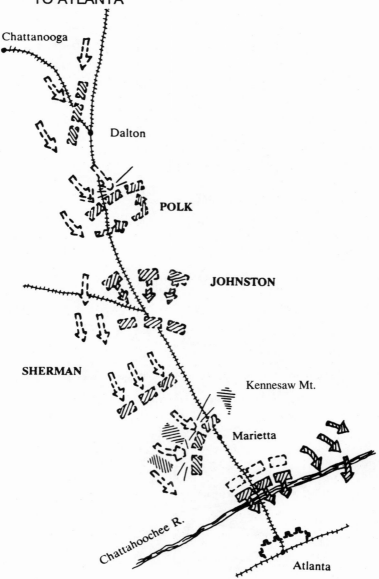

SHERMAN TURNS JOHNSTON FROM DALTON TO ATLANTA

Chattanooga

Dalton

POLK

JOHNSTON

SHERMAN

Kennesaw Mt.

Marietta

Chattahoochee R.

Atlanta

GULF CONFLICT TURNING MOVEMENT

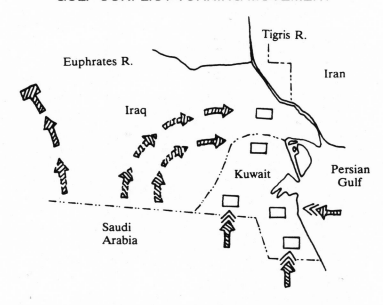

Tigris R.

Euphrates R.

Iran

Iraq

Kuwait

Persian Gulf

Saudi Arabia

NAPOLEON DIVIDES COLLI AND BEAULIEU

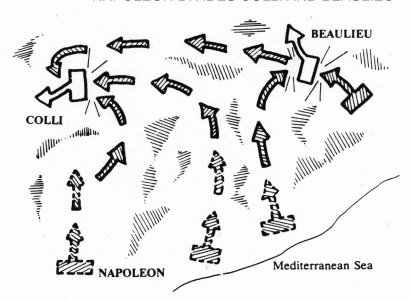

BEAULIEU

COLLI

NAPOLEON

Mediterranean Sea

DEFENSE OF MANTUA SIEGE 1

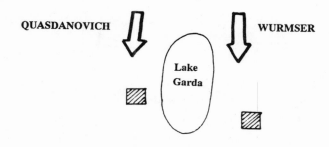

DEFENSE OF MANTUA SIEGE 2

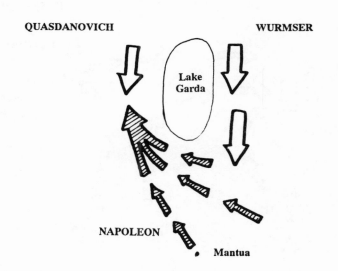

DEFENSE OF MANTUA SIEGE 3

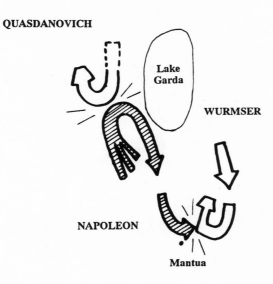

NAPOLEON TURNS BEAULIEU

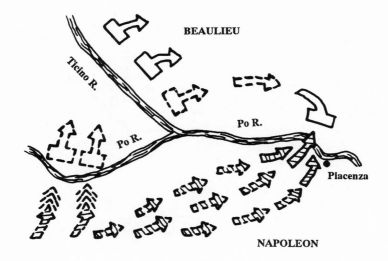

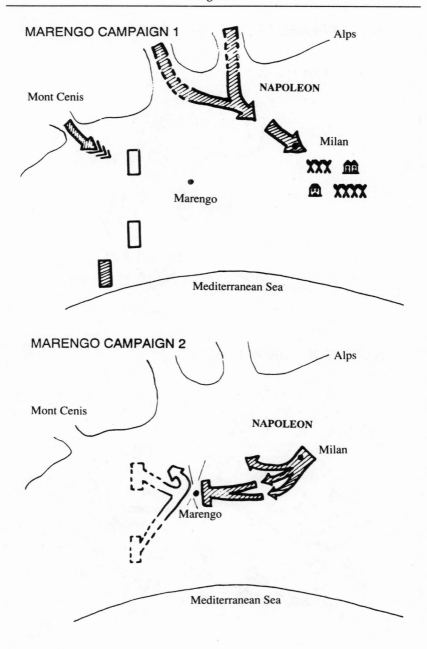

MARENGO CAMPAIGN 1

Alps

Mont Cenis

NAPOLEON

Milan

Marengo

Mediterranean Sea

MARENGO CAMPAIGN 2

Alps

Mont Cenis

NAPOLEON

Milan

Marengo

Mediterranean Sea

ULM CAMPAIGN

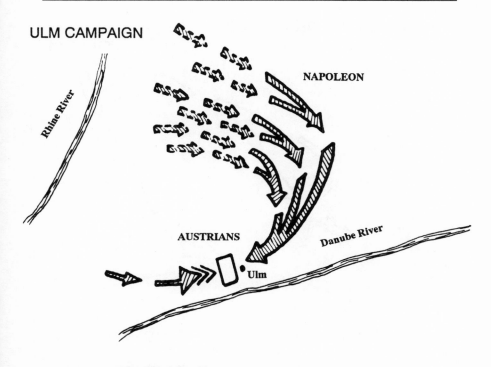

BATTLE OF MONTEREY

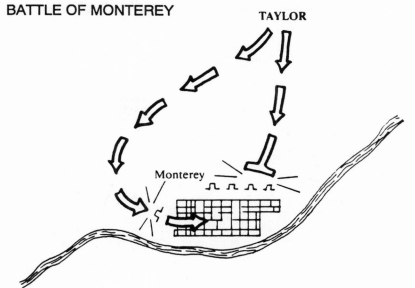

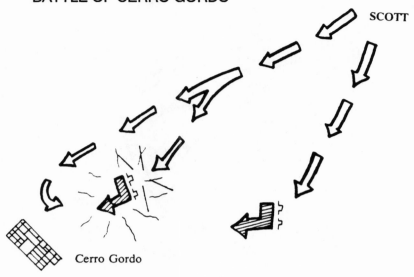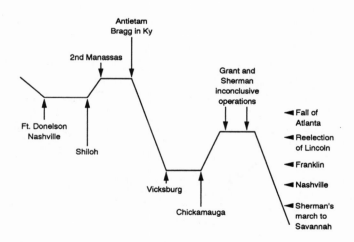

BATTLE OF CERRO GORDO

SCOTT

Cerro Gordo

DIAGRAM OF CONFEDERATE EXPECTATIONS OF VICTORY

1862   1863   1864

Aug   Sept   July   Sept   May – Aug   Sept – Dec

Antietam
Bragg in Ky

2nd Manassas

Grant and
Sherman
inconclusive
operations

◀ Fall of
Atlanta

Ft. Donelson
Nashville

◀ Reelection
of Lincoln

Shiloh

◀ Franklin

◀ Nashville

Vicksburg

Chickamauga

◀ Sherman's
march to
Savannah

Derived from Bell Irvin Wiley, <u>The Road To Appomattox</u>
(New York, 1977) between pp 34-35.

SOME RECENT BOOKS
PERTINENT TO
COMMAND AND
STRATEGY

———•—•———

This work has its antecedents in T. Harry Williams's *Lincoln and His Generals* (1952) and Frank E. Vandiver's *Rebel Brass* (1956), both outstanding works explaining Civil War command and strategy. Williams extended this interpretation in his "The Military Leadership of North and South," in David Donald, ed., *Why the North Won the Civil War* (1960), 23–48. *Rebel Brass* has stood the passage of time well, but Williams's study was controversial because of his powerful and justly influential view of Abraham Lincoln as correctly understanding that the proper military objective was to destroy the enemy army in battle; this placed the president at odds with his generals until the emergence of the like-minded Ulysses S. Grant. Herman Hattaway and Archer Jones in their 1983 *How the North Won: A Military History of the Civil War* strongly differed with this idea, presenting an alternative perspective of Grant as well as Lincoln and his generals. These are the interpretations which I have followed.

How the North Won had a similar disagreement with Stephen E. Ambrose, *Halleck: Lincoln's Chief of Staff* (1962), which used Williams's viewpoint and his complementary understanding of Antoine-Henri Jomini. Russell Weigley, in his *American Way of*

War (1973), offered his replacement for Williams's interpretation of the war and, in doing so, provided the best statement of the traditional view of Grant. This he modified markedly in his "American Strategy from Its Beginnings to the First World War," in Peter Paret, ed., *Makers of Modern Strategy from Machiavelli to the Nuclear Age* (1986). Weigley presented Grant as a practitioner of Napoleonic operational techniques, a realist about the prospects of destroying the enemy army in battle, and a believer in a logistic strategy. In noting that Grant's operations displayed a consistency with Jomini, Weigley contributed to ending a phase of Civil War historiography which had seen Jomini not as interpreting Napoleon but as expounding older strategic ideas and exercising a baleful influence on Union generals in particular. Jomini's ideas and their influence, dealt with at length in *How the North Won* and earlier, received a needed epitaph in John Shy's fine essay "Jomini," in Paret, *Makers of Modern Strategy*.

Weigley's *American Way of War* also provided the most complete and concise presentation of the thesis that Lee sought the annihilation of the enemy army and, in the process, lost more men than the Confederacy could afford. This generalization about Lee as too expensive a general received its best statement from Thomas Lawrence Connelly and became a part of his and my *Politics of Command* (1973). Initially agreeing fully with this approach, Herman Hattaway and I subsequently developed a different idea, first offered in *How the North Won* and in its Appendix B, and also presented here. Readers should be sure to note that, in his essay in *Makers of Modern Strategy*, Weigley makes a synthesis of the two interpretations, seeing Lee's turning movements not as defensive but as aiming at the enemy's annihilation.

Among the many recently published works particularly relevant to command and strategy, Grady McWhiney and Perry D. Jamieson's *Attack and Die: Civil War Military Tactics and the Southern Heritage* (1982) provided an excellent treatment of tactics and presented a tactical explanation for the war's military outcome, arguing that the Confederates lost the war because they suffered unsustainable casualties in combat. The authors found the reason for these losses in the Southerners' belief in

302

the efficacy of the frontal attack and their constant use of it. Research on Civil War combat effectiveness shown in Appendix B of *How the North Won* does not support this thesis of Confederate tactical ineptitude. Richard E. Beringer, Herman Hattaway, Archer Jones, and William N. Still, Jr., *Why the South Lost the Civil War* (1986), Appendix Two, offers more elaborate data which indicates that the Confederates did not attack more frequently than the Union. Albert Castel's "Mars and the Reverend Longstreet: Or Attacking and Dying in the Civil War," *Civil War History*, Vol. 33, No. 2, June 1987, 104–14, in giving a good conclusion to this argument, does not support the McWhiney and Jamieson thesis.

Paddy Griffith's *Battle Tactics of the Civil War* (1989), the most significant recent book on the war's military history, should command the interest and respect of all Civil War military historians, but they should beware of allowing occasional errors and overstatements to irritate or mislead them into underestimating the work. Researching published combat reminiscences, analyzing tactics and weapons, and using the profound tactical understanding exhibited in his *Forward into Battle* (1981), Griffith has broadened and deepened our understanding of the war's tactics. Further, he has changed scholars' ideas substantially by showing that Civil War tactical conditions had a far greater resemblance to those of earlier rather than later wars. From his book it is clear that J. F. C. Fuller and everyone else tended to project back into the brief era of the muzzle-loading rifle the conditions of combat with the breachloader and even the magazine rifle and machine gun. But readers must avoid misunderstanding the effect of this important new explication of tactics on our existing view of its role in command and strategy. With the smoothbore, the tactical defensive had long overmatched the offensive and, strengthened by the rifle in the Civil War, continued to dominate an offense weakened by the absence of shock cavalry.

If one had assumed that the offensive had dominated in combat between infantry armed with smoothbores, the change to the rifle would explain Civil War conditions. Such an assumption, made by occasional writers, like some other views of the Civil War, actually says more about the past than the Civil

War itself. For example, to say that William T. Sherman made the first use of turning movements and distraction or introduced the intimidation of civilians is more a novel thesis about warfare before 1861 than a commentary on these attributes of Sherman's operations. Those wishing a better understanding of Civil War operations from the standpoint of the more remote past as well as of the era since 1865 might consult Archer Jones, *The Art of War in the Western World* (1987). This book, which begins in 490 B.C., also elaborates the approach to strategy and guerrilla warfare used here.

The subject of command has its presentation scattered through the biographies of the generals and the other participants. Most recently George Green Shackelford's *George Wythe Randolph and the Confederate Elite* (1988) appraises the man and his influence. Eli Evans, *Judah P. Benjamin: The Jewish Confederate* (1988), gives a different insight into this key cabinet figure. Steven E. Woodworth, *Jefferson Davis and His Generals: The Failure of Confederate Command in the West* (1990), provides an interpretive account and ushers in a deluge of biographies of Davis, now in progress by outstanding scholars. These will fill a void, leaving us with a far better understanding of his role in command and strategy. Also valuable is Roman Heleniak and Larry Hewitt, eds., *The Confederate High Command* (1990), particularly Herman Hattaway's essay on Davis.

Recent studies of generals include Stephen W. Sears, *George B. McClellan: The Young Napoleon* (1988), which neglects the strategy of the Peninsula campaign and Michael C. C. Adams's speculation to emphasize McClellan's neurotic reaction to the stress of command. Gary W. Gallagher, ed., *Fighting for the Confederacy, Personal Recollections of General Edward Porter Alexander* (1989), provides valuable amplification of the general's original memoir. Christopher Phillips treats a brief, important career in *Damned Yankee: The Life of General Nathaniel Lyon* (1990) and Wallace J. Schutz and Walter Trenerry fill an important gap in *Abandoned by Lincoln: A Military Biography of General John Pope* (1990). James I. Robertson, Jr., *General A. P. Hill: The Story of a Confederate Warrior* (1987), illuminates the career of this important corps commander, as does William Garrett Piston's *Lee's Tarnished Lieutenant: James Longstreet and His Place in Southern*

History (1987). Christopher Losson's *Tennessee's Forgotten Warriors: Frank Cheatham and His Confederate Division* (1989) gives insight into the Army of Tennessee.

Among the many valuable new books, Stephen V. Ash's superb *Middle Tennessee Transformed: War and Peace in the Upper South* (1988) gives a comprehensive interpretation of life behind the lines. I depended upon it and his "White Virginians Under Federal Occupation, 1861–1865," *Virginia Magazine of History and Biography*, Vol. 98, April 1990, 169–92 for my account of guerrilla warfare in Tennessee and Virginia. When combined with Peter Maslowski's *Treason Must Be Made Odious: Military Occupation and Wartime Reconstruction in Nashville, Tennessee, 1862–65* (1987), the history of occupied Tennessee begins. But the story will need the two volumes B. F. Cooling, III, plans to add to his *Forts Henry and Donelson—the Key to the Confederate Heartland* (1987). Even so, East Tennessee, where Confederates occupied Unionist territory, will need the kind of treatment characteristic of Ash and Cooling. The amount of work done, and remaining to do on Tennessee alone, illustrates the extent of this major dimension of Civil War history, largely neglected in the last 125 years. The numbers of Union troops devoted to garrisoning occupied areas give a rough measure of the military significance of this story; but the South behind the lines needs more research and writing on most of the states to tell the dramatic social, political, and economic history of which guerrilla warfare is only a part. The latest among the few books concerning guerrilla warfare is Michael Fellman's comprehensive *Inside War: The Guerrilla Conflict in Missouri During the American Civil War* (1989). In *Rebel Raider: The Life of General John Hunt Morgan* (1986), James A. Ramage tells the story of one of the most important raiders.

A significant dimension of logistics receives an excellent analysis in Stephen R. Wise, *Lifeline of the Confederacy: Blockade Running During the Civil War* (1988). He conclusively supports earlier and more limited research which showed that blockade running had met the Confederacy's essential needs. Amplifying one aspect of Richard Goff's classic *Confederate Supply* (1969) is Leslie D. Jensen, "A Survey of Confederate Central Government Quartermaster Issue Jackets," *Military Collector and Histo-*

rian, Vol. XLI, No. 3, Fall 1989, 105–22, and No. 4, Winter 1989, 162–71.

In his *The American Civil War and the Origin of Modern War: Ideas, Organization, and Field Command* (1988), Edward Hagerman has contributed much to improving our understanding of the tactical and logistical underpinnings of strategy by bringing together his pioneering research on the development of trench warfare and his thorough study of the supply problems of the field armies. Richard M. McMurry, in his *Two Great Rebel Armies: An Essay in Confederate Military History* (1989), has done much for a consequential aspect of command by comparing the main Confederate armies in Virginia and Tennessee. In evaluating various explanations of their performance, he sees Lee as offensive minded, trying to win the Civil War with his army. McMurry is at his best in comparing the armies in various respects, including the source of their men and the number of trained leaders available to each.

In treating the soldiers McMurray touches on another subject relevant to command, the morale and motivation of the men, to which much besides the actions and appeal of commanders contributed. Joseph T. Glatthaar's splendid *March to the Sea and Beyond: Sherman's Troops in the Savannah and Carolinas Campaigns* (1985) is a model of the kind of research and writing which this neglected field needs. Other recent books on this important subject include Glatthaar's *Forged in Battle: The Civil War Alliance of Black Soldiers and White Officers* (1990); Gerald F. Linderman, *Embattled Courage: The Experience of Combat in the American Civil War* (1987); James I. Robertson, Jr., *Soldiers Blue and Gray* (1988); and Reid Mitchell, *Civil War Soldiers* (1988).

Larry E. Nelson, *Bullets, Ballots, and Rhetoric: Confederate Policy for the United States Presidential Contest of 1864* (1980), includes a treatment of the effect of this crucial election on Confederate military actions. Marck E. Neely, Jr., "Was the Civil War a Total War?" *Civil War History,* Vol. XXXVII, No. 1, March 1991, 5–28, thoroughly and convincingly demolishes the thesis that the Civil War was a total war in the sense that it sought unlimited victory and made civilians a particular object of its military effort.

The foregoing mentions only a few of many excellent recent books relating to the subject of command and strategy. The number available and the comparatively new lines of investigation which historians are pursuing indicate how much work they have done and how much more is needed to give a significantly more complete account and understanding of this war, whose story has so often seemed fully told and whose outcome so often apparently adequately explained.

INDEX

309

Beauregard, [Pierre] Gustave
Toutant, Confederate
general, 33, 85, 86, 101,
108, 115, 119, 122, 124,
162, 164, 167–68, 170, 172,
180, 189, 217, 220, 221,
222, 223, 226, 274
assessment of his strategy and
influence, 228
assigned to command Department of South Carolina,
Georgia, and Florida, 88
background, 28
at Battle of Manassas, 28–30, 32
at Battle of Shiloh, 52
bombards Fort Sumter, 1
in command in South, 213
connection with Abingdon-
Columbia bloc in Corinth
campaign, 56–57
and Davis, 79
defeats Butler, 193–94
defects in his strategic ideas,
120
defends Petersburg, 194–95
entrenches early, 135
extravagant statements dis-
credit plans, 120
his bloc a part of Western
Concentration bloc, 119
in Manassas campaign, 40, 41
objections to him as replacement for Bragg, 121–22
plan for a western offensive,
173
*Principles and Maxims of the Art
of War* plagiarized, 275–76
proposes 1864 strategic plans,
190
provides strategy for Western
Concentration bloc, 119
quoted on Gettysburg cam-
paign, 171

relieved of western command, 88
sent west, 50
his strategy of concentrating
in Tennessee, 119
his strategy and influence,
173–74
suitable choice to replace
Bragg, 121
summary of his tactical experience with Scott, 271
Belisarius, Byzantine general,
36, 67
Benjamin, Judah P.
Confederate Secretary of War,
75–76
Blair, Francis Preston, Jr., 17
Blockade
beginning, 7–8
difficulties fueling steamers,
139–40
difficulties in making effective, 139–41
effect on costs of the war,
234, 238
ineffectiveness in interdicting
essentials, 9–10, 142–43,
234
a persisting logistic strategy,
132, 139, 141
value of capturing ports, 141,
142
Boonville, Battle of, 17
Bragg, Braxton, Confederate
general, 97, 103, 116, 117,
118, 119, 120, 122, 124,
135, 165, 184, 200, 202,
217, 221, 222, 226, 228,
231, 235
arrived in Corinth, 51
background and character,
88–89
Chattanooga campaign,
178–80

313

his ideas, 256–59
Jones, Samuel, Confederate general, 221

Kennesaw Mountain, Battle of, 199
Kentucky
early struggle for, 18–19
Kentucky bloc
part of Western Concentration bloc, 119
Kentucky campaign, 135
account of, 89–93
military and political attrition and strategic significance, 92–93
Kernstown, Battle of
strategic significance, 65
King Cotton, initial Confederate political strategy
expectation of foreign intervention, 152–53
Kirby Smith, Edmund, Confederate general, 87, 97, 122, 220, 222
commands in East Tennessee, 78
commands in the Trans-Mississippi, 122
raids into Kentucky in coordination with Bragg, 90–92

Lee, Robert Edward, Confederate general, 79, 83, 98, 101, 112, 114, 115, 117, 124, 133, 162, 172, 182, 184, 189, 206, 220, 221, 222, 225, 229, 237, 263
Antietam campaign, 93–96
appointed chief of staff, 64, 76
appointed general in chief, 216

appointed Johnston to command in the Carolinas, 217
assessment of, 226–28
assumes command of the army in Virginia, 63
background, 63–64
in Chancellorsville campaign, 157–58
and Chickamauga campaign, 175
and the defensive turning movement, 134–35
effect of Chancellorsville campaign on his strategic thinking, 158–59
1864 spring campaign, 192–95
and 1864 strategic planning, 190–91
enunciates Confederate political strategy, 153–54
evacuates Richmond and retreats west, 217
Gettysburg campaign, 166–71
harmonious collaboration with Davis, 226
interpretation of as believing in the possibility of annihilating an army, 227–28
interpretation as seeking to win the war in Virginia, 226–27
logistic motives for fearing a Richmond siege, 136
Mine Run campaign, 177–78
the motif of his strategy, 228
notes loss of morale among soldiers and civilians, 216
operations after Antietam, 102
rationale for opposing reinforcements for Tennessee, 123–24

Lee, Robert Edward, Confederate general (*cont.*)
resolution of dissonance between army command
and strategic knowledge,
123, 226
Second Manassas campaign a
model for Meigs, 157
sends a corps to the Shenandoah Valley, 197–99
sends Longstreet to southeast
to alleviate logistic problems, 125
Seven Days' Battles campaign,
68–70
the stated objective of his
strategy, 227
surrenders at Appomattox
Court House, 217
why slow to adopt entrenchment, 134–35
Lincoln, Abraham, President of
the United States, 1, 10,
16, 20, 23, 86, 97, 110,
156, 165, 174, 194, 197,
198, 207, 212, 228, 231,
237
able to bear responsibility, 224
and Antietam campaign, 94
appoints Grant lieutenant
general, 182
appoints Halleck general in
chief, 81
assesses political attrition of
Seven Days' Battles, 71
background, 13–15
calls for 75,000 volunteers, 2
and Chickamauga campaign,
176–78
chose Hooker to command in
Virginia, 112
collaboration with Halleck,
225

compared with Davis, 24
concern about casualties,
196–97
conciliatory peace terms, 208
and the critics of the generals,
81
devotes less time to military
operations than Davis,
225
differing interpretations of his
role in civilian/military
disagreements about the
war, 224–25
diverts Banks to New Or-
leans, 104
eliminates War Board, 81
established War Board, 79
estimates political significance
of the Battle of Stones
River, 108
evaluation as military commander, 223–26
followed U.S. tradition in exercising military com-
mand, 12
and Gettysburg campaign, 169
his problem of differing military and civilian views of
warfare, 224
learned strategy and the indecisiveness of military operations, 224
likely effect of his reconstruction plan on Confeder-
ates, 239
no compunctions about relieving army commanders,
122
and operations after Antietam, 102
political factors in selection of
generals, criteria for, 111
relations with Halleck, 110–13

324

Scott, Winfield, Union general,
14, 29, 46, 89, 100, 139,
223
background, 20–21, 267–68
forecast of cost of victory using military strategy, 23
influence on the army, 232,
268
Lincoln's general in chief, 16
in Manassas campaign, 40, 41
Mexico City campaign, 269–72
proposes political strategy, 21
retires as general in chief, 43
Seddon, James A., Confederate
secretary of war, 114, 117,
118, 172, 188, 192, 203,
222, 226
appointed, 113
assessment of his perfor-
mance and contributions,
113
background, 113
and 1864 strategic planning,
190
give and take with Lee representative of command
relations in both armies,
125–26
productive collaboration with
Davis, 113
and reinforcements from Lee
for Tennessee, 123, 125
resigns, 216
wants J. E. Johnston to supersede Bragg, 121
Sedgwick, John, Union general
in Chancellorsville campaign,
157–58
Seven Days' Battles, 101, 133,
227
Seven Days' Battles campaign,
233
account of, 63–64, 68–71

evaluation of, 69–70
military and political attrition
and strategic significance,
70–71
Shenandoah Valley
base area for Lee, 135, 167
configuration aids Confederate but not Union armies,
136
defensive logistic strategy
eliminates it as a base
area, 207
1864 operations in, 198–99, 207
Shenandoah Valley campaign
account of, 64–68
evaluation of, 66, 68
objectives of, 64, 67, 68
Sheridan, Philip H., Union general, 228
commands in Shenandoah
Valley, 198–99
defensive logistic strategy in
Shenandoah Valley, 207
victories in Shenandoah Valley and their political attrition, 207
Sherman, William T., Union
general, 112, 116, 118,
159, 164, 195, 197, 201,
213, 216, 221, 228, 229,
233, 234, 235, 242
advocate of conciliation, 23–24
Atlanta campaign, 199–203,
206
background and collaboration
with Grant, 182–83
at Battle of Manassas, 30
Carolinas raid, 214, 216, 217
and Chattanooga campaign,
179
Chickasaw Bluffs attack, 105
in command in the West, 178,
187

distracted Davis with cavalry
raids, 202
meeting with Halleck, 45
Meridian Raid, 185–86
political effects of his raids,
243
role in Grant's raiding logistic
strategy, 230–31
undecided whether to raid to
Atlantic or Gulf, 208
Vicksburg campaign, 160–61
Sherman's raid to the sea
account of, 210–12
logistic damage of, 212, 237
orders for his raid, 210
political attrition of, 212–13,
218, 237
psychological effect as showing Confederates that
they have lost, 212–13,
237
Shields, James, Union general
in Shenandoah Valley, 65–68
Shiloh, Battle of, 100, 115, 121
account of, 51–52
military and political attrition
and strategic significance,
53
Shiloh campaign, 75, 190, 219,
220, 228, 233
account of, 49–55
evaluation of, 53–55
model of Beauregard's strategy, 119
Sigel, Franz, Union general, 198
Skirmishing, 251
Slavery
Confederates prepare to enlist
slaves, 208
effect of Confederate plan to
arm slaves, 237
potential effect on Confederate strategy, 236

role in southern nationalism,
238
Smith, William F. "Baldy,"
Union general, 197
attacks Petersburg, 194
contributes strategic ideas,
181, 183
South
effect on mobility of its rainy
winters, 44, 130
Spotsylvania Court House, Battle of, 193–94
Staff
Buell's effective, 52
functions explained, 41, 79
informal relations and procedures facilitate func-
tioning of Confederate,
225
Union's performs informally
as a general staff, 112–
113, 225
U.S. Army's organization, 79
Stanton, Edwin M., Union secretary of war, 82, 103,
108, 166, 224, 226, 228
appointed, 80
background and contribution,
80
publicity about Grant's spring
of 1864 operations, 195
reinforcement for Rosecrans,
177
views on the nature of military operations, 80
States' rights
contributions to the war efforts, 3, 76–78, 234–35
role in Confederate defeat,
234
Steamboats
role in Fort Donelson campaign, 46–49

Napoleonic operational
  characterized Civil War op-
    erations, 240
  explained and illustrated,
    255–60
persisting
  distinguished, 138
  implemented by Napoleonic
    operational methods,
    138
political
  anaconda explained, 21–22
  defined and distinguished,
    21, 138
  employs same military
    means as military, 138
  initial Confederate King
    Cotton strategy of foreign
    intervention, 152–53
  objections to a strategy of
    deep retreats, 144, 236
  second Confederate, to
    wear down the Union by
    the 1864 elections, 153
  summarized by Lee, 153–54
raiding
  distinguished, 138
  used by Confederate Navy
    with commerce cruisers,
    141
Union
  acknowledged stalemate in
    Virginia, 136
  conditioned by primacy of
    retreat and tactical defen-
    sive, 131
  difficulties with persisting
    logistic, 181–83
  for East and West adopted
    in 1863, 136–37
  explained, 128–34
  Grant continues persisting
    in 1864, 187

Grant's proposed changes
  and their merits, 184–85
  logistic constraints, 128–30
  logistic summarized, 232–33
  realism summarized, 225
  success of Grant's raiding
    strategy, 217
  for Virginia, 136–37
Stuart, J. E. B., Confederate
  general, 33, 41
Surprise, 65, 180
  absent in most of Grant's 1864
    turning movements, 192
  absent in most of Sherman's
    turning movements, 199
  equivalent to finding enemy
    weak, 85
  facilitated by initiative, 140
  Grant surprises Lee in his
    move to Petersburg, 194
  important for the turning
    movement, 60
  Marlborough attained by dis-
    traction, 124
  Melas gains against Napo-
    leon, 259
  Napoleon achieved, 258
  role in spring of 1863 cam-
    paigns, 172
  in Vicksburg campaign, 160

Tactics
  antecedents of Civil War sum-
    marized, 277
  armies' facility in maneuver,
    232
  cavalry had little mounted
    combat role, 240
  changes since 1800, 252–54
  Civil War distinct from Euro-
    pean, 232, 239–40
  conditions in Virginia in 1864,
    193

335